M
Adrian Moore

CCEA AS
DIGITAL
TECHNOLOGY

COLOURPOINT
EDUCATIONAL

Copyright

Colourpoint Educational
An imprint of Colourpoint Creative Ltd
Colourpoint House
Jubilee Business Park
Jubilee Road
Newtownards
County Down
Northern Ireland
BT23 4YH

Tel: 028 9182 6339
E-mail: sales@colourpoint.co.uk
Website: www.colourpoint.co.uk

The Authors

Janet Allison has a BSc in Computing & Mathematics (Queen's University Belfast) and an MSc in Information Technology (Ulster University). She currently teaches computing to Level 3 and Foundation Degree students in Northern Regional College. She works as an AS-level examiner for an awarding body.

Professor Martin McKinney has an MSc in Computer Science and Applications and is Professor Emeritus of Computing (Ulster University). He is a former Head of School of Computing & Information Engineering (Ulster University) and a former Vice-Principal of Teaching & Learning (Northern Regional College).

Dr Adrian Moore is a Senior Lecturer and Course Director in the School of Computing at Ulster University. He holds a PhD and BSc in Computing and has published widely in areas including multimedia web technologies, computer networks and computer graphics.

Publisher's Note: This book has been through a rigorous quality assurance process by an independent person experienced in the CCEA specification prior to publication. It has been written to help students preparing for the AS Digital Technology specification from CCEA. While Colourpoint Educational, the authors and the quality assurance person have taken every care in its production, we are not able to guarantee that the book is completely error-free. Additionally, while the book has been written to address the CCEA specification, it is the responsibility of each candidate to satisfy themselves that they have fully met the requirements of the CCEA specification prior to sitting an exam set by that body. For this reason, and because specifications and CCEA advice change with time, we strongly advise every candidate to avail of a qualified teacher and to check the contents of the most recent specification for themselves prior to the exam. Colourpoint Creative Ltd therefore cannot be held responsible for any errors or omissions in this book or any consequences thereof.

The answers to the questions in this book are available online in PDF format. Visit www.colourpointeducational.com, and search for this book. On the page for the book you will find details of how to download the answers. If you have any problems, please contact Colourpoint.

CONTENTS

UNIT AS 1
Approaches to Systems Development

UNIT AS 2
Fundamentals of Digital Technology

UNIT AS 1
Approaches to Systems Development

CHAPTER 1
Reasons for Systems Development

By the end of this chapter students should be able to:

- explain the impact of the 'software crisis';
- explain the need for software systems that meet the needs of organisations and/or individuals;
- explain the main factors affecting systems development: the user needs, time and cost;
- understand that a computer system consists of a user interface, processes and data;
- describe the roles of the following during systems development: the systems analyst; the project manager; and the programmer.

1.1 Introduction

To understand **systems development,** it is first useful to consider what we mean when we talk about a **system**. All of us will have come across things in the real world that we call systems. Some of these systems are extremely large and complex. Others are small – but often just as significant.

Examples of large, real-world systems are as follows.

- The **solar system** includes the Sun and all the planets and other objects that orbit it. It is an example of a naturally-occurring system.
- **The digestive system** in the human body consists of a group of organs that work together to convert food into energy and other nutrients that serve to feed the body.
- A **city transport system** includes the vehicles (such as buses, trains, trams, cars and bicycles), the associated pathways (such as roads, railway lines, tram lines and cycle lanes) and routes through the city that they serve.

- An **education system** facilitates the training and instruction of people from their infancy into adulthood. An education system itself consists of a number of smaller systems (known as **sub-systems**) such as the pre-school system, primary school system and the secondary school system.

Other systems are significantly smaller and simpler than those described above, such as:

- A **queueing system** in a café which might include an area for people to stand, different serving counters and a way for staff to bring cooked food to the correct customer.
- A **job applications** system which, at the most basic level, might simply allow applicants to submit their application online. A highly sophisticated job applications system might provide a much broader level of functionality. For example, it might also facilitate the shortlisting of applicants, the scheduling of interviews and any post-interview monitoring and reporting.

1.2 Characteristics of a System

The above examples help us to see what it is that makes something a 'system'. The three main characteristics of any system are:

- the system should have a defined **purpose**;
- the system should meet a defined **need**;
- the system should have a **number of components** which are likely to be interdependent.

Case Study

City Transport System

Consider the city transport system discussed above. We are able to state its purpose as "to enable commuters and other users to navigate around the city in a flexible, efficient and economical manner".

In doing so, this transport system meets the defined transport needs of the city and its inhabitants, namely that people and goods need to be able to move around the city in order for it to function.

The transport system has a number of components such as the buses and trains (public transport), cars, bicycles and taxis (private transport) and the roads, railways and footpaths themselves. The system can contain a number of sub-systems such as the bus system and the train system. These systems are integrated. For example, cars are dependent on the roads and trains on the tracks. There may be further interdependencies, so for example the train and bus systems may have integrated timetables to provide connecting services for train arrivals.

In summary, the city transport system meets the three characteristics of a system:

- **Purpose:** To enable commuters and other users to navigate around the city in a flexible, efficient manner.
- **Need:** So that people and goods can move around the city in order for it to function.
- **Components:** Public and private transport vehicles, roads, paths, tracks etc.

As we have discussed, large systems can generally be broken down into a number of smaller sub-systems. In some cases, a system can be so complex that it is essential to break it down in this way. An example is the system for running an airline.

Case Study

Airline System

Consider the computer system for Dalriada Airlines, which must facilitate all aspects of running the airline's operations. Rather than consider the entire system, we instead think of the 'system' as consisting of the following sub-systems:

- **Bookings system**, to facilitate booking of flights by passengers.
- **Payments system**, to facilitate the payment of flights booked by passengers.
- **Lost luggage system**, to help trace luggage that has not arrived at the correct destination.
- **Human Resources (HR)** system to deal with essential HR functions such as the payroll, hiring of staff, handling appraisal and maintaining staff records.
- **Personnel scheduler** system, to support the management of the flight rotas for staff such as the pilots and flight attendants.
- **Maintenance scheduler** system, to ensure that the planes are serviced in line with any legal/insurance requirements and to ensure that the planes are maintained in an airworthy condition.

This list in not exhaustive but serves to illustrate how complex and inter-connected systems can be.

1.3 Developing Systems

Systems development is concerned with the creation, or **development**, of systems. The term is normally used when referring specifically to **computer (software) systems**, i.e. systems where there is an element of computer processing. Hence the solar system would not be classified as a computer (software) system whereas an online banking system would clearly be classified as such.

In this context, the word 'development' is used to refer to the full range of activities from the initial identification of the need for a system, through a series of tasks that culminate in the full and final implementation of the system. This series of activities is what constitutes the systems development process and includes the following steps:

- Identify the **need** for a system by **analysing** the current system.
- **Define** the system. At this stage, the precise user requirements of the system have to be identified and agreed. Any mistakes made in the definition are likely to require a re-think at a later stage and this can be very expensive.
- **Design** the system. All systems should be carefully designed (and a systems specification produced) as any flaws in the design are difficult to alter later and can be very expensive.
- **Implement** the new software application or program based on the systems specification.
- **Test** the new system.
- **Document** the system.
- **Hand over** the system.
- **Maintain** the system.

Each of these steps will be discussed in more detail in subsequent chapters.

1.4 The Software Crisis

In the embryonic days of the software industry the process of developing software was more informal and certainly less structured than it is today. Many of the procedures that are now taken for granted had not yet been established in what was still a very young industry. For example, approaches to establishing precise requirements from customers were not as sophisticated or as precise as we would now expect. In the absence of clear and precise requirements, software often did not fully meet the user requirements.

A number of factors led to the software crisis:

- People had little historical experience of similar work on which to base future work estimates. Hence the time and cost estimates for work were often crude and inaccurate.
- The tools used to develop software were not very sophisticated and as a consequence software took much longer to produce.

- Unlike today, there were no tools to support the early identification of errors and this slowed down the process of locating and correcting faults. This also meant that systems were difficult and expensive to maintain.
- Systems were not meeting user requirements.
- Specialist testing staff were not part of the software development process, so there was no formal process for testing software for correctness.

As a consequence of these factors, the software being developed was typically of lower quality and was less robust than the systems we are familiar with today. Teams dedicated to developing the software often struggled to meet both deadlines and cost estimates. This meant that the industry was ill-prepared to meet the demand for ever larger and more complex systems. The problem became more and more acute and eventually culminated in the **software crisis**. The term was first coined at a NATO Software Engineering conference in Germany in 1968 to refer to the difficulties the software development industry was facing.

Software developers realised that in order to develop quality software on time, within budget and to more accurately meet the needs of the user, a more systematic approach to the software development process was necessary. This led to the development of **software engineering**. Software engineering is the application of a more structured approach to the design, development and maintenance of software systems, similar to the systematic approach taken in other areas of engineering such as civil engineering.

1.5 Factors Affecting Systems Development

Three main factors affect the systems development process:

- The necessity of meeting the **needs** of organisations and individuals.
- The **time available**.
- The **costs** of the project.

The needs of organisations and individuals

As previously discussed, all computer systems have both a defined **purpose** and meet a defined **need**. If we consider the example of the airline system, and focus on the booking sub-system, we can easily see that it satisfies these two criteria:

- An airline booking system has a defined **purpose** which is to allow travellers to efficiently and effectively book and pay for flights over the Internet.
- There is a defined **need** for such a system because the sheer volume of flights could not be facilitated by booking on a personal, one-to-one basis.

While it is easy to see the benefit of using software systems for organisations, organisations are also aware of the need to provide services in a manner that is easy for individual customers to use. In the case of an airline, the customers are travellers wishing to book flights. These customers are called the **users** of the system and it is important that they find the system **accessible** and **easy to use**. If they do not, they may take their business elsewhere and the system will therefore have failed to achieve its purpose. The **user interface** is how a user interacts with the system. It is considered to be of vital importance to a system's usability. Figure 1.1 illustrates how much interaction there is across the interface between the user and a simple online airline booking system.

For a system to be a success, therefore, it must meet the needs of both the organisation that operates it and the individuals who use it.

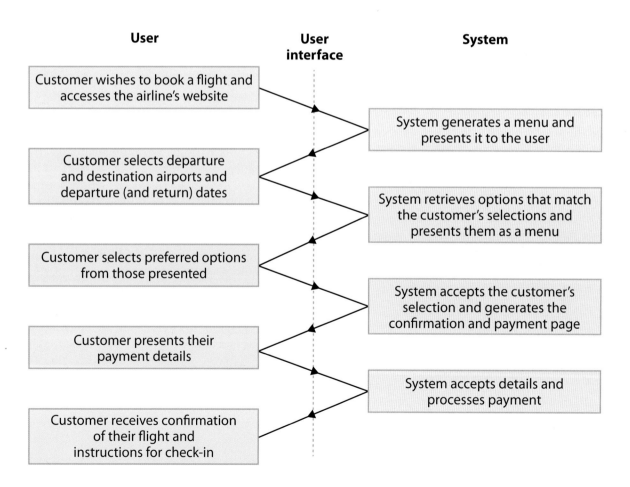

User   **User interface**   **System**

Customer wishes to book a flight and accesses the airline's website

System generates a menu and presents it to the user

Customer selects departure and destination airports and departure (and return) dates

System retrieves options that match the customer's selections and presents them as a menu

Customer selects preferred options from those presented

System accepts the customer's selection and generates the confirmation and payment page

Customer presents their payment details

System accepts details and processes payment

Customer receives confirmation of their flight and instructions for check-in

Figure 1.1: Typical online airline booking system.

The time available

The length of time available to develop a new system constrains what can be done. For example, there is little point in specifying a component that will take a year to develop if the system has to be operational within six months.

The costs of the project

Similarly, there is a limit on how much money that can be spent on a project. This will place limits on the number of people who can be employed and the type of hardware that can be purchased. Systems development must take place within the constraints of cost.

1.6 Elements of a Computer System

A computer system can be thought of in simple terms as a system that uses computing power to support a function. Typically, such systems will be characterised by the ability to:

- receive data (raw facts);
- process the data received;
- store the data received and any data generated as a result of processing;
- present the processed data as information; and
- communicate data between related sub-systems.

From this description it is clear that a computer system receives data as input, performs tasks on the data and presents processed data (information) to the user as output. Therefore, we can describe a computer system as consisting of the following distinct elements (as shown in figure 1.2):

- **Data**, provided by the user or generated by the processes.
- **User interface (UI)** which allows users to send data into the system and to view the data that has been processed.
- **Processes** which manipulate the data in the desired manner.

Each of these elements is important in its own right. For example, poor data will produce meaningless or unreliable results. A poor user interface will result in users avoiding the system, making errors and spending more time using the system. Poor processing could produce inaccurate data or take more time than necessary.

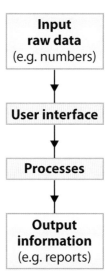

Figure 1.2: A computer system consists of data, a user interface and processes.

We can see this structure in the numerous computer systems we encounter in our everyday lives. The following case study shows how all three elements are present in a typical online banking system.

Case Study

Online Banking System

An online banking system consists of the following elements:

Data
- Account holder details.
- Transaction data.

User Interface
- Accepts user verification details (name, password and other security checks).
- Presents details of the user's account and the results of any requests that they make for information in a suitable format.
- Permits the user to enter details of transactions such as payments or transfers between accounts or transfers to other accounts.

Processes
- To retrieve our account information based on the login information.
- To analyse our data and our recent transactions.
- To allow us to make new transactions.

Task

For each of the following systems, identify examples of data, user interfaces and processes present in each case. Try to list as many as you can.

1. A fitness device worn on the wrist that continuously monitors the wearer's activity, for example their heart rate and number of steps taken, and gives feedback on the user's fitness level.

2. An automated tyre pressure monitoring system in a car, which alerts the driver if the pressure in any of the tyres drops below an acceptable level.

Computer systems are everywhere and will play an increasingly important role as time goes by. It is likely that in the future more people will live in so-called smart homes. A smart home will have a number of strategically-placed sensors about the house that can be used to monitor the behaviour of the occupant. Hence there may be a sensor on the door of the refrigerator or on the kettle. These sensors might be used to monitor the kettle being switched on or the refrigerator door being opened. Should any of these sensors be activated due to 'unusual' behaviour then this can trigger a message to the relevant parties. Unusual behaviour might even be the absence of input – hence if the kettle and refrigerator sensors have not been activated (say) by mid-morning it might be indicative that the occupant is still in bed and may be unwell.

1.7 User Interfaces

We have already seen that the needs of the user are vital to the success of a software system. Therefore, the user interface is a vital element of the computer system. The user interface forms the gateway between the system and its user. It allows the user to enter data and, after processing, it outputs the results to the user.

There are many ways of interacting with computer systems and indeed these have changed significantly over the years. In the past, much of this interaction took place via a combination of a mouse and keyboard. In more recent times user interfaces have become more sophisticated and now include elements such as voice control and touchscreen technology.

Many organisations with high security needs have replaced physical key access to restricted areas of their buildings with swipe-card access, using a card with a magnetic strip that holds encoded information. As the card is swiped through the slot, the encoded information is interpreted and, if the user is authorised, they are given access. It is likely that, in the future, interaction using gestures will become increasingly commonplace for such applications.

A common user interface used by supermarkets is the barcode. Many supermarkets today are almost totally reliant on barcodes on the packaging of their products to process sales at the checkout desk. A barcode consists of a series of parallel black and white lines and each product's data is uniquely encoded by varying the thickness of and spacing between these parallel lines. As a customer passes through the checkout, specialised barcode readers are used to scan and interpret these barcodes in order to display the product's details on the screen and process the sale. From a supermarket's point of view this:

- speeds up the checkout process;
- significantly reduces the possibility of human error;
- maintains an up-to-date record of stock levels which is vital for re-ordering from suppliers.

A barcode reader is a very different user interface from a keyboard and mouse. Indeed, every system will have a different interface. The decision of what type of interface to provide for a computer system is dictated by:

- the application;
- the environment in which it operates;
- the characteristics of its users.

Whatever the choice of user interface, it must be simple to use and extremely intuitive. Figure 1.3 contrasts two systems with very different user interface needs. Typically, users of an airport check-in kiosk only have to supply small amounts of data, so a touchscreen interface is appropriate. By contrast, a

	Airport Check-in	Hospital
Application	Check passengers onto particular flights	Update patient records
Environment	Kiosk in a busy airport	Hospital
Reason for using the system	To notify the airline that the passenger has arrived at the airport	To record patient data
Interface	Touchscreen	Screen, keyboard and mouse

Figure 1.3: Comparison of two typical user interfaces.

system used by staff in hospitals to record patient information requires many fields of data to be completed. The interface therefore needs to allow more sophisticated input, and hence a screen, keyboard and mouse are appropriate. While such a system would likely appear difficult to use to members of the public, it is only intended to be used by trained hospital staff and hence serves its purpose.

User interfaces change and evolve over time. This can happen rapidly, depending on the needs of the user that moment, or it can happen slowly as technology and society evolve. The following two case studies show two ways that this can happen.

Case Study

Satellite Navigation System

Consider a car satellite navigation (satnav) system that provides the user (the driver) with information on the route to a specified destination. The system has a number of different interfaces. The first interface the driver encounters when they turn on the satnav allows them to enter details of their desired destination. The driver must be able to concentrate fully on providing accurate destination information, so naturally this data must be entered when the car is not moving. At this point, **accuracy** is important and since they can focus their attention on the task the user will probably use a touchscreen keypad to enter details of the destination.

Once the destination has been entered and the system has calculated the appropriate route the driver can commence their journey. The satnav system will provide the driver with a series of instructions as to the precise route to be followed. However, as the driver is now focusing primarily on **driving safely** the user interface changes

dramatically. A satnav interface that simply displayed the route instructions as text on a screen and required the driver to read it while driving would be dangerous. Instead, instructions are issued both visually (via an on-screen map) and orally (via a voice commentary). The main reason for the audio interface is that the user can receive instructions without taking their eyes off the road.

Case Study

Toll Road System

Toll roads are typically constructed by private organisations to provide an alternative and faster route between two locations. To pay for their investment, a fee is paid for the use of the road – this is the toll. Toll roads are increasingly common in Ireland.

In the early days of toll roads, the toll was collected manually. A barrier was constructed at some point on the road to prevent road users from progressing until their toll was paid. The toll transaction involved the driver physically handing over payment before the barrier was raised and the driver permitted to proceed with their journey.

An initial attempt to speed up the process was to have unmanned coin baskets at the barrier, that drivers simply dropped their coins into. The baskets did not issue change and were quicker to use, though drivers still had to have their coins ready in advance and wait for the barrier to rise.

As toll roads became ever more popular it was observed that the time taken for the payment process was still too long, resulting in long queues of traffic waiting to pay. Such delays were slowing down journey time and thus defeating the purpose of the roads, so an alternative mechanism was devised to speed up the payment process. On the M50 in Dublin number plate recognition is now used to identify users as they pass the toll point. Users do not have to stop and instead go online to pay their toll within a particular time frame.

1.8 System Development Roles

The development of any complex computer system requires a team of people with different skills to analyse the problem. Three of the most common roles are the **systems analyst**, the **project manager** and the **programmer**.

Systems analyst

The main role of the systems analyst is to identify the **user** and **data processing requirements** for the new or modified computer system.

Typically, the systems analyst will:

- carry out a feasibility study and produce a feasibility report;
- liaise with the client (user);
- undertake some fact-finding (using interviews, observation, questionnaires or document sampling if there is an existing system);
- define the system specification, i.e. the specific proposals for a new, modified or replacement system.

Project manager

The project manager is responsible for the **planning**, **management**, **co-ordination** and **financial control** of the project. They must ensure the project is completed on time and within budget, that the project's objectives are met and that everyone else is doing their job properly. Project managers oversee the project to ensure the desired result is achieved,

the most efficient resources are used and the different interests involved are satisfied.

Typically, the project manager will:

- plan the project's schedule;
- split the project up into suitable tasks/subtasks;
- allocate resources such as personnel, hardware and software to each task/subtask;
- identify risks to the project;
- monitor the progress of the project;
- ensure the project is delivered on time and within budget;
- report back to the client.

Programmer

When creating a new system, the role of the programmer is to **develop** and **test** the system designed by the systems analyst to meet the particular needs of the client.

Typically, the programmer will:

- write or amend source code (using a high-level programming language such as Java) for the proposed system based on module specifications, algorithms or flowcharts;
- document the code (add meaningful comments) to help other programmers when the code needs to be modified;
- debug the code to correct any errors that may have been found during testing;
- ensure integration of existing software systems (if these exist);
- test the new system using a test plan;
- write operational documents for the new system; and
- work closely with the **systems analyst** and **project manager** to ensure the user requirements are met within the expected time frame.

A programmer involved in the development of code for a particular system would be well-placed to be involved in the future maintenance of code for that particular system. However, their expertise would not be confined to that one system and so they are likely to be of great value in the enhancement and/or maintenance of code for other systems that they were not originally involved in developing. The more experienced a programmer is, the more likely they are to be involved in the development and maintenance of more complex systems.

CHAPTER 1 – REASONS FOR SYSTEMS DEVELOPMENT

Questions

1. List three characteristics of any system. Consider how a pupil information system within an educational organisation that you are familiar with operates. Identify these three characteristics for that system.

2. In the late 1960s there was a crisis in the software industry. List four reasons why this crisis occurred. What was the software industry's response to this crisis?

3. What is meant by the term 'software engineering'?

4. A computer system can be thought of as a system that uses computing power to support a function. List three functions that a computer system must be able to do.

5. (a) Three elements of any computer system are the data, the user interface and the processes which need to be carried out. Describe each of these elements.
   (b) A computer system is used for stock control in a supermarket.
       (i) Suggest why such a system is needed. Within this system identify:
       (ii) what data needs to be stored in the system;
       (iii) what processes take place so that the quantity of each item of stock is always up-to-date;
       (iv) what user interfaces are needed to manage the data and processes in the system.

6. The following three categories of staff have specific roles during the development of a computer system:
   • systems analyst,
   • programmer,
   • project manager.
   For each category, explain what their primary role is and list three specific duties they would be expected to perform.

CHAPTER 2
Analysis

By the end of this chapter students should be able to:

- describe the purpose of analysis;
- evaluate different fact-finding techniques: interviews, questionnaires, observation and document sampling;
- distinguish between functional and non-functional user requirements in systems, such as stock control, reservation, payroll and billing;
- explain the purpose of a data flow diagram (DFD); and
- produce context and level 1 DFDs for simple scenarios.

2.1 Introduction

The main purpose of the **analysis** (or investigation) phase of systems development is to ensure that the existing system is fully understood and that the **user requirements** of the new system are agreed prior to proceeding with the next phase. Historically, this has proven to be an extremely useful part of the process. Not only is it essential that the analysts fully understand the existing system – in terms of inputs, processing and output – but also that they are able to identify strengths and weaknesses of that system and may even identify opportunities for improvement or for the addition of new features.

2.2 Gathering Data

In order to understand an existing system it is first necessary to gather data about it. This data normally has to be collected by the analysts. The sources that they use can be categorised as either **direct** or **indirect**.

Direct and indirect data sources

> **Note:** At the time of writing, the CCEA specification does not require you to have knowledge of direct and indirect data sources. However, it is very useful to be aware of.

A **direct data source** is one from which data can be gathered from without having to go to a third party for confirmation, and can be used for a specific purpose. For example, an analyst might ask visitors to a shopping centre to complete a questionnaire about their shopping preferences. The questionnaire is intended to acquire very specific data and the questions will be tailored to acquire this data. So, for example, there may be questions asking how much the customer typically spends weekly on confectionary and newspapers. These questionnaires could be reviewed to inform a decision as to whether there might be sufficient demand to open a newsagent in the shopping centre.

The ability to acquire specific, targeted data is the main advantage of direct data sources. However, the main disadvantage is that they incur a high cost. For example, because a questionnaire has to be designed with a specific purpose in mind, it will take the designer time to establish precisely what information is required and then to formulate the questions so that they provide the data used to uncover this information. In addition, it also takes time to carry out the questionnaire.

An **indirect** data source is one that is already available and is being used for a purpose for which it was not originally intended. For example, all hospitals hold patient records. These records could be analysed to extract the postcodes of patients with a particular illness, and this data could be used to identify regions with higher than expected incidents of the illness. In this example, the analyst has used the patient records as an indirect data source. Similarly, in the example of the shopping centre questionnaire, the data obtained might also be useful in reviewing the healthy eating habits of the shoppers based on their confectionary spend even though this was not the intended purpose of the questionnaire.

The main advantage of indirect data sources is that they can be very cost effective since the data already exists and is likely to be available immediately. The main disadvantage is that, since it was initially designed and the data acquired for a different purpose, the source may not provide the exact data required by the new user. Consequently, some additional filtering or data processing, for example removing irrelevant data.

Case Study

Leisure Club

A town's leisure centre is closing down and a local hotelier sees an opportunity to develop his hotel's leisure facilities. He is planning to set up a membership-only Leisure Club and is currently considering providing a large, state of the art, unisex fitness suite complete with an extensive range of fitness machines. A friend has suggested that this might not be a good idea and suggested that he reduce the size of the suite and use the remaining space to operate a small sports hall that would allow indoor activities such as yoga, Pilates, spin classes and Zumba. The hotelier wishes to establish what the likely demand for the leisure facilities might be from the local community.

The hotelier decides to use a **direct data source** by surveying the residents in the area and asking them whether they would be interested in becoming a member of the hotel's Leisure Club and, if so, what their likely usage pattern would be.

He also decides to use an **indirect data source** by approaching the Council for data on the existing membership of the leisure centre and usage statistics of its facilities. This data will require some work as it will contain a lot of data irrelevant to the hotelier's needs. It will also need some effort to extract useful information.

Task

A businesswoman currently operates a juice bar that specialises in selling a range of the more popular, healthy fruit juices within a local sports club. She is aware that many of her customers are females in the age range 14–45 years and she also notices that she is particular busy on weekdays (11am to 4.30pm) and on Saturdays. She is planning to open a second juice bar in a similar sports club in an adjacent town but has received conflicting advice from her business partners. One of them has advised her that she simply replicate the model she currently employs. The other business partner has suggested that she should extend the range of healthy drinks she sells, although these additions are more exotic and hence more expensive.

She is not quite sure what to do as she believes that one of the strengths of the business is promoting a reasonable range of drinks at affordable prices. Suggest two direct data sources and two indirect data sources that the businesswoman could use to decide which approach to take.

Fact-finding techniques

Systems analysts can use a number of techniques in order to gather data about a system. The four main methods are:

- interviews;
- questionnaires;
- observation;
- document sampling.

Interviews

The staff who use an existing system are often the most knowledgeable about how it works, and therefore interviewing them is an excellent opportunity to acquire data. Conducting such interviews is a time-consuming activity and requires significant planning and scheduling to produce accurate information.

The analyst's first step in planning interviews is to determine precisely what it is they need to know. Interviews can be used to:

- confirm the analyst's understanding of the system;
- fill in the gaps in the analyst's basic understanding;
- delve deeper into certain aspects of the system in which the interviewee is an expert.

Interviews are most effective when the analyst is suitably prepared and is already knowledgeable about the type of people who use the system. Therefore, time must be spent planning the interviews. This preparation will include crafting questions in such a way that the answers will provide the necessary information. Questions should be targeted at the interviewee's areas of expertise and should allow the interviewee an opportunity to expand on their answer if they feel the question does not fully address the subject under discussion. The systems analyst may ask the questions on a one-to-one basis or to a group of people.

Some interviewees may be suspicious of the process and may feel that their role within the organisation could change or even be made redundant by a new system. Sensitivity and respect must therefore be shown during the process and time should be spent at the start to provide the interviewee with clarity about the process and reassurance on the possible outcomes. To keep the information organised it is a good idea to use a response sheet with a standardised format for all the interviews.

Generally, it is neither necessary nor possible to interview every single user of the current system so it is important to select the people to be interviewed with care. It is also important that those chosen are told why they have been selected, what the purpose of the interview is, how it will be structured, how long it is likely to take and what the analyst intends to do with the information. Questions can be structured or unstructured, with the possibility of follow-up questions to encourage conversation and fact-finding. While it may be tempting to record the conversation, interviewees may be reluctant to speak freely if they know their words are being recorded. It is preferable to have a free-flowing conversation, listening and taking notes, paraphrasing the responses to check they have been understood and then clarifying any issues with the interviewee.

After the interviews the analyst can evaluate the information. This is where the interview planning has maximum benefit. To provide confidence that the responses are accurate and that the questions have been fully understood, answers can be cross-checked by triangulating their responses. For example, if an interviewee indicated they had possessed an HGV driver's license for more than five years but their employer records indicated that they were only 22 years of age, this would clearly be a problem since it is not possible to obtain such a license before the age of 18. Another example might be someone who claims to be vegetarian but later states that their favourite meal is spaghetti and meatballs.

Questionnaires

Questionnaires are particularly useful for reaching mass audiences, where one-to-one interviews would be impractical. Since most questionnaires are now conducted online, they have the additional advantage that they can be conducted in total privacy and at a time convenient to the respondent. Many software tools are available for the preparation and presentation of the questions and, crucially, for analysing the responses.

Questionnaires can have a rich mix of questions and are becoming increasingly sophisticated.

Questions are usually of one of the following styles:

- **radio buttons,** where the user may select only one answer from a predefined set of options, for example to select which of the 11 council areas in Northern Ireland they currently live in;
- **checkboxes,** where the user may select multiple answers from a predefined set of options, for example the genres of music they like to listen to;
- **sliders,** where the user can indicate a percentage value by dragging a slider across a designated range, for example what proportion of their income is spent on renting accommodation;
- **free text response,** where the user can provide additional textual information, for example their address or for adding comments, observations or opinions.

As with interviews, well-crafted questionnaires often contain additional questions that can be used to verify consistency with previous responses. These can be used to filter out spurious responses. For example, one question may ask the user to enter their age, while a later question may ask for their date of birth. These can be cross-checked for consistency.

Observation

Sometimes the best way of acquiring information is to actually observe the process at first hand. Observation can be extremely informative since users in the real world may undertake their duties in a different manner than that described in the documentation. These alternative methods are often, though not always, a more efficient and effective way of operating and it is important for the analyst to discover cases where this is happening.

Observation can be fruitful but can be problematic if the person being observed is aware that it is taking place. If this is the case, they are likely to modify their behaviour and may not undertake the task as they normally would. For example, a machine operator may take greater safety precautions if they know they are being observed than if they are not. Consequently, it helps if the observation is as unobtrusive as possible, can cover multiple operators and can be conducted over a period of time. The analyst should therefore select a representative sample of employees and 'shadow' them as they carry out their daily tasks so that they can identify:

- the **processes** involved;
- the **data needed** to perform each process;
- the **data generated** by each process.

Observation can be particularly useful when everything takes place at a single, central location, but it may be unsuitable in an organisation where people are doing similar, but not necessarily identical, work at different locations. For example, a mail order company may distribute their sales items using a number of different distribution depots. The work at each depot may be undertaken by a number of operatives and

involves receiving orders, retrieving the goods from store and then packaging the goods and delivering them to a post room for final distribution. In the larger depots, a supervisory operative is given responsibility for reviewing each order as it is received and passing the details on to the other operatives. However, there may be no designated supervisory operative in a smaller depot. In addition, there may be local practices that improve the efficiency of the operation at each specific depot. For example, as the layout of each depot is likely to be different, the distance between the store and the post room will vary and may be quite some distance in larger depots. In such depots, the operative may agree to take it in turns to visit the post room with a number of orders. Even though this is not the designated process, it may have proven to be a more efficient way to work at that depot.

Document sampling

Many existing systems have documented processes. Consulting this documentation can prove to be a useful initial starting point in the fact-finding process. It is likely to identify:

- the key users of the system (or sub-systems);
- the data the organisation needs;
- how the data flows through the organisation;
- the volume of data being processed;
- the output data required by the organisation.

Reading through the essential documentation includes examining existing documents, forms and files related to the current system, for example invoices, sales receipts, orders and reports. The process can be extremely time consuming but can provide a useful insight into how the need for the system initially arose, and perhaps how it later evolved. It can also serve to more clearly identify the part of the organisation to which the existing system applies.

Task

Identify which of the four data gathering techniques would be most suitable for each of the following scenarios. Justify your answer in each case.

1. To find out about an invoicing system that is currently used in an office with three office clerks.

2. To investigate the breakfast-time eating habits of first-year undergraduate students in Northern Ireland.

3. To find out how staff are using an existing computerised control system in a factory.

4. To investigate the fire evacuation procedures within an office block.

5. To identify what the procedures are in a school for storing and handling hazardous substances (such as bleach, acids, chemical substances and radioactive material).

6. To establish the social media habits in a class of Year 13 students.

7. To find out pupil views on teaching in a school (assessing aspects such as punctuality, clarity of presentation, provision of support material, homework and feedback).

8. To identify the procedures in an organisation for lifting heavy loads.

Task

Select one of your answers from the previous task and:

- design a questionnaire, or
- prepare a set of interview questions

that could be used in the scenario.

2.3 User Requirements

Once the collection of data has been completed, the **user requirements** can be identified and documented as a **system specification.** The system specification is really the plan as to how these user requirements will be met. It is very important because it specifies in a precise way what the user expects the software to be able to do and the schedule for its production.

In the past, this document would have formed the basis of the contract between the procurer of the system and the system vendor. It was a two-way agreement: a client could not at a later date demand additional or alternative features to those described within the system specification, while the vendor was required by the contract to meet the specification. Changes to the requirements would result in penalties or revised charges and hence it was extremely important that the document was precise so that what was being agreed was clearly understood by both parties.

This worked well in the days when there was a limited number of software vendors because they knew precisely what was to be delivered and within what timeframe, allowing them to plan ahead and ensure that the workforce was suitably deployed over time. In more recent years, however, the number of vendors has greatly increased and software development skills are much more prevalent than in the early days of the industry. This means that companies can be more flexible. Furthermore, recent trends towards a more Agile approach to software development (see Chapter 5) means that such documents today are less prescriptive and have built-in safeguards that allow more flexibility in the final product.

Functional and non-functional requirements

The system specification differentiates between **functional** and **non-functional** requirements. A good way to think of the difference is that a functional requirement is something the system *must* do, while a non-functional requirement describes additional conditions which the system *should* meet.

For example, the following are all examples of functional requirements, things that a system should do or allow:

- The system should provide routines to allow approved administration staff to add/edit customers.
- The system should provide routines to permit authorised staff from within the finance department to create invoices.
- The system should provide a facility to back up transactions regularly and on demand.

Non-functional requirements specify additional conditions for how the system should behave. They are essentially *constraints* upon the system's behaviour, specifying criteria that judge the behaviour of a system, rather than the behaviour itself. For example, the requirement that "modified data in a database should be updated for all users accessing it within two seconds" is a non-functional requirement. Non-functional requirements can be considered to be a specification of the system's **quality characteristics** or **quality attributes.**

The following are all examples of criteria that could be covered by non-functional requirements:

- System availability, including response times.
- System reliability.
- Security issues, such as who has access, who has priority, password and password changes, frequency of data backups.

- Performance, such as response time, throughput rates, utilisation of processors and computer memory.

Case Study

Building Supplies Stock Control

A company that supplies materials to the building trade currently operates a paper-based stock control system. It is vital to the operation of the company that it never runs out of stock as this would give it a reputation for being unreliable and its customers would take their business to another supplier. A software company was asked to develop a computerised stock control system. They identified some functional and non-functional requirements. Examples of the requirements that the software company produced are as follows.

Functional requirements
The system should:

- allow the company to keep track of current levels of all of its stock, (including any impending orders);
- keep a history of stock to facilitate "first-in, first-out" stock movement;
- alert the company whenever current stock levels of any item falls to its reorder level; and
- provide a range of reporting utilities.

Non-functional requirements
The system should:

- accurately reflect the current stock level of all items;
- be available at all times;
- be secure and accessible only to specified staff;
- be backed up daily; and
- handle multiple users simultaneously.

Worked Example

Dalriada Airlines operates a basic online reservation system to allow people to book flights between a number of destinations. The system is designed to accept personal data from the user first, before proceeding to the actual booking process. This personal data includes things such as the person's name, address and telephone number. The user is then asked to identify the relevant flight details – departure and arrival airports, preferred dates, nature of journey (one-way or return) and the number of passengers.

Once this basic information has been entered the user is presented with possible flight times and costs and invited to make their selection. Once this has been done, the customer is then prompted to enter the personal details of others flying (if appropriate) and any hold luggage requirements. At this stage the user may also be offered the chance to reserve actual seats on the flight for an additional fee; otherwise the seats will be randomly allocated. The system then provides an opportunity for the user to pay for the flights (credit or debit card) and once the payment has been approved a confirmation message is displayed and an email is sent to the user. To make future bookings easier, and to allow the airline to promote future sales/discounts, the user is invited to register their details with the airline as a 'member'. If the user agrees they will be allocated an airline account complete with membership number and a temporary password which they are free to change at any time. The details used for the current booking will be saved to this account.

Identify three functional and three non-functional requirements of the system from the **airline's** perspective.

The question asks for requirements from the point of view of the airline, so your answer must consider what the airline wants from the system, not what customers want from it. There are many possible answers. Four examples of each type of requirement are given below.

Functional requirements
The system should:

- allow the airline to present users with flights in accordance with their stated preferences;

- monitor current bookings for all of its flights;
- change the price details of flights as they approach their maximum capacity;
- maintain a history of flights booked by each person who has become a member.

Non-functional requirements

The system should:

- be secure and accessible only to specified staff;
- be available at all times;
- be backed up daily;
- handle multiple users.

Task

Consider the worked example of Dalriada Airlines' online reservation system above. Identify three functional and three non-functional requirements of the system from the **customer's** perspective.

Data flow diagrams (DFDs)

When describing the user requirements for a system it can be useful to illustrate its operations as a series of **flows of data.** The concept is that the user is providing data which flows through the system, where processes perform tasks on the data. New data then flows back out of the system. As the name suggests, data flows can be modelled using **data flow diagrams** (DFDs). DFDs are an excellent way of illustrating the flow of data throughout a system. They can be drawn with minimal detail, to provide an overview of the data flow, or in great detail, providing a much more detailed view of the flow of data. They are quite simple in nature, relying on a small number of symbols. Because of this, a system described using a DFD can easily be understood, even by someone with only a limited knowledge of DFDs.

DFDs can have different levels of detail, or granularity. A DFD with a coarse degree of granularity can be used to give a high-level overview of a system. This is sometimes called a **Level 0** DFD, but is more often referred to as a **context diagram** because it provides the context or boundaries within which the system under consideration operates. More detailed DFDs can then be drawn at **Level 1** and so on down into more and more detail.

Context diagrams

Context diagrams typically do not contain very much detail and are used primarily to provide a graphical representation of the limits or boundaries of the system under consideration. They are most useful for providing a high-level view and are likely to be of most benefit to management.

For example, consider a system being designed for the sales department of ABC Ltd. This company accepts orders for goods from its customers and, once confirmation has been received from the warehouse that there is sufficient stock to facilitate the order, dispatches the goods to the customers. At this level we do not consider more detailed matters such as checking that the customer is credit worthy or generating invoices. The context diagram for this system would include the ordering of and distribution of the goods. However, the parts of ABC Ltd in which the company acquires the goods to sell and carries out the marketing would be outside the scope of the context diagram.

Context diagrams are drawn using the five basic elements shown in figure 2.1. Since context diagrams exist to delimit the system in question, data stores should be used sparingly at this level.

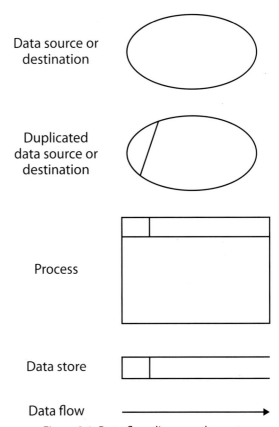

Data source or destination	
Duplicated data source or destination	
Process	
Data store	
Data flow	

Figure 2.1: Data flow diagram elements.

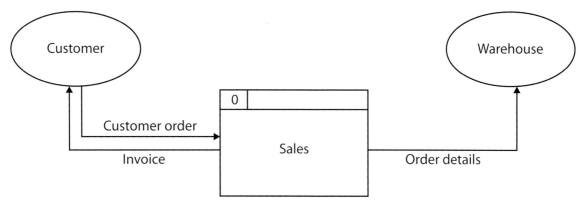

Figure 2.2: Example context diagram.

An example of a context diagram (Level 0 DFD) is shown in figure 2.2. In this example, we have identified a single process – Sales – and two external entities – Customer and Warehouse. When thinking about external entities, we sometimes differentiate between sources and sinks. In this case, the Customer is the source of the data (i.e., a Customer will initiate an order) while the Warehouse is the sink that receives the data (i.e., the Sales department will send shipment requests to the Warehouse).

Level 1 DFDs

Once a Level 0 DFD has been created, the processes can be described in more detailed in a **Level 1 DFD**. In doing so, we say that the Level 0 DFD has been

exploded into more detail. This process can be continued indefinitely, i.e. a Level 1 DFD can be described in more detail by exploding it in a Level 2 DFD and so on. Hence, as we increase the level of the DFD we introduce more detail. Each level is essentially the content (or a part thereof) from the previous level but showing more detail (i.e. with a finer degree of granularity). We can think of this detail as describing the sub-systems that make up the initial system. With each sub-system we introduce more precise and relevant details while maintaining consistency.

Note: At the time of writing, the CCEA specification only requires you to be able to produce context diagrams and Level 1 DFDs.

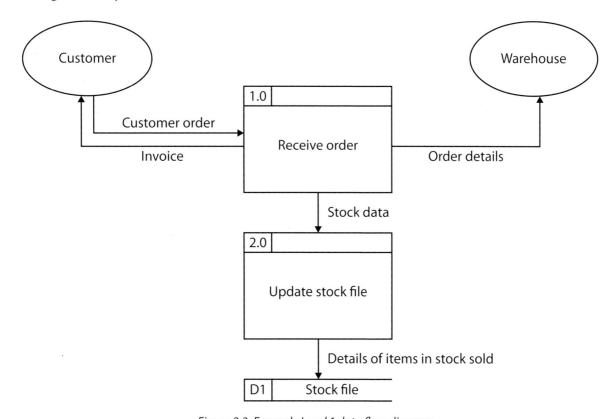

Figure 2.3: Example Level 1 data flow diagram.

As we move through the various levels, it is essential that we maintain a consistency between them. Hence, if we consider figure 2.2 we note that there is a data flow from the Customer entity to the Sales process and a data flow back to the Customer entity from the Sales process. At the next level, this two-way flow should still be present in the more detailed 'explosion' of the Sales process, as shown in figure 2.3.

Advantages of DFDs

DFDs are highly effective visual tools providing a pictorial representation of a system. They are extremely useful in providing an agreed, common understanding of the nature of the existing system. Carefully drawn, they can highlight issues such as potential bottlenecks and problematic data flows within the existing system.

Case Study

Road Grippers Ltd

Road Grippers Ltd specialises in selling car tyres to the general public. The company also sells larger tyres that are suitable for farm machinery (for example, tractors), public transport buses and industrial vehicles (for example, bin lorries and road sweepers). The company has just one depot at present but has plans for expansion in the future. The depot manager looks after the management of the company and one of his jobs is to ensure that stock levels are kept at an optimum level to service the requests for tyres.

The owner of the company feels that the current paper-based system is placing the company at a disadvantage. In particular, there are concerns that the company's stock control system is not working as it should. The owner would like to computerise the part of the system that involves its customers and warehouse. The owner believes that with such

a system the depot manager will have a better understanding of the stock levels and can better maintain these at an optimum level.

Following a meeting with a company tasked with carrying out this work a Level 0 Context diagram has been produced. This is shown in Figure 2.4.

The company has identified just one process – the Tyre Ordering System. It has also identified three sources and sinks – Customers, Warehouse and the Depot manager. Note again the difference between a source and a sink: a source is an external entity that supplies data to the system, while a sink is an external entity that receives data from the system.

In this simplistic view of the system a Customer places a Customer Order and this order enters the Tyre Ordering System as data. The Tyre Ordering System process needs to ensure that an order for tyres is made to the Warehouse (as Tyre Order data). It also produces Management Reports for

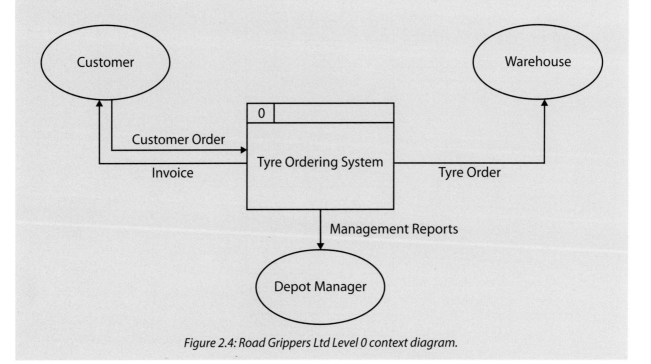

Figure 2.4: Road Grippers Ltd Level 0 context diagram.

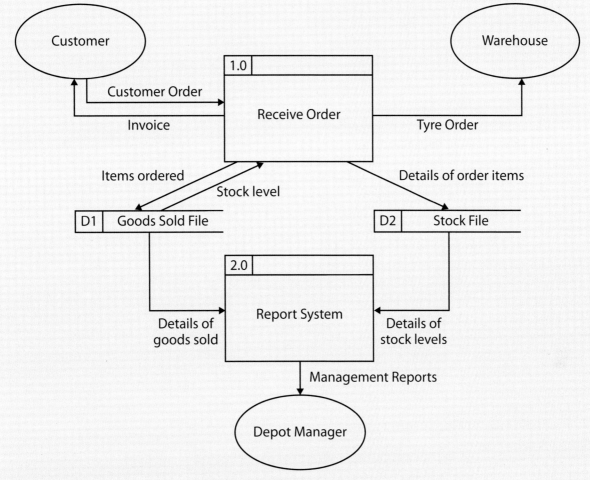

Figure 2.5: Road Grippers Ltd – Level 1 data flow diagram.

use by the Depot Manager.

The system analysts now explode the context diagram into a more detailed Level 1 DFD, shown in figure 2.5. In this case, the data stores required for the organisation have been identified. Note that the three sources/sinks (Customers, Warehouse and the Depot Manager) remain unchanged. This is not surprising since they are regarded as being outside the system. However, this diagram introduces significantly more detail for the Tyre Ordering System effectively replacing the single Process (Tyre Ordering System) with two smaller processes.

These two smaller processes are as follows:
1.0 Receive Order, the process by which an order is processed, a tyre order sent to the warehouse and records updated.
2.0 Report System, the process which pulls data from the list of goods sold and goods in the warehouse and generates Management Reports.

In this diagram, we also introduce two data stores (files) – the Goods Sold File and the Stock File. These files are then used to support the work of the Depot Manager, by contributing information to the Report System that generates management reports.

What has been described in this case study is very simplistic and many things have not been detailed such as:

- An initial check to see whether the customer is 'acceptable'. The definition of acceptable will vary but is likely to include checks to ensure that the customer has an account, has not exceeded their credit limit and has a good credit rating.
- Engagement with the customer to identify more precise requirements or to see whether they would be willing to accept alternative options.
- Payment arrangements, for example to decide if the customer has to pay on delivery or has 30 days of credit.

Task

A company's order processing system is described below. Draw a context diagram and a Level 1 DFD for this system.

The Customer (which lies outside of the organisation) places an order which arrives with the Sales department. A member of the Sales department reviews the order and depending on the nature of the order will instigate one or more discussions with the organisation's internal departments. If the order is for 20 widgets the internal discussion will be with the Warehouse department to see whether there are sufficient widgets in stock to complete the order. If the order is for a bespoke piece of furniture, then the internal discussion will be with the Manufacturing department of the organisation to see whether the necessary items/materials are in stock and whether there is space in their work schedules to manufacture/assemble the requested item within the requested time frame.

Once an order is confirmed, the Sales department will request that the Finance department raises an invoice with the customer. The Finance department will raise an invoice and process all aspects of the payment. If the item was out of stock, the Sales department will request that the Manufacturing department assemble the order and send the finished item to the Warehouse. Once the items for the order are ready it will be prepared for delivery and dispatched to the Customer.

Questions

1. Carrie Anderson runs two news agency shops in Ballymena and Limavady. She would like to open a third news agency in Coleraine. In order to find out if this would be profitable she decides to do some research. She could get data directly or indirectly.
   (a) Explain the difference between a direct data source and an indirect data source.
   (b) State one benefit and one drawback of a direct data source.
   (c) State one benefit and one drawback of an indirect data source.
   (d) Data could be used from any of the following sources. Indicate whether each of these is a direct or indirect data source:

   (i) Statistics about the population of Coleraine available on the Northern Ireland Statistics Agency (NISA) website.
   (ii) Create a questionnaire which people shopping on the main street in Coleraine on a Saturday afternoon will be asked to complete.
   (iii) Use data from an online survey about weekly expenditure sent to all Northern Ireland residents who have a Tesco loyalty card.
   (iv) Data from the Northern Ireland newspapers' websites showing circulation of each newspaper in Northern Ireland.

2. A fast food outlet wishes to computerise their system for taking customer orders, stock control and payroll system. It employs a team of specialists to carry out some fact finding.
   (a) Before computerising the system, the systems analyst needs to do some fact-finding. Why is it necessary to carry out some fact finding?
   (b) There are four main methods of fact-finding – interviews, questionnaires, observation and document sampling. State the main features, one benefit and one drawback of each of these methods of fact-finding.
   (c) The systems analyst needs to identify the functional and non-functional requirements for each part of the new system. What is the difference between functional and non-functional requirements? Give two examples of functional requirements and two examples of non-functional requirements of the payroll system.
   (d) The team wants to produce data flow diagrams (DFDs) during the design of the information system. Describe the purpose of a DFD.
   (e) Customers can only place orders in person. When an order is received by the attendant, it is sent to the kitchen. When the food is ready it is given to the attendant who asks the customer for payment. When payment has been made the attendant gives the food to the

customer and also hands them a paper receipt. Draw a context diagram (level 0 DFD) for the ordering system.

3. The diagram below shows a level 1 data flow diagram (DFD) for a system which records pupils' exam results. Identify the components A to D.

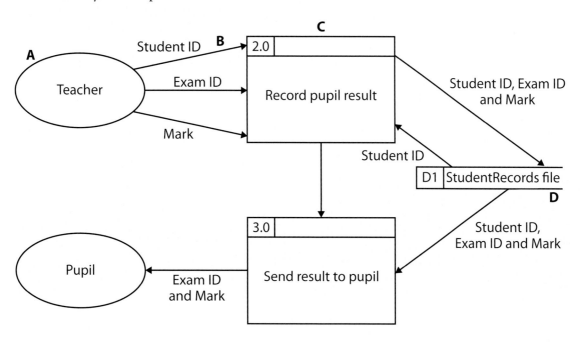

4. Draw a Level 0 (context diagram) and Level 1 data flow diagram (DFD) to authenticate a user's ID and password. Authentication is processed as follows:
   • User enters their ID.
   • A check is made to ensure this is a valid ID (details of valid user IDs and corresponding passwords are held in a Users file).
   • If it is an invalid ID, the user is informed and asked to re-enter their ID.
   • User enters their password.
   • A check is made to ensure this is the correct password for this user ID.
   • If it is an invalid password, the user is informed and asked to re-enter their password.
   • If both are valid, the user is sent a message "Valid Login".

5. What is the relationship between a context diagram and a Level 1 DFD? Describe the process of creating a Level 1 DFD from a context diagram.

6. Analysis is the first stage of the software development process. During this stage the analyst will interview the client.
   (a) Why is it necessary to interview the client?
   (b) Name two other techniques the analyst could use during the analysis stage.
   (c) At the end of this stage a document is produced. What is the name of this document?

CHAPTER 3
Systems Design, Development and Testing

3.1 Introduction

Systems design is a creative process which results in an outline description of the system to be developed. Systems design requires a thorough understanding of what the system is to be used for – hence it is only possible after the analysis phase. Crucially, the design must meet the user requirements that were identified in the analysis phase.

The output from the design phase will be a **design document** that includes:

- the design of the user interfaces;
- the specification of the data structures to be used;
- identification of any data validation or verification required;
- the design of any reports to be produced by the system.

Following the completion of the **system specification**, the **development** phase can begin. This is the phase in which the system specification is implemented and the code is created by software developers.

Because the system is developed as a series of inter-related software modules, these must be **tested** to ensure that they comply with the **system specification**. Testing must take place on the modules individually, and as they are integrated with each other.

In this chapter, we will explore the main principles and techniques used in the systems design and testing phases. Programming will be explored in more detail in chapter 8.

3.2 Systems Design

Two techniques that are used extensively in the systems design phase are **storyboarding** and **prototyping.** We will examine each in turn.

Storyboarding

The storyboarding technique can be used during the design and development of the user interface. The term 'storyboarding' has its origins in the film industry when the storyline for a film would have been illustrated as a series of sketches. This simple technique made it easier for those involved in the film to visualise what was happening and to identify any problems they were likely to encounter or any resources they were likely to need (for example, access to a particular filming location).

System designers are able to use the storyboarding technique to assist discussions with the users about the proposed user interface. Just as the technique can highlight issues in the film world, the use of storyboarding can identify issues in the software system. For example, during the development of a mobile application (or app), the following steps could be carried out:

- Diagrams would be produced for the user interface showing the contents of each screen of the app.

- All inputs and outputs would be identified.
- Details of navigation through the system would be recorded.

The main advantages of storyboarding are as follows:

- Storyboarding promotes early communication between designers and users.
- Storyboards can be used to obtain feedback on many aspects of the system early in the development cycle, including functionality and navigation.
- Storyboards can be created quickly and easily.
- Storyboards do not require specialist knowledge to understand.
- Changes can be more easily implemented earlier in the process.

Some disadvantages of storyboarding are as follows:

- Storyboards are unable to provide the higher-level interactive quality of other methods (such as prototyping – see below).
- Storyboards provide only limited detail.
- Storyboards do not accurately convey aspects of the user interface such as speed, system responsiveness or usability.

Case Study

Recipe Manager
Recipe Manager is a proposed smartphone app that allows a user to manage a collection of favourite recipes. Once a user has logged in, they are presented with a list of their recipes under various categories (for example, fish, beef or vegetarian) where the name of each recipe is presented as a clickable link. When the user clicks on a recipe name, a screen showing the list of ingredients and method is displayed, as well as a button that links to a page where the user can add a comment to the recipe text. The screens are linked as shown in the storyboard in figure 3.1.

Figure 3.1: Initial storyboard for the Recipe Manager app.

When the storyboard is presented to a panel of test users, it is reported that testers are irritated that they are required to click a link on the "Show Recipe" page to add a comment. Furthermore, once the comment has been added, they need to click two links to return to the list of recipes.

After considering the issue, the designers modify the navigation by incorporating the "Add Comment" functionality into the "Show Recipe" page, resulting in the simplified structure shown in figure 3.2.

Figure 3.2: Modified storyboard after user feedback.

Prototyping

In everyday life we understand the term **prototype** to mean a developmental or experimental entity. We often hear of a prototype car which has been developed for thorough testing and experimentation prior to possible mass production. Prototypes provide an opportunity for potential users to give their opinions. In the case of the car, this could include comments on space, aesthetics, road-handling capabilities, comfort and visibility. This allows for early user feedback and is likely to identify compromises or changes that need to be made to the specification.

Software prototyping is similar in that it involves creating early, experimental versions of software applications and sharing these with the users of the system to give them a 'look and feel' experience. By their nature, software prototypes are incomplete and can encompass a wide range of options. For example, they can be used in the following ways:

- To provide an exemplar of the proposed interface for the system, to determine whether this is acceptable to the users. Various arrangements of menus and colour schemes can be explored and the prospective users can give their feedback on these important aspects of the system. The client and the software vendor can use the prototype to check whether the proposed system meets the agreed user requirements.
- To help design the data model by focussing on what input is required, what output needs to be produced and what processes are needed to get the desired output. This allows the identification of required data tables and relationships.

While software prototypes are not full-blown systems, it is not uncommon for them to provide some limited functionality. They may well have menu systems that do not actually work (known as stubs) and even those that do work may only do so if provided with 100% accurate input as they may lack any significant error checking. For example, in the case of a database system, perhaps only the 'add' and 'delete' features in an add/edit/delete menu may be programmed and, even then, details such as the validation of email addresses are left to the imagination.

Both the software designer and the programmer can be involved in the prototyping process and both benefit from getting early user feedback prior to committing to the full development of the system.

The main advantages of prototyping are as follows:

- Prototyping can improve the quality of the user requirements and specifications provided to developers.
- Problems can be identified earlier in the development of the system.
- Refinements and enhancements can be identified and introduced earlier in the development of the system.
- Prototyping requires users to be involved and this interaction allows them to provide better, and more complete, feedback.
- The presence of the prototype can reduce the possibility of misunderstandings.
- Users can be involved in the user interface design resulting in an enhanced product.

Some disadvantages of prototyping are as follows:

- Depending on the time expended, the use of prototyping can be expensive and this can result in an unwillingness to make significant changes to the prototype.
- If a user indicates apparent satisfaction with an early prototype, better alternatives may be rejected too early.
- Prototyping may lead to insufficient reflection on possible extensions or enhancements.
- Users can be swayed by the aesthetics of the prototype and lose sight of more crucial elements such as accuracy and security.
- Excessive development time can be spent on the prototype.
- Seeing a prototype can lead to unrealistic expectations of how quickly the finished system can be implemented.

3.3 Testing

Software **testing** should be thought of as an ongoing activity that takes place at all stages of the system development process. Software is likely to be developed as a series of units, so each of these units has to be tested individually, and any errors detected addressed. However, this is not the end of the testing process. Once the various units have been tested and corrected, it is time to commence the **integration** process, where the units are put together. Just because each individual unit works satisfactorily in isolation does not mean that they will integrate seamlessly.

Case Study

Testing

The design for a new accounting software system requires the development of two units of software. The two units have been individually tested and each works correctly on its own. However, when integrated the system does not function as intended.

Each unit uses dates as part of its functionality. However, it is found that:

- the first unit stores and displays the date in a day:month:year format (for example, 12:10:2018 representing 12 October 2018).

- the second unit stores and displays the date in a month:day:year format (so 12:10:2018 will represent 10 December 2018).

Independently the two units work well and each displays dates in an understandable format. However, when the two units are brought together the different approaches to storing and displaying dates invalidates the integrated system.

The above case study illustrates how integration can throw up issues that would not necessarily be apparent at the unit testing stage. One way to reduce the chances of this type of error occurring would be to agree a consistent approach to data formats at an earlier stage. Nevertheless, errors of this nature – **integration errors** – often come to light only when elements of a system are brought together. Hence, it is not sufficient only to carry out testing of individual software units. Further stages of testing must be employed before the system can be regarded as complete.

The key steps in the testing process are:

- **Unit testing**, where the various software units are tested individually.
- **Integration testing,** where the effects of bringing together the individual software units are checked.
- **System testing,** to ensure that the system meets the agreed user requirements.
- **Alpha and beta testing,** which is carried out by the developers and end users to confirm that the system works as intended.
- **Acceptance testing,** carried out prior to the handover to the organisation. This final phase of testing is designed to ensure that the system integrates correctly into the organisation's other systems.

Each of these steps will be discussed in turn.

Unit testing

Unit testing is intended to check that the individual parts of a software system are correct and work appropriately under all circumstances. When done well, unit testing provides confidence that an element of software works. This greatly reduces the scope of any errors that are detected when integrating the unit into the system. Conversely, when unit testing is not done thoroughly it provides only limited confidence in the correctness of the unit when integration errors are detected. The two most common approaches to unit testing are black-box testing and white-box testing.

Black box testing

Black box testing is so called because it treats the software as a 'black box', i.e. the testing examines whether the functionality of the code is satisfactory without having any access to or knowledge of the source code. The code is effectively invisible to the tester, as if it is enclosed within a box. All that the software testers are aware of is what the software is supposed to do and their job is to confirm this is indeed the case. This means that testers can be non-technical and are not required to have a detailed understanding of the system being tested.

For example, consider a module of code that takes the number of electricity units consumed by a household and generates a bill for the consumer. A black box test might involve entering a series of values for the number of electricity units into the module and reviewing the bills produced against the bills expected. The module would obviously fail should there be any discrepancy between the actual bill and the expected bill.

White box testing

In white box testing the tester has access to the internal structures of the code and is consequently able to consider the various pathways through the code and can structure their testing to accommodate that. Conceptually one might consider the code as being enclosed within a glass box which allows the tester to view inside. White box testing requires an understanding of the code in use. The tester will review the code and look at the areas where errors might potentially occur. The tester will specifically focus on these areas to see whether the module behaves as expected.

Consider again the example of the module of code that takes the number of electricity units consumed and generates a bill. The code might calculate the bill in three different ways depending on the type of customer – for example using the standard domestic rate, the discounted domestic rate or the business rate. In this case, the white box test will specifically check each of these three sections of code to ensure each one generates a correct bill.

Integration testing

Integration testing takes place when the various units that have been tested individually are brought together, or integrated, into a single system. Typically, integration problems will occur at the interface between units and this may be due to inconsistencies in the data that each of them expects to receive. Where integration testing locates errors they need to be fixed, which may involve modifying individual units and carrying out further unit testing before returning to the integration process.

System testing

System testing (sometimes referred to as **application testing**) is performed on a complete, integrated system in order to assess and evaluate the system's compliance with its agreed system specification. System testing is essentially black box testing, but applied to a complete system rather than to an individual component and so the tester does not require technical knowledge of the implementation of the system. The testing requires **test plans**, discussed in the next section.

Alpha and beta testing

Alpha testing is the final phase of testing before the software is handed over to the organisation. This testing is conducted 'in-house' by the software developers. It will involve unit, integration and system testing and will follow a test plan. Minor changes can still be made to the system before the software goes to beta testing.

Beta testing comes after alpha testing and can be considered a form of external user acceptance testing. A group of potential users are given a pre-release version of the software which they test in a realistic environment. These beta testers undertake testing without the developers being present, to ensure that the product has as few faults (or bugs) as possible.

Acceptance testing

Acceptance testing is the final test of the system and is performed when the software is ready to be released, or handed over to the client, after system testing. It is intended to give the end users the confidence that the software meets their requirements. End users test the system in a 'live' environment with real volumes of data. The group then provides feedback on any problems. Upon the successful completion of acceptance testing, and assuming all problems have been satisfactorily resolved, the users 'sign off' the software and the contract is regarded as being formally completed.

Test Plans

Testing is not a random function. If we were asked to test out a new car, or a newly designed keyboard, we would expect to be provided with a list of criteria or features against which we are being asked to test or assess. In the case of a car, we might be asked to assess driver rear-view visibility or the ergonomics of the instrument layout. For a new television remote control, we might be asked to assess it in terms of the responsiveness of keys, or the ease of understanding. To undertake this, or any, testing we must first develop a **test plan**. This involves selecting the criteria under which the item is to be assessed and indicating how each criterion will be tested.

For example, suppose a new car is being tested. The testers decide that in one test the criteria under which the car is to be assessed is the rear-view visibility. They then need construct a test plan.

At first, the testers consider asking 20 people selected at random to test the visibility. Each person would be asked to adjust the driver's seat to give them a comfortable driving position and then comment on their rear-view visibility. However, this test plan is unlikely to guarantee a sufficiently wide range of drivers to ensure that all driving seat positions are tested. A better plan would be to systematically identify a range of drivers of various heights and builds, thereby ensuring that people with a wide range of physical attributes can comment on the visibility. In the revised test plan, the testers carefully select a range of drivers of different heights and builds. As before, each person is asked to adjust the driver's seat to give them a comfortable driving position and then comment on their rear-view visibility. However, by carefully selecting their test drivers, they can ensure that the full range of positions is tested.

In this case, the test might show that drivers taller than 1.90 m have a significantly restricted rear-view visibility when in their normal driving position. This information can then be fed back to the designers and they can revise the design of the car accordingly.

In the above example, the observation that very tall drivers had a restricted view did not come about by trial and error. The testers had developed a systematic plan to test the full range of possible scenarios, especially its vulnerable points, in this case very tall drivers. The purpose of a test plan, therefore, is to ensure that systems are tested **thoroughly.** The case study below contains a more detailed example of the development of a test plan.

Case Study

Examination Mark System
Consider an examination mark system with a number of components. The system takes marks in exams and converts them into grades (Fail, Pass, Commendation or Distinction). The system is used in three key phases, namely:

1. Data input: where a pupil's marks are entered.
2. Grade calculation: each pupil's marks are converted into grades.
3. Data output: the system prints out the names of the pupils together with their grades.

The system has been developed with three modules, one for each of the above phases. Even in this simple system, there are many areas where things could potentially go wrong.

Testing the data input module
In the test plan for this module, we need to incorporate a number of checks to see whether the data entered is a legal entry. If we assume that a pupil's marks must be integers in the range 0 to 100 inclusive, we need to test to see that our system deals correctly with marks that lie on the edges of or outside of this range. In other words, we have to **validate** the mark to ensure that the system will respond appropriately if the user enters marks that lie outside of this range. This does not mean that the system will be able to detect marks entered incorrectly (such as typing 56 instead of 65) but it can check to see whether the value entered is a legitimate mark. Thus figures such as 132, –20 or 69.5 will get rejected as illegal, whereas values such as 0, 72 and 100 will be accepted.

Testing the grade calculation module
When testing this module, we need to be clear that the mark is correctly converted into the appropriate grade. Suppose we have just four grades, such that:

- Fail = 0 to 39
- Pass = 40 to 59
- Commendation = 60 to 69
- Distinction = 70 to 100

A good test plan will check that marks such as 39 and 40 are converted correctly. These are known as the boundary values. We should always test at the boundary values, in this case 0, 39, 40, 59, 60, 69, 70 and 100.

Testing the data output module
The test plan for this module needs to check that the results are output correctly and that the grade calculated by the grade calculation module is output correctly in all circumstances. So again, we would check the full range of marks, including boundary values, and check that the grade that appears on the screen is correct each time.

Integration testing
What has been described so far is all basic unit testing. We must then test the interfaces between the various modules as they are integrated. For example, there is no point in the data input module deciding that the value entered is illegal, if it still

allows that illegal value to pass through to the grade calculation module of the system. In other words, it is pointless to conduct extensive 'intra-phase' (unit) testing if we ignore the 'inter-phase' (integration) testing.

Components of a test plan

The **test plan** usually takes the form of a detailed document which a team of testers must follow carefully. It will set out every single test they are to do on the system, what data they should enter and what result they should expect to obtain. Therefore, for each individual test, the test plan indicates:

- the part of the system to be tested;
- what is being tested;
- the test data to be used;
- the expected outcome.

Figure 3.3 provides an example of a typical test plan. The purpose of this test plan is to check that the system only accepts an initial data input number in the range 0 to 100.

This example identifies six tests, numbered 1 to 6

in Column A. The real test plan would contain more tests and be much longer than shown, so in reality the table would extend down to N tests. For each test, a total of seven columns (A to G) must be completed. The first five columns (A to E) are prepared by the person charged with developing the test plan. Column A is simply the test number while columns B to E provide details of what is being tested and what the expected results will be. The two remaining columns (F and G) are initially left blank.

The test plan is then handed to the person conducting the actual testing, the tester. Their task is to conduct the test and populate the two blank columns (F and G) with the results. If all is well, the expected outcome should be the same as the actual outcome. If this is the case the word PASS will be recorded in Column G. Column G will only receive the word FAIL if there is a difference between columns E and F, which indicates that the expected outcome differs from the actual outcome.

The test plan should ensure that the testing covers:

- the system requirements;
- how the system actually performs against the design;

Test	The part of the system being tested	What is being tested	Data to be used for the test	Expected Outcome	Actual Outcome	PASS / FAIL
A	B	C	D	E	F	G
1	Initial Data Input	Valid data – to check the system accepts a number within range	40	Accept		
2	Initial Data Input	Boundary data – to check the system accepts the lower limit	0	Accept		
3	Initial Data Input	Boundary data – to check the system accepts the upper limit	100	Accept		
4	Initial Data Input	Invalid data – to check the system does not accept a negative number	–34	Error Message		
5	Initial Data Input	Invalid data – to check the system does not accept a number with decimal places	5.9	Error Message		
6	Initial Data Input	Invalid data – to check the system does not accept a character	'X'	Error Message		

Figure 3.3: Example of a test plan.

- the various pathways through the system;
- all validation (data checking) routines.

In the case study above, we noted that it was necessary to test not just normal data but boundary values too. In fact, when formulating a test plan, we generally have three categories of test data:

Normal/valid test data values

These are test values representing what would normally be entered into the system. This is data, probably entered by the user, which is correct in both nature and format. In the examination mark case study this would include acceptable values such as 43, 55 and 89. Use of this test data allows us to confirm that the system behaves as expected when correct data is entered.

Extreme/boundary test data values

These are test values that also represent what would normally be entered into the system, but which lie at the boundaries. The data is again correct in both nature and format but is designed to test correctness at these boundaries. In the examination mark case study this would include values such as 0, 1, 99 and 100. Use of this test data allows the tester to confirm that the system behaves as expected when boundary values are entered.

Invalid/exceptional test data values

These may be thought of as data entered by the user that is not correct in terms of nature and/or format. In the examination mark case study this would include values such as 55.6, the character 'X' or the string "sixty". Use of this test data allows the system to confirm that it behaves as expected (in this case, trapping errors) when abnormal (incorrect or inappropriate) data is entered.

Questions

1. The design phase in producing any software system results in the production of a design document. List four features you would expect to find in the design document.

2. (a) Why is storyboarding useful when designing a user interface?
   (b) State two advantages and two disadvantages of storyboarding.

3. (a) What is prototyping and how can it be used in designing the user interface and the data model of a computer system?
   (b) State two advantages and two disadvantages of prototyping.

4. (a) Why is testing important?
   (b) What happens during each of the following phases of testing?
       (i) Unit testing
       (ii) Integration testing
       (iii) System testing
       (iv) Alpha testing
       (v) Beta testing
       (vi) Acceptance testing

5. (a) Define the main components of any test plan.
   (b) A travel booking system needs to determine if travellers are infants, children, adults or senior citizens to calculate the cost of any holiday. The age range for each category is as follows:

   Infant – Less than 2 years of age
   Child – 2 to 17 years of age
   Adult – 18 to 64 years of age
   Older Adult – 65 years or older

   Suggest suitable test data for each of the following categories:
   (i)   Valid infant
   (ii)   Valid child
   (iii)   Valid adult
   (iv)   Valid senior citizen
   (v)   Extreme infant
   (vi)   Extreme child
   (vii)   Extreme adult
   (viii) Extreme older adult
   (ix)   Two invalid test data values.

6. Explain how a systems analyst could be involved in the testing phase of a project.

CHAPTER 4
System Implementation

4.1 Introduction

While a new system is being developed, it is important to consider how the new system will be introduced and how it will replace the old system. This must take into account the resources – such as personnel, hardware and software – which must be in place before the new system can become fully operational. This usually also involves converting data from the old system into a format compatible with the new system. Once it is time to introduce the new system, a variety of changeover methods can be employed: parallel, direct, pilot and phased.

Another key part of the implementation phase is the provision of documentation, both to explain the system to the end users and to provide technical descriptions of the system for use during future maintenance. It is inevitable that periodic maintenance will be required on a system once it is in use, for a variety of reasons: to correct errors, to adapt to changing user requirements or to perfect its functionality.

4.2 Changeover Methods

In most cases a new computer system is intended to replace an existing system. This may be an older computer system, or perhaps a paper-based system. There are four different methods of managing the changeover from one system to another:

Parallel changeover

Parallel changeover is a very common method. It involves operating both the old system and the new system together until the new system has been proven to perform all of the required tasks. Each transaction is performed twice: once for the old system and once for the new system. The two systems are then compared to make sure the new one is producing the correct results. Once the new system has been found to work reliably, the organisation can stop using the old system and carry on operating with the new system only.

The main advantages of parallel changeover are as follows:

- It is a very safe changeover method because if the new system is found to have flaws then the old system will be there as a backup, avoiding unfortunate consequences of the failure.
- Changeover can take place over a period of time to allow staff to familiarise themselves with the new system.

The main disadvantages of parallel changeover are as follows:

- It is expensive and time-consuming to maintain two systems simultaneously.
- Time is also required to check the two systems against each other to ensure the new system is producing the correct results.
- Two duplicate sets of data must be maintained which can mean that the two systems are not always synchronised.

Direct changeover

Direct changeover is a riskier changeover method than parallel changeover. In this 'big bang' approach there is a specific date on which the old system is switched off and the new system introduced immediately. There are no parallel systems. This is an unusual approach because, should the new system fail, the organisation may have to revert back to the older system and this may not be easy; indeed, it may not be possible.

Figure 4.1: A street in Stockholm at the moment of changeover on 3 September 1967. Many people came onto the road to experience the change.

Organisations would only use this approach if there was no realistic alternative. For example, direct changeover was used on 3 September 1967 when Sweden switched traffic from driving on the left-hand side of the road to the right (an event known as Dagen-H, shown in figure 4.1). Clearly this was not something that could be introduced using a parallel changeover. It had to be extremely well-planned months in advance since the consequences of failure would be so high. There were some very strong arguments for change:

- all of the neighbouring countries (including Norway and Finland, with which Sweden has land borders) drove on the right;
- five million vehicles crossed the Swedish border each year; and
- approximately 90% of Swedes drove left-hand drive vehicles.

Although the proposal was unpopular with the general public, the Swedish government decided to make the change. As Dagen-H got underway, all non-essential traffic was banned from the roads for five hours between 01:00 and 06:00 to allow essential changes to be made, for example road signs moved to the other side of the road. All vehicles had to stop at 04:50, then carefully change to the other side of the road and stop again before being allowed to proceed at 05:00.

The main advantages of direct changeover are as follows:

- There is no duplication of resources.
- The new system is available to everyone at the same time.

The main disadvantages of direct changeover are as follows:

- It is very risky: if the new system fails, there is nothing to go back to.
- There may be a period of time between the old system being switched off and the new system being operational during which no system is available.

Pilot changeover

The **pilot changeover** method is where the new system is first tested in one department or section of the organisation. Once the users are convinced that the system is fully operational it can then be rolled out to the rest of the organisation. A good example of this might be a new system for a bank or building society. The new system could be piloted in a particular branch and then, once the system has been shown to be successful, it can be rolled out to all the other branches. Users in the pilot section can often be used to help train the remaining personnel to use the new system. This method of changeover is suitable when an organisation has a number of sections that are similar to each other.

The main advantages of pilot changeover are as follows:

- Only one section of the organisation is affected – the rest continue working on the old system until the new system is proven to work.
- Users from the pilot section can help to train new users.
- Any problems identified in the new system only affect one section of the organisation.

The main disadvantages of pilot changeover are as follows:

- Extra resources are required as two systems have to run concurrently in different sections of the organisation.

- It may not be easy to share data from the new system with sections which are still running the old system.

Phased changeover

This changeover method involves the gradual introduction of the system by activating different components one at a time. For example, if a business wanted to introduce a new financial system they may activate the new payroll system first and then, once they have ensured that that part of the system works to their satisfaction, they may activate the invoicing system, and so on. Over a period of time the whole system is gradually introduced.

The main advantages of phased changeover are as follows:

- Staff are introduced to changes in stages, which can be less stressful.
- If a problem occurs, it should only affect one section of the organisation.

The main disadvantages of phased changeover are as follows:

- The changeover can take a long time.
- One section of the organisation may ask for changes to the system after it has been introduced, which can slow down the implementation in other departments.

Choosing a changeover method

Most organisations are likely to seek the most cost-effective and low-risk approach they can to perform a changeover, given that the consequences of failure are often costly. Taking everything into consideration, the pilot method is therefore often seen as the most appropriate method of changeover. However, as we have seen, this is not always feasible. In such cases the direct changeover approach may need to be considered – but it is high risk and should be avoided whenever possible.

In an environment where the consequences of failure are catastrophic – for example, where serious injury or huge financial loss may result – the parallel approach might be the best option for reducing risk, despite the higher changeover cost. Finally, certain circumstances can lend themselves to a phased changeover – for example, where a system has many discrete elements. This approach can be a good choice when the various elements can be introduced independently.

4.3 Documentation

Documentation is produced at each stage of the software development process, for a number of reasons, including the following:

- To provide a starting point for the next stage of the development process.
- To provide a record of the work done at each stage.
- To aid maintenance by keeping a record of changes made.
- To track any changes of personnel in the development team.

Two main types of documentation are produced:

User documentation

User documentation is intended to be of use to the end user of a system. User documentation is typically made up of the following components:

- An introductory section that provides an overview of the system.
- A guide to the relevant hardware and software requirements for the system together with any supporting installation instructions.
- A user guide.
- A troubleshooting section.
- A FAQ (frequently asked questions) section.
- Additional training materials.
- An outline of backup and maintenance procedures.

Technical documentation

Technical documentation is intended to be of use to the administrator of the system, their maintenance staff and end users with good technical knowledge. Such documentation is typically made up of the following components:

- System specification/user requirements.
- Data models and data flow diagrams (DFDs).

- Input/output design.
- Report specifications.
- Query designs.
- The program code.
- Test plans with the data used and the results.
- Detailed hardware and software configuration.

4.4 Data Conversion

Data conversion relates to the task of converting the data used under the old system into the correct format for optimal use with the new system. When introducing a computer solution for the first time, this might involve converting an old paper-based system (such as forms, reports, orders and invoices) into electronic format. This will typically mean:

- creating a new database structure;
- employing people to manually type or scan its paper-based records into the new database;
- verifying and validating the data which is entered into the new system.

The amount of data could be quite large if, say, scanned images are to be included. Should the new system be simply an upgrade to an existing computer-based system, the transfer of data is likely to be a much quicker process, although it may require specialised and/or bespoke software to perform the task.

4.5 System Maintenance

In the same way that cars need to undergo regular maintenance, so too do computer systems. The term **system maintenance** refers to any change applied to a system over its lifespan.

No matter how carefully the design and implementation of a system, or how rigourously the application has been tested, there will always be a need for ongoing maintenance and adjustment.

This can be due to a number of factors including the following:

- A software error which has been uncovered during use.
- Some aspect of the organisation's business processes have changed and the system must be modified to reflect the new process.
- A security vulnerability has been discovered which must be addressed.
- A potential improvement has been identified.
- The operating infrastructure – such as the hardware or network – has been improved and the system should be changed to take advantage of it.

There are, therefore, many kinds of maintenance and system modification. They can, however, be categorised into three general areas:

Corrective maintenance

Corrective maintenance is undertaken to fix flaws or weaknesses within the system.

For example, an invoicing system may, despite extensive testing, still be found to issue bills to its customers for meaningless amounts such as £0.00. Alternatively, a security flaw that leaves the system open to attack may have been identified. Such flaws must be corrected before they cause difficulties.

The term **software patch** refers to a piece of software used to update, fix or improve a computer program or its supporting data. We say we 'apply' a software patch when we use it to correct a flaw in the system. Software patches are typically downloaded by the user and are often installed automatically.

Corrective maintenance is most important when the system has become insecure and/or does not perform the basic tasks as required. It is most often performed by the original programming team and, if the problem has been caused by programmer error, will be typically covered free of charge. Otherwise, the work may be covered by a rolling maintenance contract. Over time the amount of corrective maintenance ought to decrease as more and more errors are removed, leaving fewer and fewer undetected errors.

Adaptive maintenance

Adaptive maintenance means changes to the system in response to some change in circumstance. The change may be external (for example, a change in the rate at which VAT is charged) or internal (for example, a revised discount policy). Either way, the outcome is that the system can no longer perform its basic tasks and needs to be adapted to take account of these changes.

Adaptive maintenance is generally paid for by the client organisation, as the software is gaining new functionality that was not part of the original specification. A small amount of adaptive maintenance can be expected (and is probably inevitable), but too much may be a sign that the user requirements were not properly defined during the analysis phase.

Perfective maintenance

As the name suggests, the goal of **perfective maintenance** is to improve the performance of the software product after initial delivery. The system will have been operational for a period of time but some relatively minor changes have been identified that could improve it. Some examples of perfective improvements are as follows:

- Re-designing input forms to make them easier or faster to use.
- Improvements to the help system or the wording of error messages.
- Providing keyboard shortcuts to help experienced users navigate the system more quickly.
- Re-organising data (possibly archiving older records) to enable faster searching.
- Taking advantage of the space available on larger monitors.
- Redesigning interfaces for use on mobile devices.

Questions

1. Parallel running, direct changeover, pilot changeover and phased changeover are four ways of implementing a new system. Describe each of these, identifying one benefit and one drawback of each method.

2. When implementing any new system four types of changeover could be considered – **direct**, **pilot**, **parallel** or **phased**. Consider the situations below and suggest what method of changeover has been used in each case.
   (a) A restaurant chain tries out a new menu in one outlet before launching it in every restaurant.
   (b) A bookshop moves to new premises 200 metres away from their current location over a weekend.
   (c) An accounting firm keeps the manual system of recording transactions for clients for two months while simultaneously recording the transactions electronically.
   (d) A television company decides to commission one episode of a popular news discussion programme in a completely different format to test its popularity with the viewers.
   (e) A person gets a new laptop but still keeps their old laptop until they are happy that everything works as it should on the new machine.
   (f) A retail chain changes the layout of one store every week until all outlets have the same 'new look'.
   (g) A building society replaces its software system overnight.
   (h) A bank installs a new software system but also runs the old software system at the same time for a defined period.
   (i) A family decides to decorate their house on a room-by-room basis during the summer holidays.

3. Explain why it is necessary to produce documentation at each stage of the software development process.

4. (a) User documentation is intended to be of use to the end user of a system. List three components of user documentation.

(b) Technical documentation is intended to be of use to the administrator of the system, the maintenance staff and any end user with good technical knowledge. List three components of technical documentation.

5. Jane is the sole owner of a small florist business and specialises in providing different types of flower arrangements for individual customers. Although Jane enjoys creating the arrangements, the administrative side of the business takes a lot of time. Jane is heavily reliant on her paper diary which she carries with her at all times. When a customer telephones with an order Jane checks her diary to see if she is able to fulfil the order. If she can, she writes the customer's details (name, address and telephone number) as well as the details of the arrangement in her diary. Every Wednesday evening Jane reviews her diary and identifies what flowers she will need in order to complete the following week's arrangements. She then orders these flowers online from her dependable supplier who makes sure they arrive on the following Monday morning. Jane also uses her diary to records all costs and expenditure. When an order is completed, Jane prepares an invoice for the customer. This consists of the customer's details, the number of arrangements provided and the total cost. When Jane receives payment from a customer, she provides them with a paper receipt from her receipt book. Jane has noticed that she has a lot of repeat customers and that she is regularly recording the same contact details whenever she takes an order. Jane would like to make the system electronic.

   (a) With reference to the above system, explain how "data conversion" is necessary if an electronic system is to be introduced.

   (b) Suggest a suitable changeover system (direct, pilot, parallel or phased) for the florist business and justify your choice.

6. Define each of the following types of maintenance, giving an example of each:
   (a) corrective;
   (b) adaptive;
   (c) perfective.

7. The following list is a set of changes that have become necessary after a new software system has been deployed to a bank. Identify whether each one constitutes **corrective, adaptive** or **perfective** maintenance:

   (a) One year after installing the new financial software the bank opens some new branches. To accommodate this expansion, the software must cope with 60 bank tellers accessing the system simultaneously, rather than the current 40.

   (b) Just after starting to use the new system, a bank cashier has discovered that the system can only process bank accounts of exactly eight digits. However, some older back accounts which are still in use have only six digits.

   (c) In an ever more competitive market the bank decides that they must process cheques more quickly. Currently the bank guarantees that a cheque will be processed within 6 working days by running the batch software for cheque processing on a weekly basis. The bank would like all cheques processed within two working days.

   (d) Although the new software system provides clients with the ability to access their bank accounts online, the bank would like to re-design the user interface so that relevant information appropriate to that client appears when they first log in.

   (e) Six days after the system was installed, a customer informed the bank that they were not able to transfer £100,000 to another account. The finance team investigated this and discovered that the maximum amount that could be transferred between accounts was £65,535.

CHAPTER 5
Alternative Development Approaches

By the end of this chapter students should be able to:

- describe the main features of different approaches to systems development: the waterfall model, Rapid Application Development (RAD) and Agile; and

- evaluate different approaches to systems development: the waterfall model, RAD and Agile;

5.1 Introduction

The process from identification of a need to the successful installation of a new system is a complex one. There is no single, perfect method for developing systems, and the methodologies that do exist are regularly under review. All methods have both strengths and weaknesses that make them more suitable in some circumstances than others. In this chapter we will examine three distinct approaches to developing computer systems: the **waterfall model, Rapid Application Development** (RAD) and **Agile.**

5.2 The Waterfall Model

The classic methodology for systems development is the waterfall model, which dates back to the 1970s. The traditional waterfall model is made up of five distinct stages, each of which must be completed and verified before moving on to the next. Each stage results in an end product or **deliverable**. Progress flows from one stage to the next, like a waterfall. These stages are shown in figure 5.1.

Requirements (analysis) stage

During this stage, the analyst seeks to establish precisely the essential requirements of the new system. Their role is to fully understand these requirements and document them in a clear and consistent manner. Should the system in question be a replacement for an existing system, the analyst will look at the existing system and attempt to precisely identify the operation of the current system. This is known as fact-finding (see chapter 2).

In addition, the analyst will also establish a comprehensive list of requirements from the **users** of the system. For new systems (i.e., those that are not replacement systems) no current system is in existence, so there is effectively nothing to analyse. In these cases, the requirements of the users are of additional significance.

The end product (deliverable) of this initial stage of the waterfall model is a set of user requirements, usually referred to as the **system specification**, that is well-documented, clearly defined, unambiguous and complete. This last criterion is particularly important – if any significant user requirements are missed at this point it may prove to be difficult (and expensive) to include these requirements at a later date.

Design stage

This stage begins with the system specification from the first stage and leads to the production of a software design that will fully comply with it. The design identifies the various processes required as well as the

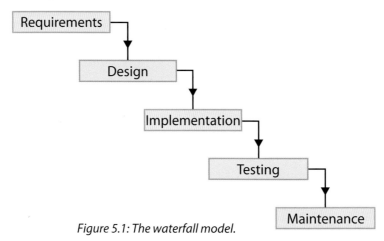

Figure 5.1: The waterfall model.

data inputs and outputs for each of these processes. Hence, the design includes both the software units and the interaction between them. It also involves the design of user interfaces and identification of hardware needs. The deliverable of this stage of the waterfall model is a **design document** (see chapter 3). In the coding stage precision is critical, so the design document must be as precise and unambiguous as possible.

Implementation (software development) stage

Following the design stage, the work can now be passed over to the software developers who will write the code and implement the final solution. The software developers work in accordance with the design document provided. This stage is typically performed using a team of programmers, each of whom is assigned particular tasks. For example, a project might have a team of twelve programmers who work individually, or they may be organised into four sub-teams of three.

Consider a real-world analogy. When a house is being built there will be many workers, organised into teams (for example, bricklayers, electricians and plumbers). Each have their own tasks to perform, yet each is working precisely to the architect's plan.

Programming will be discussed in more detail in chapter 8.

Testing (verification) stage

During this stage of the waterfall model the system that has been implemented is **tested** to make sure that it meets the system specification. The developed system must be tested to demonstrate that it works in accordance with the specifications to ensure there has been no misinterpretation or misunderstanding of the requirements (see chapter 3). While testing is

seen as a separate stage within the traditional waterfall model, significant ongoing testing often occurs during the previous (software development) stage, for example during unit testing of individual components.

Maintenance stage

Once a new system has been developed it needs to be installed (see chapter 4). In the short term this may involve the migration of existing data from an old system. In the longer term it will involve support and maintenance of the completed system. This final stage also covers any improvements or refinements made to the software, either in the period immediately following installation or over an extended period of time.

Advantages and disadvantages

The main advantages of the waterfall model are as follows.

- There are distinct stages, which means that work can be signed off from one stage before being passed on to the next stage. In earlier times, this was seen as highly desirable as work could be easily broken down into a number of clearly defined **deliverables**. This meant that work could be invoiced in stages. Compartmentalising the work into these stages supported this methodology.
- As each stage is likely to require staff with different skillsets, staff within a software company can be asked to work on a project for a period of time, before passing the project on to staff with different skills to carry out the next stage. This means that the same staff can work on the same stage of a range of different projects.

The waterfall model also has a number of major disadvantages as follows.

- Having staff that focus on a particular stage means that they are limited in the work they can perform. Modern software development often uses Agile methods (see section 5.4) which require staff to be multi-skilled. Having a team of multi-skilled staff means that they can support work in a range of different stages and can also be moved around from project to project to equalise workloads. This is more efficient and cost-effective for the software company.

- The waterfall model introduces a critical handover interface between stages. Any misunderstandings introduced at this interface may travel through the system for quite some distance before being detected. A good example of this might be a misunderstanding introduced at the requirements definition stage. Analysts involved in establishing requirements may feel that the client fully understands what they are asking for, and the client may feel that they have conveyed their thoughts unambiguously to the analysts. Nevertheless, what is agreed at this stage may not be entirely correct and this misunderstanding might only be detected at the implementation stage. Similarly, something that appears to be innocuous at the requirements gathering stage may cause disproportionate disruption at a later point. For example, should different rates of (say) VAT apply to goods destined for EU customers over non-EU customers, and this has not been identified as a system requirement, then the resultant software will not function as required and this may require major work to fix at a later stage.

Summary of the waterfall model

- It consists of a sequence of distinct stages (analysis, design, implementation, testing and maintenance).
- Each stage must be completed before the next stage begins.
- Deliverables are produced at the end of each stage.
- An earlier stage may need to be revisited if an error is found at a later stage of development.
- The user is only involved in the analysis stage (to find out user requirements) and the testing stage (to ensure the developed system works as the user intended).

Case Study

London Ambulance Service Computer System

In 1990 the London Ambulance Service (LAS) commissioned a software system to aid the dispatch of ambulances to incidents within the 600 square mile area which it covered. However, problems started just a few hours after the system was deployed in October 1992. Multiple ambulances were arriving at some locations, whereas no ambulances arrived at other locations. The system generated such a large number of error messages on the dispatchers' terminals that calls got lost in the system. People started calling back when ambulances they were expecting did not arrive, which made the problem worse. The LAS switched back to a part-manual system the following day.

Although there were problems with the selection of the vendor, re-use of existing hardware and a requirement to have the project completed within an 11-month timescale, there were a number of further key problems during the different stages of the development of this piece of software, including the following.

- At the requirements stage, key stakeholders (ambulance operators, dispatchers etc) were not consulted.
- There was no sign-off on the design document and it was later updated during the development of the project.
- During the implementation stage no quality assurance was performed and agreed changes were not tracked.
- No test plans were produced to verify the system.

The LAS failure demonstrates the serious consequences that can result from using the waterfall model in a haphazard or imprecise way.

5.3 Rapid Application Development (RAD)

Rapid Application Development (RAD) refers to a specific approach to systems development made popular by James Martin in the 1980s. As its name suggests, this methodology produces applications rapidly by dividing the project into a series of 'builds'. It enforces a strict timescale that cannot be overrun. Requirements are ranked in priority order, so not all the requirements may be implemented if time runs out, with those deemed merely 'desirable add-ons' sacrificed. The RAD methodology requires more user input than the waterfall methodology with prototypes frequently being produced and delivered to the users for their feedback. The RAD methodology consists of four phases, shown in figure 5.2.

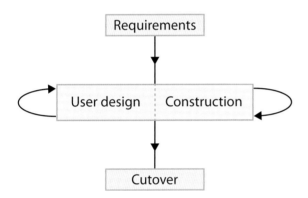

Figure 5.2: The Rapid Application Development model.

Requirements phase

This is the planning and investigative phase during which all interested parties meet and agree on the key elements of the project. This includes the scope of the project, as well as the various requirements of the project. This phase is similar in nature to the requirements phase of the waterfall model. However, unlike in the waterfall model, where it is essential that the requirements are fully thought through and agreed prior to the start of the project, RAD projects are often more flexible. It is generally easier to make modifications during software development than it is, for example, when building a bridge. RAD is particularly able to accommodate such modifications, and indeed encourages them, because the user is constantly involved in regular communication in subsequent phases.

User design phase

This phase is characterised by regular interaction between users and systems analysts with **prototyping** playing a key role in these discussions (see chapter 3). Because prototypes are simply mock-ups, with little functionality, they can be used to show the user what the system might look like at an early stage without having to wait until all the functions have been completed. This methodology is very useful for designing the necessary functionality as well as testing out a variety of alternative user interfaces.

Construction phase

This phase deals with the actual programming of the software. However, the software is continually being refined, adapted and enhanced in response to further user input. Users continue to participate in the process and can still suggest changes or improvements as actual screens or reports are developed. Furthermore, testing and the integration of the various software modules also takes place during this phase.

Cutover phase

The cutover phase is concerned with the transition from the old system to the new system. During this phase, the new system is brought into use. This involves a significant degree of further testing as the changeover of the system is effected.

Advantages and disadvantages

The key advantages of RAD are as follows.

- As its name suggests, when compared with traditional methods, RAD can shorten the timeframe within which the entire systems development process is completed. As a result, the new system is often built, delivered, and placed in operation much sooner.
- Continual involvement of the users. Prototypes are produced frequently and delivered to the user so that errors can be identified at an early stage.

Some disadvantages of RAD are as follows.

- RAD can usually only be undertaken by skilled practitioners trained in the methodology.
- RAD is often used when time is of the essence and a system must be developed quickly, and it can therefore be expensive.

Summary of Rapid Application Development

- It consists of four distinct phases (requirements, user design, build, cutover).
- Requirements are prioritised, so if time runs out the desirable add-ons may not be included.
- A new system is often built, delivered and operational much sooner than with other development methods.
- Can be expensive to develop as it can only be undertaken by skilled practitioners.
- There is more user involvement than in the waterfall method as prototypes are produced and delivered to the user for feedback.

5.4 The Agile Methodology

The Agile approach to systems development was popularised with the publication of *The Manifesto for Agile Software Development* in 2001. The Agile methodology seeks to bring together the best concepts from several different existing methodologies and techniques. Some of the key concepts used in the Agile methodology are discussed below. Agile prioritises early and continuous delivery of software, close collaboration between team members and the customer and welcomes changes to the requirements throughout the project.

Product backlog

When embarking on the project, an initial 'wish list' of what the product should be able to do is identified. This is referred to as the **product backlog** and the maintenance of this list is central to the Agile methodology as we shall see below.

Release backlog

At the start of each phase of the project **release planning** is carried out. The product backlog is reviewed and a set of features are identified for inclusion in the next increment of product functionality, called a **release**. These features are removed from the product backlog and put into a **release backlog**.

The product backlog is thus reduced in size and the release backlog now consists of those elements that have been extracted from the product backlog. As progress is made through the project and more and more work is completed, the product backlog becomes less of a 'wish list' and more of a 'to-do' list of features still to be completed.

The release backlog is then used to produce a list of work items that need to be carried out to complete the release. These work items may simply be tasks required to implement a particular piece of functionality (for example, to add a user help feature) or to improve some existing functionality. However, the release backlog can also include other project-related tasks such as things that need further investigation or to make an adjustment to the design.

Sprints

Once the release backlog has been created for the next phase of the project, an estimate is made of the time needed to complete each task and these are put into a priority order. This list is then used to produce one or more **sprints.**

Each sprint lasts for a few weeks and seeks to deliver a release. Hence the initial sprint will result in some very limited functionality, while each of the subsequent sprints will either add a new feature or improve the overall functionality. Over time the product is developed incrementally. Sprints are small enough to allow for effective time management, so ensuring that the project is kept to schedule. Once each task has been completed it is removed from the release backlog.

Scrum and Scrum team

Central to the Agile methodology are the **Scrum** and the **Scrum team**. The term Scrum refers to the overall framework for carrying out a project in sprints. It is a flexible development strategy where the entire development team works as one unit.

The **Scrum team** is made up of a number of people with the necessary skills to undertake all aspects of the work they are assigned. It consists of developers, testers and customers and has the capacity to analyse, design, develop and test the software. While most staff will have a particular specialist expertise, they will also be able to perform other functions so that they can contribute to other aspects of the work rather than focus entirely on their primary skills.

Members of the Scrum team are encouraged to meet in groups and everyone is allowed to have an input to the discussion. Staff are thus empowered to play a full role in proceedings rather than having the more passive roles often found in more traditional techniques.

A pivotal member of the team is the **Scrum master** whose role is one of responsibility and accountability. They are there to ensure that the team functions appropriately and to remove any obstacles getting in the way of progress. The Scrum master arranges meetings and will monitor the progress of the work being done. In many respects the Scrum master is in the role traditionally occupied by the project manager.

One member of the team is designated the **product owner** whose role is to act as the voice of the client. They are likely to be a member of the development team and are accountable for ensuring that the team delivers value to the client. They are also responsible for looking after tasks in the backlogs and establishing their priority. They monitor items being added to the product backlog to ensure that nothing spurious or unachievable is added.

Daily Scrum

Monitoring of Sprints is pivotal to the success of an Agile project and this is achieved by the use of **daily Scrums.** A daily Scrum is a brief meeting (around 15 minutes) during which all team members are asked three questions:

1. What did you do yesterday?
2. What are you planning on doing today?
3. What obstacles are in your way?

The Scrum master takes overall responsibility for resolving any problems identified, though everyone in the meeting has an input to the discussion.

Burn down charts

Burn down charts are a day-by-day measure of the amount of work that still needs to be done in a sprint, and are used to monitor whether work is keeping to schedule. A typical burn down chart for a sprint lasting 15 days is shown in figure 5.3. If the sprint progression was uniform over time (i.e. the team is moving in a constant manner from 100% of the work to be completed down to 0% of the work to be completed) then the graph should be a straight line from 100% to 0% over the 15 days, as shown. In

reality, unforeseen difficulties mean some tasks take longer than anticipated, so the graph of actual progress may deviate from the ideal path, as shown. The burn down chart allows the Scrum master to identify when the project is at risk of going over schedule and that corrective action may be required.

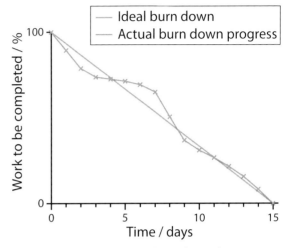

Figure 5.3: A typical burn down chart.

Case Study

National Bank Computer System
A software company is working on a new computer system for The National Bank. The system is already partially completed and it is time to plan the next release. The team start with a release planning meeting which takes up most of a morning. At this meeting, work items are selected from the product backlog for inclusion in the next sprint. The product owner directs what is selected, and this work becomes the release backlog.

Because some of the tasks in the product backlog are described only in loose terms, the Scrum team meets to define them more fully. They then estimate the effort required to complete each of the tasks in the release backlog, and decide who is going to do what. The team members are aware that these are provisional allocations of tasks, and that it may change later in the sprint.

The team then begins work on the release with team members working alone or in groups as necessary to carry out their tasks. Each morning they have a short daily progress meeting of 10–15 minutes and these are led by the Scrum master. Everybody stands during the meetings to encourage efficiency. At each meeting the burn down chart is updated and discussed, which sometimes leads to people being shifted from one task to another to overcome difficulties.

After three weeks, the sprint finishes with two meetings facilitated by Scrum master.

The first of these meetings – the sprint review – takes a few hours and allows the team to review their completed work on the actual product. They also take note of any planned work that was not completed on time for this release. The completed work or release is then presented to the product owner.

Later the team holds the second of these meetings – the sprint retrospective meeting – which is dedicated to reviewing the process itself (not the product) with all team members reflecting on the past sprint and identifying what went well, what could be improved in the next sprint and so on.

Advantages and disadvantages

The Agile approach to systems development is currently very popular. Its main advantages are as follows.

- The project can start quickly, with important requirements being given highest priority, and then evolve.
- Deliverables are created at an early stage.
- Ongoing communication with the customer means it is less likely that there will be misunderstandings.
- It is flexible because the team members are multi-skilled and can be moved around in order to support work that is taking longer than estimated.

The main disadvantages of Agile are as follows.

- It can prove difficult to accurately estimate the time needed to complete activities and the subsequent allocation of the team members to undertake the work.
- The accuracy of the time estimates are often dependent on the experience and skill of the Scrum master, so it is important to choose someone for this role carefully.
- Documentation may be of poorer quality or less detail when compared to systems developed using more traditional techniques.

Summary of the Agile methodology

- The project is undertaken in a series of iterations called sprints.
- A product backlog (wish list) is produced at the start of development.
- As features on the product backlog are selected for implementation, these are moved to the release backlog.
- The release backlog is used to provide early deliverables.
- The Scrum master co-ordinates members of the Scrum team to develop the project.
- The user is continually consulted throughout the development of the project.

Task

Robinson Parts Ltd is a small business which sells car parts to members of the public. The business is run from a small office with an adjoining store in John Robinson's back yard. Currently, customers can visit the business directly or telephone with their order.

Customers who visit the office first ask for the required part(s). One of the two order clerks checks the ledger (which contains part name, quantity in stock and price per part) to see if the order can be serviced. The order clerk then prepares an invoice which the customer takes to the store manager who gives it to one of three store operatives who get the parts for the customer. The order clerk then updates the quantity in stock in the ledger.

When a customer telephones the business, a receptionist writes down the order and passes it to one of the order clerks who checks the ledger to see if the order can be serviced, then prepares an invoice. A copy of the invoice is given to the store manager who gets one of the store operatives to gather up all the parts on the order and box them ready for collection. When the customer comes to collect the order, he or she goes to reception, pays for the parts and is given a receipt which they take to one of the store operatives who hands them the boxed order.

When new parts arrive from suppliers they are sent to the store where one of the store operatives checks the list and places the items onto the shelves. They then give the list of parts which have arrived to one of the order clerks who will update the stock level of the newly acquired parts in the ledger.

When the price of a part changes one of the order clerks updates the price in the ledger.

Mr Robinson has recently discovered that some customers, whose orders have been successfully processed, arrive to collect their goods at the store only to find that the part is out of stock. This has usually happened because the stock level in the ledger has not been updated. Mr Robinson has decided to invest in a bespoke computer system. He would like the system to provide the following facilities:

- To maintain a record of all parts that the company sells, including the sales price and quantity in stock and, if possible the name of the supplier and the time it takes for that part to arrive once ordered (there is only one supplier for each part).
- To produce receipts automatically.
- To record a stock re-order level (the number which indicates more stock needs to be ordered).
- To maintain a list of supplier details.
- To create a list of customers so that the company can offer a mail order service.

Consider each of the three development methodologies (waterfall, RAD and Agile) and decide which of these would be most suitable methodology for creating this computerised system. Justify your answer.

Questions

1. The waterfall model is often used to develop an information system.
   (a) Describe the main features of the waterfall model.
   (b) Briefly describe each stage of the waterfall model.
   (c) Describe the users' involvement in producing a software system using the waterfall model.
   (d) List two advantages and two disadvantages of the waterfall model.

2. Rapid Application Development (RAD) is a model of systems development.
   (a) Describe the main features of RAD.
   (b) Briefly describe each phase of the RAD model.
   (c) Describe the users' involvement in producing a software system using the RAD model.
   (d) List two advantages and two disadvantages of the RAD model.

3. The Agile approach to systems development has become very popular in recent years.
   (a) Describe the main features of the Agile approach to systems development.
   (b) Describe the users' involvement in producing a software system using the Agile approach.
   (c) List two advantages and two disadvantages of the Agile approach.

CHAPTER 6
Software Projects

By the end of this chapter students should be able to:

- describe the main elements in the organisation of a software project: resources, constraints and risks;
- explain the main features of project management for a software project;
- evaluate the use of project management tools: Gantt charts and critical path analysis; and
- describe the importance of version management during systems development;

6.1 Introduction

Regardless of whether one is using the waterfall model, RAD, Agile or some other methodology, the central task in a software project is to meet the project objectives by deploying **resources** within given **constraints** while managing **risks**. In this chapter we will look more closely at these elements, and then look at the role of software project management and its associated tools.

6.2 Elements in the Organisation of a Software Project

Resources

The resources available to a software project can be **human** (for example, programmers, graphic designers and database administrators), **technical** (for example, network bandwidth and processing power), **financial** (for example, the available budget) or **physical** (for example, available accommodation and transport links).

However, resources can also be classified in terms of the way they can or cannot be used for the project, as follows.

- **Availability** – Resources are **recurring** if they do not reduce in quantity as they are used, for example staff dedicated to the project, or **depleting** if they diminish over time, for example time and money.
- **Location** – Resources are **fixed** in location if they cannot readily be moved, for example

computing resources, or **movable** if they can be shifted from one location to another, for example staff.
- **Elasticity** – An **elastic** resource is one that can be increased or decreased in size. For example, it is theoretically possible to invest more money or assign more staff to a particular project (though this may not be possible in practice; see the next section on Constraints). The volume of an **inelastic** resource, however, cannot be changed, for example the amount of time in a project with a hard deadline.
- **Ownership** – A **dedicated** resource is assigned solely to the project for its entire duration, whereas a or **shared** resource is also used on other projects. Human resources can fit into either of these categories. For example, a programmer may be dedicated solely to the project, while a graphic designer may work on multiple projects at the same time. Funding, by contrast, is normally dedicated to a particular project.

It is important that resources are managed correctly to maximise the benefit that they bring to the project. **Resource management** is concerned with the following activities.

- **Planning** – This task is usually carried out ahead of work commencing. The software project manager makes an estimate of the number of units of each resource required, and these resources are requested from those who control them. They then schedule the use of each resource so that it is sufficiently available at each stage of the project.
- **Deployment** – Once the project is actually underway, the schedule is implemented and

the resources are physically allocated to the various development activities. Deployment also requires the software project manager to monitor the project to ensure that each development stage is completed on target and, if not, to manage resources sufficiently to correct the problem.

- **Release of resources** – Once a particular stage is completed, the software project manager compares the resources actually consumed against those planned. If a stage has consumed more or less of a resource than anticipated, then this is documented so that lessons can be learned for the future.

Constraints

Every software project manager would prefer an unbounded supply of resources to deliver their project. Unfortunately, in the real world, projects are restricted by **constraints** that have to be taken into account when planning a project. These constraints usually fall into one of three categories.

- **Scope** – The characteristics of the final product may be limited by the client. For example, at project commencement the client might have specified the number of users that must be able to have simultaneous access to the system, the response speed of the system, the compatibility of the system with different web browsers and/or mobile platforms. These are constraints because they have been taken out of the hands of the developer.
- **Time** – The project will normally be time-limited with a fixed deadline by which the final system must be delivered. It is important that the project manager pays careful attention to the timeframe available when signing off on the scope of the project to ensure that the work is actually achievable in the available time.
- **Resources** – There is generally a limit to the volume and availability of resources for a particular project. Even resources that are theoretically elastic in nature are likely to be limited in practice. For example, there is generally a ceiling to the amount of money that can be allocated to a project.

It is important that constraints are clearly and unambiguously set out so that they are understood by all parties. For example, it is inadequate for a client to request that a system be delivered "as quickly as possible" or "as cheaply as possible" as this wording is open to many different interpretations. It is much better to be explicit with statements such as "the latest acceptable delivery date is 31 December" or "the maximum budget available is £100,000".

Risks

Everything we do in life carries an associated **risk**. Risks may be trivial (causing minor annoyance), more serious (having a pronounced effect on health or wealth) or potentially fatal. In the context of software projects, risks are anything which could have a detrimental effect on the project or even cause the project to fail. It is vital, therefore, for the software project manager to identify the sources of risk and take steps to manage them. Some of the main risks faced by a software project are as follows.

- **Time** – The project will have an agreed deadline that must be met. Missing this deadline may have a negative effect on the client (for example, losing market share to a trading customer) and may also be disastrous to the developer who may have to fund the cost of additional development if a fixed price for the project has been agreed. There is also the risk of reputational damage on both sides.

- **Requirements shift** – It is important that the developer and the client are clearly agreed on exactly what will be produced at the outset of the project. If the user is not involved sufficiently at the analysis stage, this can result in changing requirements and runs the risk of missing the deadline and/or increasing costs.
- **Staff turnover** – When a developer has to leave a team (for example, moving to another job or going on maternity leave) they may take vital knowledge with them. It is important that the software project manager minimises this risk

by insisting that the team collaborate and, as far as possible, to share knowledge.

- **Productivity** – On a task that has an extended timeframe, it is human nature to start slowly, safe in the (perhaps false) assumption that there will be sufficient time to catch up later. The software project manager should guard against this risk of complacency by splitting the task into a number of smaller sections, each with their own deadline, to keep the project on track.

6.3 Software Project Management

Software project management first emerged as a specific role in the 1970s, following a series of high-profile software project failures (see the software crisis in section 1.4). Although it shares many characteristics with general project management, there are some important differences, as follows.

- Software is **intangible**. In a traditional engineering project, it is difficult to claim that a building is nearly finished if there is no visible sign of the building rising from the ground. However, it is harder for an observer to judge the progress on a software project that they cannot see.
- Software is **bespoke**. Most large software systems are 'one-off' projects, having been built for a specific customer for a specific purpose, with experience gained in one project being of little benefit in another. A project manager for the building of a small housing development is likely to have had prior experience in managing a similar development. They will, therefore, be aware of potential pitfalls. While a software project manager is likely to have experience of managing other software projects, the bespoke nature of the work means that it is less likely that specific problems will have been encountered previously. Similarly, solutions devised for previous projects are less likely to be relevant to the bespoke system.
- Rapidly changing **technology**. The reason that many software projects are undertaken in the first place is to take advantage of new developments in computing technology. Given the pace of technological change, it is possible that new or improved technology will become

available during the life of the project and the software project manager may then instigate changes to take advantage of them. This flexibility and agility is, of course, important as it helps to futureproof the project. However, a software project manager is more likely to encounter such change than a project manager for the construction of a building, since it is less likely that a brand-new technique for a routine task such as installing wiring or plumbing will appear during the lifetime of the project.

The role of the **software project manager** is to control all aspects of system analysis, development and deployment. This involves developing a realistic plan that describes the software to be produced, the acceptance criteria to be used and how the system will be maintained. The software project manager also has responsibility for scheduling the project development activities and managing the project risks.

The key to ensuring the success of a software project is establishing clear project objectives, agreed between all parties, at the start of the project. Each objective should be made up of the following elements.

- A clear **statement** of what the objective is intended to achieve. For example, a local furniture showroom may want to replace a paper-based customer records system and define their objective as: "to produce a software program to keep track of up to 10,000 customer accounts with up to 100 transactions per customer, to be deployed by December".
- **Performance indicators** (metrics) that will be used to measure whether an objective has been met. For example, the time taken to produce the system, the resulting increase in productivity, the reduction in errors or a measure of user satisfaction.
- A list of the **values** for each performance indicator that would be sufficient to regard it as a 'success'. For example, deployment within five months, a 30% reduction in user errors over a six-month period, or a user satisfaction score of at least 80%.

It is important for objectives to be precisely specified so that each party has the same view of what will represent 'success'. It is often tempting to specify a range of acceptable values (for example an increase in sales of between 10% and 20%), but this can lead to one party considering the objective to have been fulfilled by a 10% outcome, while the other party may only consider the higher figure to be a success.

A useful mnemonic for setting objectives is to remember the letters of the word SMART, where each objective should be:

- **S**pecific – clearly defined with no possibility for misinterpretation.
- **M**easurable – each objective should have a clear, quantifiable metric that can be used to assess success (for example, time, money or size).
- **A**greed – the objectives should be signed off by both sides before development begins. If objectives are not agreed, then they should be revised until agreement is reached.
- **R**ealistic – the project should have objectives that the development team believes they can meet with the resources available.
- **T**imed – each objective should have a target date by which it will be achieved.

6.4 Project Management Tools

The task of the software project manager is complex, requiring the oversight and coordination of many different aspects of the project at the same time. The task is further complicated by the fact that, very often, one element of project development is dependent on the completion of one or more other elements. This creates a critical point where a delay at one stage can have significant knock-on effects on other stages.

Consider a real-life project of a team of workers constructing a garden shed. If we assume that the garden shed comes in a 'flat pack' we can easily identify the main tasks for the team. These might include:

- Task 1: Prepare the **groundwork**.
- Task 2: Insert the **wall supports**.
- Task 3: Insert the **actual walls**.
- Task 4: Put on the **roof**.
- Task 5: **Paint** the shed.

The order of the tasks for the construction of the garden shed is Task 1 then Task 2 then Task 3 etc. The starting point is Task 1 (groundwork) and the team cannot commence Task 2 (wall supports) until this task has been completed. Once the wall supports are in place, the team can then commence Task 3 (actual walls) and once these are in place, they can commence Task 4 (roof) before, finally they perform Task 5 (paint). This order is important and there is an obvious dependency between the tasks. Clearly, the team cannot insert the actual walls until the appropriate wall supports are in place. Similarly, the team cannot undertake Task 4 (roof) until all the walls have been completed.

It is important to note, however, that there may be occasions when some tasks (or parts of some tasks) can be undertaken in parallel. In our example, the team need not necessarily wait until a task is fully completed before they start the next task. For example, suppose the team has completed part of Task 2 and inserted the wall supports for the first side of the shed. Other members of the construction team might be able to commence Task 3 and insert the actual walls on the first side while their colleagues are inserting the wall supports for the second side of the shed. Those working on Task 2 (wall supports) will effectively be working 'one side ahead' of those working on Task 3 (actual walls). There may, therefore, be some overlap in the work schedule for Tasks 2 and 3.

Project management tools are software programs that help the project manager organise, plan and monitor the progress of a project. Typically, these tools facilitate the following tasks.

- Planning each task required to complete the software project.
- Delegating members of the software development team to particular tasks.
- Monitoring the progress of the project.
- Providing the analytical capability to identify possible future problems.

These tasks should ensure that there is optimum deployment of resources so that the project is kept on schedule and within budget.

In the rest of this section we shall look in more detail at two particularly useful project management tools: **Gantt charts** and **critical path analysis**.

Gantt charts

One of the most widely used project management tools is the **Gantt chart**, which is a form of bar chart that tracks tasks against time and allows the manager to keep track of the tasks, milestones and interdependencies. Gantt charts represent each task as a horizontal bar, where the position and length of the bar reflect the start date, duration and end date of the task. This allows the manager to see easily:

- what each task is;
- when each task is scheduled to begin and end;
- how long each task is scheduled to last;
- the degree of overlap between tasks; and
- dependencies between activities.

The Gantt chart shown in figure 6.1 describes a project consisting of seven tasks (named A, B, C, D, E, F and G). Note the column on the left labelled 'depends on' showing which tasks need to be completed before this one can begin. In this project, task A is carried out first. Once task A has been completed tasks B and C can commence, so both tasks can be carried out independently and concurrently. Once task B is complete, task D can begin while task E can begin once task C is complete. The remaining tasks (F and G) run in sequence as soon as all the other tasks are finished.

The Gantt chart provides a clear visual representation of the overall duration of the project, as well as the duration and relationship between the individual tasks. It can also be used to see the knock-on effects of delays. For example, it can be seen from figure 6.1 that task D can overrun by up to three days with no effect on the overall project duration (since task F cannot begin until **both** D and E are complete), while any overrun on (say) Task E will have an adverse effect on the overall project duration.

Critical path analysis

The above discussion allows us to identify the concept of **critical tasks**. Critical tasks are those tasks for which any delay will have an adverse effect on the overall project schedule. The **critical path** is the chain of critical tasks whose schedule is essential in order that the project is not delayed. It is important for the project manager to identify the critical path as they may need to pay particular attention to these activities to ensure the deadline is met. The critical path is not always clear from a Gantt chart, but a process called **critical path analysis** (CPA) allows a software project manager to analyse all the project tasks to identify it so that delays can be minimised and any potential conflicts resolved.

In CPA, a project is presented as a circle and arrow diagram, where circles (known as **nodes**) represent events within the project (such as the start and finish

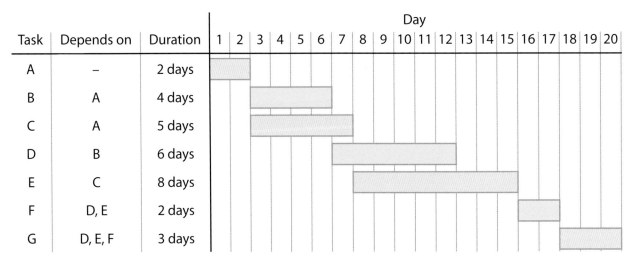

Task	Depends on	Duration	1	2	3	4	5	6	7	8	9	10	11	12	13	14	15	16	17	18	19	20
A	–	2 days																				
B	A	4 days																				
C	A	5 days																				
D	B	6 days																				
E	C	8 days																				
F	D, E	2 days																				
G	D, E, F	3 days																				

Figure 6.1: A Gantt chart.

of tasks) and arrows represents the tasks themselves. An example is shown in figure 6.2, showing how task A from the Gantt chart in figure 6.1 would be shown under critical path analysis. Node 1 represents the start of task A, and node 2 the end of that task two days later. The arrow represents task A itself, labelled with the duration of two days.

Figure 6.2: Circle and arrow diagram for task A.

The right-hand side of each node is divided into two sections displaying the **earliest start time (EST)** for the activity in the upper section and the **latest finish time (LFT)** in the lower section. The EST is the earliest time that an activity can commence, based on the completion of the previous activity, while the LFT is the latest time by which that activity must be complete.

To complete the CPA for the whole project, we first connect the tasks according to their dependencies.

For the previous seven-task example, this results in the structure shown in figure 6.3. Observe that task B and task C both begin at the node that marks the end of task A, because tasks B and C depend on task A, and so forth.

Next, we assign the **EST** to each node by working from left to right and calculating the earliest time that each activity can begin, based on the completion of previous activities. For example, node 1 (the start of the project) can begin on day 0 while node 2 (start of tasks B and C) cannot begin until day 2 (that is, after task A is complete). Where there is a conflict, we take the **highest** value. So, for example node 5 (the start of task F) must wait on the completion of task D (day 12), but also on completion of task E (day 15), therefore node 5 has an EST of 15. The addition of all the ESTs results in the diagram shown in figure 6.4.

Next, we add the **LFT** to each node, this time working from right to left. The LFT is the latest time that a task can be completed without affecting the overall project duration. So the first step is to set the LFT of the final node (node 7) to the total project duration (20 days). Then we subtract the duration of

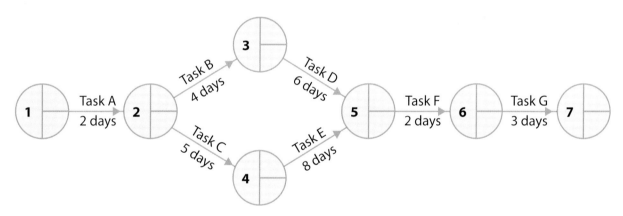

Figure 6.3: Initial critical path analysis for the whole project with all nodes and tasks added.

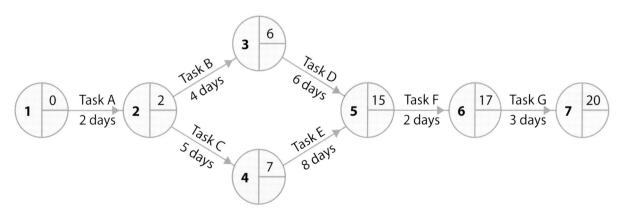

Figure 6.4: Critical path analysis for the whole project with ESTs assigned to each node.

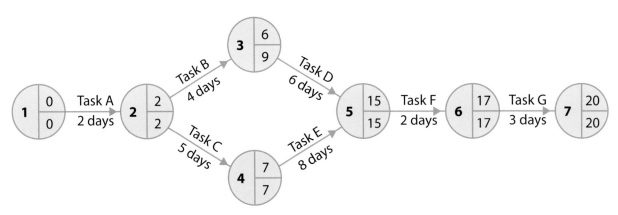

Figure 6.5: The completed critical path analysis for the whole project with LFTs assigned to each node.

the previous task (3 days for task G) to get the LFT of the previous task (node 6, 17 days). Where we have conflict, we take the **lowest** value. So, for example at node 2 the path through node 3 gives an LFT of 9 – 4 = 5. However, the path through node 4 gives an LFT of 7 – 5 = 2. Therefore node 2 has an LFT of 2. The final CPA diagram, with all LFT value completed, is shown in figure 6.5.

Once the diagram has been completed, we can use it to identify the critical path for this project. Look for every node where the EST and LFT values are the same. These represent the nodes where there can be no delay between completing the previous task and starting the next one without prolonging the overall duration of the project. The critical path is the set of tasks that connect these nodes. In this example, the critical path is through tasks A, C, E, F and G. This is indicated on the CPA by striking two short lines across the activities as shown in Figure 6.6.

It is also easy to see from the diagram that the pair of tasks B and D could be delayed by up to three days without affecting the total duration of the project. If task B runs three days late, it will complete on day 9, which still leaves six days which is sufficient to complete task D. Alternatively, if task B runs to

schedule, it will be completed on day 6, allowing a maximum over-run of three days for task D.

Advantages of using Gantt charts and critical path analysis

Gantt charts and critical path analysis are valuable tools in the management of software projects. Their key advantages include the following.

- When a project is made up of a number of more manageable tasks, they can help the project manager identify which elements can be completed in parallel, thus minimising the overall project duration.
- They can help with resource planning and allocation, allowing the project manager to schedule the acquisition of resources to coincide with the EST of the task for which they are needed and to schedule their release to coincide with the task's LFT.
- CPA can help to identify bottlenecks and resolve conflicts. It also allows the project manager to respond to delays by intelligently reallocating resources so that the overall delay is kept to a minimum.

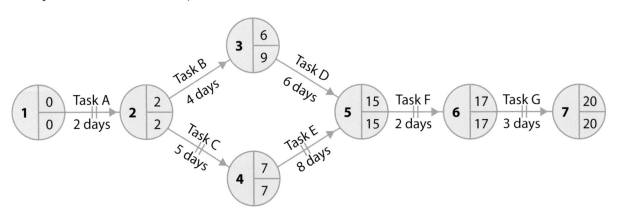

Figure 6.6: The completed diagram with the critical path for the whole project marked.

6.5 Version Management

Version management is the process by which a team of developers keeps track of changes to their code files over time. It provides a means by which they can return to a previous working version of a program if an error is discovered. They are particularly important in large systems with teams of programmers collaborating on a shared set of program files, where allowing anyone to change any file in an unrestricted manner would quickly create chaos. Version management systems require all code files to be kept in a file **repository**, where access is monitored and every change made to the code is tracked. For each change, the system records:

- who made the change,
- when the change was made, and
- a note for the developer to describe the details of their change and any knock-on effects that require action as a consequence.

A system being managed via version management is often represented as a graph structure, with each new revision represented by a new node on the graph, as shown in the following example.

Worked Example

Figure 6.7(a) represents a code file, F, in its initial version, v1. Suppose a developer makes a revision to this file and saves it back to the repository. This will result in the creation of a new version of the file, which we will call v2. We represent this on the graph by drawing a second node for v2, and connecting it to v1 via an arrow, as shown in figure 6.7(b).

(a)   (b)

Figure 6.7: Version management graph showing (a) a code file, F, in its initial version and (b) after a second version of the file has been created.

Sometimes multiple developers are working on the same code file at the same time. Suppose that:

- Aoife makes amendments to F v2 and creates F v3.
- Barbara also makes amendments to F v2 and creates F v4.

The new situation is illustrated in figure 6.8 which now shows two different versions existing side-by-side. These will need to be merged so that both sets of changes are incorporated in a new (single) version. In our example, versions v3 and v4 are merged back into a single consolidated file v5. This process is automatically performed by the version management software.

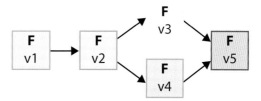

Figure 6.8: Version management graph showing the situation after two versions are created in parallel, and then merged to form a fifth version.

At any stage it is possible to rewind to a previous version and develop further from there. Suppose it is discovered that Aoife, the developer who produced v3, has introduced a serious error and it has been decided to go back to v4 and treat that as the new stable version from which to work. As a result, the next version created is v6, which incorporates the work from v1, v2 and v4 but discounts the problematic elements from v3. This is shown in figure 6.9.

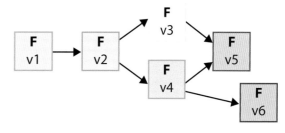

Figure 6.9: Version management graph showing the situation after version 5 and version 3 are both discarded and a new version is created from version 4.

Version management requires commitment from the developers to co-operate with the system. It only works successfully if:

- there is a consistent method of tracking changes, recording all version numbers,
- that it is possible to reverse changes, and
- all members of the development team use the same version of each code file when making changes.

Questions

1. The following factors must be considered when planning a software project. Explain what is meant by each one, and give three examples of each.
   (a) Resources
   (b) Constraints
   (c) Risks

2. Software project objectives must be clearly stated and agreed between all parties. The mnemonic SMART is useful for establishing these objectives. What project objective does each letter of the word SMART refer to?

3. The timetable for each task in a software project is provided in the following table:

Task	Depends on	Duration (days)
A	-	3
B	A	2
C	A	5
D	B	4
E	C, D	2
F	D, E	3
G	E, F	4

   (a) Draw a Gantt chart to illustrate the schedule for the project.
   (b) Draw a critical path analysis diagram for this project and identify the critical path.

4. Gantt charts, critical path analysis tools and version management software are used in the management of many software systems.
   (a) Explain the purpose of Gantt charts and critical path analysis tools.
   (b) Describe the key advantages of using Gantt charts and critical path analysis.
   (c) Explain why it is important to have version management during the development of a software project.

5. Joan and Eoin are developers working together on a project which involves modifying the existing software used by a chain of warehouses so that it can introduce a web-based ordering facility. They are using version management software to maintain a record of all changes made to the existing system. Joan takes the original system (v1) and re-designs the database structure (v2). In parallel, Eoin designs template web pages for the new system (v3). Joan then links the new database structure to the web page templates created by Eoin and tests the system (v4) while Eoin further develops the web pages (v5). Joan then incorporates the new web pages into the system (v6). At this point, Joan realises there has been a mistake in the re-design of the database (v2), so she must go back to her initial proposals (v2) and make some changes (v7). The re-designed database (v7) and the complete web pages are then merged to give the final version of the software (v8).

Construct a version management graph to represent this project. Include all the versions described (v1 to v8).

CHAPTER 7
Security Issues

By the end of this chapter students should be able to:

- explain why data is archived;

- explain the need for backup and recovery;

- evaluate methods of backup: full backup, differential backup and incremental backup;

- explain the purpose of a disaster recovery plan; and

- describe the contents of a typical disaster recovery plan.

7.1 Introduction

Data is a crucial element of any computer system and it is essential that this data is protected from loss, accidental damage or deletion. In this chapter we will explore various ways that data can be kept in a secure manner. We will first focus on archiving inactive data for possible future reference, before moving on to discuss the importance of backing up current data. Finally, we will consider the importance of disaster recovery plans which provide a way for organisations to recover from a catastrophic incident.

7.2 Archiving Data

In any organisation that processes data – such as a bank, educational institution or sports club – some data is required for immediate current use. However, there is other, inactive, data that is either not required or no longer requires immediate access but may be useful at some future point in time.

For example, a sports club might maintain details of its current membership and players. This data must be available for immediate use so that the club can selectively mailshot members and players to notify them of general club activities, collect membership fees, advise of forthcoming fixtures and so on. However, the club may also maintain records of previous members and past players. There may be a number of reasons for maintaining this inactive data. For example, someone might wish to write a history of the club, or some genealogist might wish to investigate their grandparents' contribution in forming the club. The club needs to store this data, but it is not required for immediate use.

The main difference between these two sets of data is **the immediacy of availability**. One set of data must be made immediately available to support the day-to-day operation of the club while the other (historical) set is rarely used but must be available if required. Data in this second category can be **archived.**

One might reasonably ask "Why not just make all data immediately available at all times?" The main reason for archiving data not required for immediate use is that it is then possible to optimise the performance of the resources required to operate the system. For example, if one considers the club membership example outlined above it would make sense to archive details of former members. This is because there may be thousands of these former members and it is more efficient to perform day-to-day procedures (such as mailshots or requests for payments) with the much smaller number (perhaps a few hundred) of active members.

Data archiving refers to moving inactive data to a safe and secure storage device. Although not needed for immediate use, it is nevertheless important that we are able to find the data again at some point in the future. This is usually achieved by maintaining some kind of index and making sure that searching the index is as easy as possible. It is also important that the archived data is complete and has been suitably structured so that it makes sense when referred to.

In our own lives, we might choose to archive our financial records on an annual basis. Until recently, many of these records were in paper format and included things such as bank statements, invoices, receipts and payslips. In this case, a suitable 'index' might take the form of a lever-arch file using dividers.

In today's more paper-free society, many of these records are now available in electronic format but the same indexing principles apply. In the digital world, the 'index' might take the form of a number of folders on an external hard drive, or the search facility provided by the operating system.

Case Study

Archiving at Provincial University

Students join Provincial University and remain enrolled until the successful completion of their studies. From the moment a student joins the university until they leave, the university will gather and maintain data on the student. This data will be broad-ranging and includes sensitive personal data (for example, address and phone numbers), academic performance (for example, examination and coursework marks), financial records (for example, tracking the payment of tuition fees), records of attendance at class and other relevant data.

At the end of each academic year, a large number of students will complete their studies and graduate from Provincial University, typically to take up employment. While the staff at the university need immediate access to data from students who are still studying, there is no longer any need for them to have immediate access to the records of students who have graduated.

However, the University does not simply dispose of this information. For legal reasons, they are required to maintain student records for a period following completion of studies. They also want to be able to refer to the data in the future if they need to prepare for an inspection or audit. The archived data is potentially a rich source of information for management, for example to track historical trends in student performances or subjects studied.

Hence, the University captures this data and moves it to safe storage through the process of data archiving. This involves assembling and storing the data relating to the entire student cohort who are leaving at the end of the academic year.

Advantages and disadvantages of data archiving

The key advantages of data archiving are as follows.

- It allows organisations to keep older data which might be needed at a later date for reference or regulatory compliance.
- Records are indexed to allow easy location and retrieval.
- Records are stored on cheaper storage devices as users are rarely likely to use them for prolonged periods, thus saving the organisation money.

Some disadvantages of data archiving are as follows.

- Data is not immediately available, so time must be spent searching for it.
- Once located, data access speeds may be poor.

7.3 Data Backup and Recovery

Backing up data is a distinct activity from archiving. While archiving refers to the long-term storage of inactive data, backing up data refers to a regular (perhaps daily) activity whose aim is to ensure that the organisation's **current** data can be recovered and restored should it become corrupted or destroyed. Because the loss of current data would have an immediate negative effect on an organisation, backing up is a high priority and must be carried out frequently. It normally involves making a copy of the data and storing it in a different location, as shall be discussed in this section.

Case Study

Backing up at Provincial University

Each student at Provincial University is allocated space on a computer server to store their academic work. Students are likely to work on their assignments over a period of days or weeks, regularly saving their work to the server and returning to it at a later stage. Students are advised to make personal backups of the data held in their allocated space, in case the worst happens and their work is lost. This could be a result of an error on the server, or by the student accidentally deleting their work. The backup will ensure that they can always restore their work from their most recent backup. Clearly, the more frequent the backup process, the less damage is done in the event of a data loss.

The system administrators at the University also play a role in this backup process as they make regular backups of the work of all the students on the server. With a backup made every night, they are able to restore the system to the state that existed at the end of the previous day. This process is usually automated, and therefore provides the main backup support for students who do not have backups of their own.

Data recovery refers to the activity of using backed up data to restore the system to a previously correct state after a data loss has occurred.

A key concept is that of **restore points**. A restore point is a record of what a system looked like at the precise moment in time it was backed up. Using this information, it is possible to restore the system to the state it was in at that point. Moreover, if the system has changed since the last restore point (perhaps a number of transactions have been carried out), then if we still have copies of these transactions we can re-apply them to the system and thus fully restore the system. In Microsoft Windows, the program System Restore automatically creates **restore points**, allowing users to restore their computer if a data loss occurs.

As systems are now so vital to many organisations' operations, there is an increasing need to perform backups much more frequently than once per day. For example, should an airline lose online bookings made even over one hour, the economic and reputational consequences could be disastrous for the company.

There are three main types of backup.

Full backup

A **full backup** occurs when a comprehensive copy is made of all of the data on the entire system. In important institutions, a full backup might be made daily or even more frequently. However, for many organisations a weekly full backup is sufficient. A full backup is often used as the starting point for the other two kinds of backup discussed below.

The main advantages of a full backup are as follows.

- Everything is backed up at the same time.
- The complete system can be restored from the one backup.

The main disadvantages of a full backup are as follows.

- It can take a long time to create the backup and a long time to restore a complete system.
- In most systems, only small amounts of data change from one day to the next, which leads to a lot of unnecessary work.

Differential backup

With a **differential backup**, only those files that have changed since the last full backup are copied. With each differential backup, there are likely to be more files to back up as more files will have changed since the full backup. Hence over a period of time the number of files that need to be backed up will increase quite considerably. This is illustrated in figure 7.1 which shows a differential backup that takes place once per day.

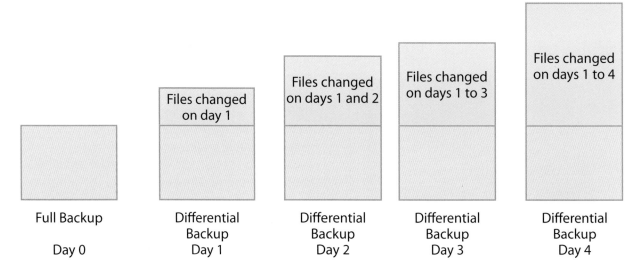

Figure 7.1: The operation of a differential backup.

The main advantages of a differential backup are as follows.

- Only files which have been changed since the last full backup are copied, so it is faster to create than a full backup.
- It has a faster restore time than an incremental backup (see next section), since there are at most two copies of each file. This is important where downtime (the time a system is not operational) is unacceptable.

The main disadvantages of a differential backup are as follows.

- It takes longer to restore files than a full backup because here are two possible locations for each file – the full backup or the most recent differential backup – and the correct one has to be identified.
- Requires more storage space than a full backup, as there may be two versions of the file.

Incremental backups

With an **incremental backup,** only those files that have changed since the last backup, either full or incremental, are backed up. Like a differential backup the process begins with a full backup. With the first incremental backup the only files that are backed up are those that have changed since the full backup. However, the next incremental backup will only back up those files that have altered since the previous *incremental* backup. This is illustrated in figure 7.2 which shows an incremental backup that takes place once per day.

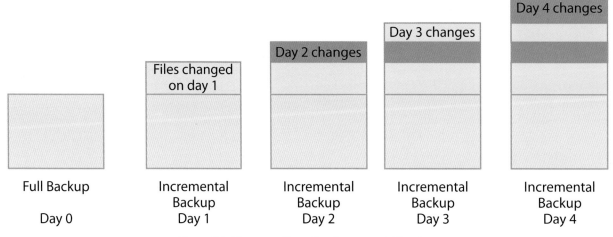

Figure 7.2: The operation of an incremental backup.

The main advantages of an incremental backup are as follows.

- It only copies files which have been changed since the last backup of *any* type, so it is the fastest backup method.
- Requires the least amount of storage space of all backup types.

The main disadvantages of an incremental backup are as follows.

- It takes longer to restore than any other type of backup as multiple copies of each file may have been copied since the last full backup.
- Problems can occur if any of the incremental backups have been corrupted as every incremental backup created since the last full backup is required to restore the system.

Restoring systems

It is important that organisations develop an appropriate backup policy to enable them to restore their computer systems to an earlier correct and stable position. Such a policy will generally be in accordance with one of the backup methods already described. However, the restoration process itself must also be performed effectively and efficiently. Restoring a system can be a lengthy process and must be carefully planned to ensure that any system downtime is kept to a minimum.

How the restore is performed will depend on the backup method employed.

If an organisation uses the **full backup** method, the restoration process will require the entire system to be restored. This is easily performed and involves replacing the existing file(s) with a full copy of the most recently-made backup. This restoration operation is therefore quite straightforward and is generally the most efficient in time terms.

If the organisation uses the **differential backup** method the process of restoration is a little more complex. The most up-to-date version of each file needs to be identified and this involves considering the files from the last full backup as well as the most recent copy of files that have been changed. As shown in figure 7.1, we can think of the most recent differential backup as having two parts – the 'last full backup' part and the 'differential' part. Files that have not been changed can be sourced from the last 'full backup' part while files that have been changed can be sourced from the 'differential' part of the most

recent backup. However, as there will be two copies of any changed file (one in each part), time will be spent checking for the most recent copy of each file.

Restoring data for an organisation that uses the **incremental backup** method generally results in the most complex, and hence the lengthiest, process. To identify the most recent version of a file, we need to consider the files held in the last full backup together with those files in each of the incremental backups. We should bear in mind that some files may have been changed more than once so there may be multiple copies of this file across the various incremental backups. Furthermore, a change to a file can have occurred at any stage. Thus, as shown in figure 7.2, we have to review all the previous incremental backups (including the full backup) to identify the most recent version of each file. An unchanged file will be located in the most recent full backup. A changed file could be located in any of the interim incremental backups and therefore the most recent version needs to be located and used.

7.4 Disaster Recovery

As its name suggests, **disaster recovery** is the way in which an organisation recovers its systems from a catastrophic incident. This usually refers to something more serious than a hard disk failure or the accidental deletion of an important file. Unfortunately, disasters are unavoidable and can include accidents (fires or widespread data corruption), natural events (earthquakes or storm damage) or deliberate acts (malicious hacking, espionage or terrorism). Organisations must be able to recover from a disaster and resume their activities as quickly as possible and with limited disruption to their customers. To do this, organisations must put in place a **disaster recovery plan**.

Disaster recovery plans

It is important to note that a **disaster recovery plan** is not about disaster *avoidance,* which is impossible. Rather, disaster recovery plans define policies, procedures and practices aimed at minimising or offsetting the *effects* of a disaster. The plan must be set up and fully documented as soon as possible after setting up a computerised system. As a minimum, the disaster recovery plan should identify:

- critical data,
- key personnel,

- backup and recovery processes,
- an alternative site from which the organisation can operate.

9/11 and Disaster Recovery

Following the 9/11 terrorist attack on the World Trade Center in 2001, companies based in the twin towers were faced with the sudden and complete destruction of all of their computer systems and the loss of all customer data. Each company's ability to re-build their business was entirely dependent on the robustness of their disaster recovery plan. The experience of two law firms clearly demonstrates the importance of having a good plan.

One company stored their backups in a secure, off-site location and were able to re-build their systems and recommence trading within two days. Another company had meticulously followed a regular backup policy, but made the mistake of storing the backups within the company premises. When the building was destroyed in the attack, so were the backups and they spent over a year rebuilding their databases by trawling through paper files in warehouses and manually contacting clients.

To go about developing a disaster recovery plan, an organisation must establish a list of the parts of the system that will need to be restored – the **recovery point objectives (RPOs)** – and the time limit for achieving the recovery of each of these – the **recovery time objectives (RTOs).**

These metrics will be decided in accordance with the key business processes of the organisation, with the most critical functions being given the highest priority. Examples of RPOs and RTOs that a business might produce are shown in figure 7.3. This organisation clearly regards the re-opening of their online shop as their highest priority, whereas they are prepared to wait for a week before needing to operate their payroll system.

Once the RPOs have been identified, the organisation determines the best way in which they can be achieved within the RTO timeframe determined for each one. Common techniques might include:

- Selection of an appropriate backup scheme, which might include storing regular backups off-site.
- Use of private online storage for instant restoration of data in the event of a local disaster.
- Full online deployment with servers and databases hosted by a third-party service provider, with the ability to activate new servers and databases when required.
- Staff employed on standby basis so that they can be deployed quickly in the event of disaster.

The RPOs and RTOs form the basis of a disaster recovery plan, but it is vital that the plan is tested regularly so that weaknesses can be identified and rectified before a disaster occurs. Disasters can take many forms, from localised hardware failure to multinational catastrophes and it is important to consider all eventualities. There may even be different

Recovery Point Objective (RPO)	Recovery Time Objective (RTO)
Re-open online purchase facility	24 hours
Operate payroll system	7 days
Examine electronic inventory of stock	48 hours
Generate management reports	5 days

Figure 7.3: Examples of recovery point objectives with associated recovery time objectives.

plans in place for different types of disaster.

Testing can be theoretical or simulated. In a theoretical test, participants walk through items on the recovery plan to ensure that employees know their roles in the event of an emergency. In a simulated test, working systems are disabled so that the recovery process can be thoroughly evaluated and changed if required.

Questions

1. What is a 'restore point' when dealing with data recovery and when is it used?

2. There are three main types of backup: full, differential and incremental. Explain how each of these backups works and state two advantages and two disadvantages of each.

3. A supermarket chain has been running a loyalty card scheme for over 20 years. Customers are awarded points for each purchase and these points can be redeemed in-store or online. Thousands of customers are registered on the scheme. Each customer's personal data and details of all their purchases are recorded. The supermarket chain uses the data to target customers with special offers which are relevant to them. Recently the system has seemed to take a long time to generate the daily reports on sales trends which management require and a long time to back up the system. Full backups are performed every Sunday at 6:00 am and incremental backups are performed daily at 10:00 pm. The chain's IT manager thinks this is due to the large volume of data stored. Many of the customers recorded on the system are inactive, i.e. they have not used their loyalty card for at least five years.

   (a) The IT manager thinks that a lot of the data could be archived. What is meant by the term 'data archiving'?
   (b) List two advantages to the supermarket if it were to archive some data.
   (c) List two disadvantages to the supermarket if it were to archive some data.
   (d) A major hardware problem occurred one Wednesday at 3:20 pm. Explain how the supermarket chain would recover their data files should a disaster occur.

4. 'DHA @ Your Service' is a small company supplying electrical parts and services to members of the public and larger companies. The company has grown considerably over the last two years. Currently, records of all stock and all work carried out is recorded on an in-house computer system. Although backups are made regularly, everything is stored at one site. The managing director sees the need for a disaster recovery plan.

   (a) What is meant by 'disaster recovery'?
   (b) List four things which should be identified to create a 'disaster recovery plan'.
   (c) When developing a disaster recovery plan, what are meant by the terms 'recovery point objectives' (RPO) and 'recovery time objectives' (RTO)?
   (d) Suggest two ways in which this company could achieve their recovery point objectives within the recovery time objectives.

CHAPTER 8
Algorithms

By the end of this chapter students should be able to:

- describe the purpose of a computer program;
- explain the term algorithm; and
- describe how algorithms can be represented using flowcharts.

8.1 Introduction

Computer programs are known as **software** to differentiate them from the physical, or hardware, components of a system. The purpose of a software program is to perform some task. The task can be quite trivial or extremely advanced. Software programs are ubiquitous in modern society and we often take them for granted. For example, if we purchase a new laptop, it will come with software pre-loaded. Some of this software (the computer's operating system; see chapter 13) provides us with a suitable interface in order to communicate with the computer. Other pre-loaded software typically includes a word processor, spreadsheet or presentation software. Software that is designed to perform a specific task, such as creating text documents, is often known as an **application** program.

8.2 Algorithms

An **algorithm** is a set of step-by-step instructions designed to solve a problem.

Real-world examples of algorithms are the recipe for baking a cake, or a set of directions to a particular location. When writing algorithms, it is very important to specify the set of instructions in the correct order. You will expect users to adhere to that order so that they end up baking a perfect cake or arriving at the desired destination. It is also important to be very precise with the instructions. It can help to imagine that the algorithm is being carried out by a robot which cannot apply common sense to the instructions. So, for example, a recipe may contain the instruction "*put two spoonfuls of sugar in a bowl*". In this case, additional precision is required to indicate whether a teaspoon or tablespoon is intended. Indeed, it may also be necessary to specify the size of the bowl required. Similarly, a set of directions might contain the instruction "*take the first left turn after the church*". However, this could be ambiguous if there were two churches on the road.

Properties of algorithms

In order to be useful, an algorithm must exhibit the following properties. In this discussion we will refer to the example of a recipe for baking a cake.

- **Be in a specific order.** The individual instructions of an algorithm have an implied order. We must start with the first instruction and perform them in the order provided. For example, we would not put an empty cake tin into an oven or place a full cake tin into an oven that had not been heated to the required temperature.

- **Each instruction should be precise.** For example, the cake algorithm might include an instruction "*stand the bowl containing the cake mixture in hot water for a few minutes*". This is imprecise because there are a wide range of possible interpretations of the phrase "*a few minutes*". The instruction to "*stand the bowl containing the cake mixture in hot water for 5 minutes*" is a very clear and precise instruction.

- **Each instruction should be clear and unambiguous.** Suppose that the cake algorithm included the instruction "*stand in hot water for 5 minutes*", i.e. omitting the reference to "*the bowl containing the cake mixture*". This could theoretically be interpreted to mean that the baker should seek out the nearest bath, fill it with hot water and stand in it. While it is unlikely a human would actually do this, computers do not have the common sense to interpret ambiguous statements like this. A good algorithm is unambiguous.

- **Algorithms must terminate at some point.** This is referred to as the 'finiteness' property. In the case of the cake, this might mean finishing with an instruction such as *"Leave the cake to cool for 15 minutes. Your cake is now ready to eat"*. If it had ended with the instruction *"Leave the cake until it rises"*, then the algorithm might never terminate if, for some reason, the cake failed to rise.

- **Algorithms may have zero or more inputs, may do some processing and must have at least one output (which is related to these inputs).** In the example of the cake, the ingredients of the cake and the various utensils (teaspoon, bowl, oven etc) are the inputs. The output is the finished cake.
- **Correct and effective.** Each algorithm should work under all circumstances and successfully perform the task is it intended to solve. This means that the algorithm should always produce some output, even when there are errors in the input. In our cake example, following the instructions precisely will result in an output, i.e. a perfect cake. It may be, however, that there are errors in the input. For example, the cake tin used may be too deep to fit between the oven racks. The algorithm should trap this and either propose a suitable remedial action (for example, rearrange the oven racks to make sure there is room for the tin) or finish elegantly (providing precise details of the error). Correctness and effectiveness are particularly important properties for computer algorithms.

- **Efficient.** Each algorithm should be written in an efficient manner. It should not include unnecessary steps or use a time-consuming method to carry out a task that can be carried out just as effectively in a quicker way. For example, there is no need for the cake recipe to insist that the ingredients must be mixed by hand if an electric food mixer could do the job just as well and with less effort.

Algorithms and computers

When a programmer writes a computer program, the first task is to define the algorithm for solving the problem. Algorithms are generally written in simple, everyday English, and this means that they can be easily understood by people who have little or no experience of computer programming. Hence the 'correctness' of the algorithm can be discussed with non-programmers.

Nevertheless, algorithms intended to be turned into a computer program are generally written in a manner that is closer to the resultant program by the use of **structured English** or **pseudocode.** The advantage of using structured English or pseudocode is that they are more helpful to the programmer but with the downside that they are slightly more difficult for the non-expert to understand.

The following algorithm is written in pseudocode and is designed to read in two numbers, add them together and print out the result.

```
START
GET Number1
GET Number2
CALCULATE Sum = Number1 + Number2
PRINT value of Sum
END
```

In the above algorithm we can identify:
- **input**: two numbers,
- **process**: add the two numbers, and
- **output**: sum of the two numbers.

Task

Extend the above algorithm to add three numbers.

It is important to appreciate that algorithms are not written for a specific program language – they

Symbol Name	Symbol	Description
Flow Line		Single-headed arrows with solid lines show the direction of flow of instructions. They start and end at another symbol. By following the arrow, we move through the various elements of the algorithm.
Terminator		Terminators usually contain the word "START" or "END". An algorithm will have one at the start and one at the finish.
Process		Processes or sets of instructions are represented as rectangles. This shape of the symbol tells us that a task is performed, while the text within it describes what is performed, for example "ADD 1 to Counter" or "SET total to 0".
Decision		A diamond shape (rhombus) shows where a decision is necessary, commonly a Yes/No question or True/False test. The decision symbol has **two** labelled arrows exiting from it: one corresponding to Yes or True (normally positioned at the bottom of the diamond), and one corresponding to No or False (normally positioned at the right side of the diamond).
Input/Output		The parallelogram represents inputs and outputs, for example "GET a number" or "PRINT the total".

Figure 8.1: Principal flowchart symbols.

are written to solve the problem and are language independent. Presented with an algorithm for solving a problem, a programmer would then be able to write the equivalent program in any desired programming language (for example C, C++, C# or Java).

Flowcharts

Flowcharts can be used to represent algorithms in the form of a diagram. In constructing a flowchart to represent an algorithm, a number of shapes are universally accepted as having a particular meaning. The principal flowchart symbols are shown in figure 8.1 – they can be combined to represent any algorithm.

It is possible to trace through the algorithm by starting at the START terminator and following the flow lines in the direction of the arrows until ultimately arriving at the END terminator. The flowchart for the algorithm to add two numbers (discussed previously) is shown in figure 8.2.

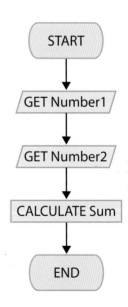

Figure 8.2: Example of a flowchart.

Worked Example

Consider an algorithm to add together five numbers and print out the result. We could extend the previous algorithm (by getting Number1, Number2, Number3, Number4 and Number5, adding them together and printing out the result), or by repeating the process of getting a number five times. This is shown in the algorithm below and the flowchart in figure 8.3:

```
START
SET Total to 0
SET Number Count to 0
REPEAT 5 times
        GET a Number
        ADD Number to Total
        ADD 1 to Number Count
END REPEAT
PRINT the value of Total
END
```

Note: in the above algorithm, 'Number Count' is used to control the REPEAT loop.

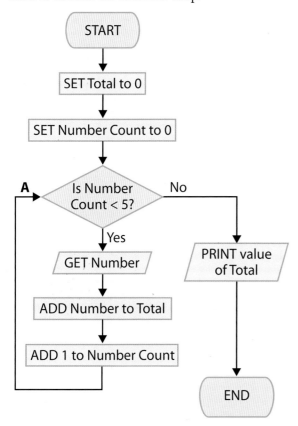

Figure 8.3: Flowchart for the algorithm that gets and adds five numbers.

If we commence at the START terminator and follow the flow lines, then the algorithm progresses as follows:

- Commence at the START terminator.

- SET Total to 0.
- SET Number Count to 0.

- We are asked the question "Is Number Count < 5?"
    - Answer is yes, so follow the YES path.
- GET a Number (the user enters 55).
- Add this Number to Total.
    - Total now has the value 55.
- Add 1 to Number Count.
    - Number Count now has the value 1.
    - We re-join at point A (note: the label 'A' is for illustration only).

- We are asked the question "Is Number Count < 5?"
    - Answer is yes, so follow the YES path.
- GET a Number (the user enters 45).
- Add this Number to Total.
    - Total now has the value 100.
- Add 1 to Number Count.
    - Number Count now has the value 2.
    - We re-join at point A.

- We are asked the question "Is Number Count < 5?"
    - Answer is yes, so follow the YES path.
- GET a Number (the user enters 20).
- Add this Number to Total.
    - Total now has the value 120.
- Add 1 to Number Count.
    - Number Count now has the value 3.
    - We re-join at point A.

- We are asked the question "Is Number Count < 5?"
    - Answer is yes, so follow the YES path.
- GET a Number (the user enters 30).
- Add this Number to Total.
    - Total now has the value 150.
- Add 1 to Number Count.
    - Number Count now has the value 4.
    - We re-join at point A.

- We are asked the question "Is Number Count < 5?"
    - Answer is yes, so follow the YES path.
- GET a Number (the user enters 20).
- Add this Number to Total.

- o Total now has the value 170.
- Add 1 to Number Count.
    - o Number Count now has the value 5.
    - o We re-join at point A.

- We are asked the question
"Is Number Count < 5?"
    - o Answer is no, so follow the NO path.

- PRINT out the value of Total (which is now 170).

- Finish at the END terminator.

Note that this is a very simple example. In particular, notice that the phrase "GET a Number" is used. This does not say how this action is performed, thus providing some flexibility as to how this operation could be implemented in an actual computer program.

Questions

1. Write a simple algorithm and draw a flowchart for the task of making a cup of tea. The system should ask if milk and/or sugar is required. The amount of milk or number of spoonfuls of sugar does not need to be considered at this stage.

2. Write an algorithm to calculate the total cost of posting parcels using the Fast Delivery Company. The company charges are based on the total weight of all the parcels posted. The algorithm should:

    - Get the number of parcels.
    - Get the weight (to the nearest kg) of each parcel.
    - Calculate the total weight of all the parcels and work out the postage as follows:

Total Weight	Cost
Less than or equal to 8 kg	£5
More than 8 kg	£10

CHAPTER 9
Fundamentals of Programming

By the end of this chapter students should be able to:

- describe the main features of an interactive development environment (IDE);
- explain the process of translation;
- explain the terms syntax, data type and variable; and
- describe the fundamental programming concepts of sequence, selection and iteration, including count-controlled and condition-controlled loops.

9.1 Introduction

In chapter 8 we looked at the process of writing an algorithm to solve a problem. In this chapter we will look at the process of writing an algorithm in a programming language such as C#. An algorithm that we have expressed correctly in a programming language is referred to as **source code**. Source code is our written program and is readable to humans, as shown in figure 9.1. We will begin by looking at the integrated development environments that computer programmers use, and then look in more detail at the fundamental concepts of programming.

9.2 Integrated Development Environments (IDEs)

An **integrated development environment (IDE)** is a sophisticated software application that provides computer programmers with a wide range of tools to facilitate the development of software. An IDE typically includes the following tools.

Editor

At the most fundamental level an IDE provides editing and file management facilitates which allow the developer to write, edit and save their source code. However, most IDEs provide a wide range of additional facilities. These include smart editors (which use colour and indentation to make the flow of the program easier to see); syntax checkers (which point out when the programmer has typed something that is not correct program code); and syntax suggestions. Most IDEs can be used with a range of programming **languages** so one of the first things that the developer will have to do is specify which language they are using. A line of program code might be valid in one programming language but not another, so the IDE needs to know which syntax to expect.

A screenshot of a computer program within a typical IDE is shown in figure 9.1. Closer inspection shows that a range of colours is used for the text of the program. Moreover, the program code itself is arranged using suitable **indentation.** For example, the code on lines 1, 3 and 12 commences at the extreme left while the code on line 5 is indented (that is, starts a few spaces along the line) while that on lines 7 and 9 is indented even further. This visual aspect of the code (often

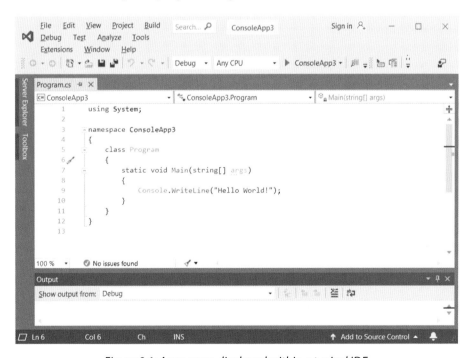

Figure 9.1: A program displayed within a typical IDE.

referred to as the 'layout') is important as it makes it easier to read and understand.

Preferences

When developing code, programmers need to make it easy for others to read their code and understand it. Hence, a team of programmers might decide that they are going to lay out their code in a particular way to improve its readability. An IDE will provide a facility to allow these agreed preferences to be set so that the team's code is laid out in a consistent manner. Indeed, the IDE can often apply the style to existing code automatically. Once written, the programmer will be able to save the work and, if necessary, share it with colleagues.

```
Program.cs  ⇥ ×
C# ConsoleApp3                    ▼ ⁴⁴ ConsoleApp3.Program            ▼
    1       using System;
    2
    3     ⊟namespace ConsoleApp3
    4      {
    5     ⊟    class Program
    6 🖉     {
    7     ⊟        static void Main(string[] args)
    8              {
    9                  Console.WriteLine("Hello World!");
   10              }
   11          }
   12      }
   13
```

```
Program.cs*  ⇥ ×
C# ConsoleApp3                    ▼ ⁴⁴ ConsoleApp3.Program            ▼
    1       using System;
    2
    3     ⊟namespace ConsoleApp3 {
    4
    5     ⊟    class Program {
    6
    7     ⊟        static void Main(string[] args) {
    8                  Console.WriteLine("Hello World!");
    9          }
   10
   11          }
   12
   13      }
   14
```

Figure 9.2: The same program displayed with two different code styles.

Compare the two screenshots in figure 9.2, which both show the same computer program. There is one slight difference between the two and that is the positioning of the left-brace { characters. In C#, braces come in left/right pairs i.e. for every left brace there will be a corresponding right brace. The program in the upper screenshot uses a convention where the left brace is positioned on a line on its own (see lines 4, 6 and 8). Note that the IDE has automatically positioned the left brace appropriately on the line. The program in the lower screenshot uses a different convention and places the left brace at the end of the

preceding line (see lines 3, 5 and 7). It is important that teams of programmers agree which convention to adopt and they can then set their preferences in the IDE to monitor this.

While developing code the IDE is likely to provide facilities that improve the programmer's productivity. For example, it may provide a facility similar to predictive texting. So, for example, the programmer may be entering code and after a few letters, the IDE recognises that the programmer is likely to be typing in a certain word and the system will provide the user with the option to accept or reject the prediction. If the prediction is correct, the user may accept the word and continue with the remainder of the program.

Compiler

An IDE will allow programmers to **compile** their source code – converting the program from the programming language into a form that the computer can understand – the **object code**. The **compilation** process is what converts source code (written by the programmer) into object code (for use by the computer). The IDE will also allow the programmer to run the program once it has been successfully compiled.

Debugging tools

Debugging refers to the process of correcting errors in a program. This can be a difficult exercise as the errors in the code can be difficult to detect. However, most IDEs provide a range of tools that support the programmer in this activity. For example, the IDE may allow the programmer to add **break points** to their program. When the program reaches a break point it pauses, and the IDE then allows the programmer to examine the contents of variables at that point and/or step forward through the code one line at a time. This allows the programmer to narrow down the region within the program where the error occurred, thus making it easier to determine the cause of the problem and fix it.

9.3 Translation

Computers operate by manipulating the **binary** values (a series of 0s and 1s; see chapter 11) representing the instructions and data that form the solution to a problem. In the earliest days of computing, operators entered instructions directly in binary, manipulating switches on the front of the device to specify each 'word' of memory to be input. This made programming a very difficult and error-prone process as the programmers had to perform the conversion to binary themselves in order to present commands to the machine. The development of **higher-level** languages was driven by a need to specify program code in a human-readable form so that programmers could work in a more natural way, using familiar characters and keywords to describe the program being input. However, these commands still need to be translated to the binary form (object code) required by the computer.

The first code translators emerged in the 1950s and were known as **assemblers**. These accepted input in a textual form that provided a one-to-one mapping between programmer instructions and their object code equivalent. For example, the instruction:

```
LDA 10
```

would specify that the value 10 should be loaded into the CPU's **accumulator** (a special **register** or word of memory used in calculations; see chapter 13). The assembler would translate this into a pair of binary words as follows:

```
10110001
```

the operation code (op-code) for "Load accumulator", and

```
00001010
```

the binary equivalent of the decimal value 10.

The next generation of languages (for example, FORTRAN, COBOL and ALGOL) allowed the programmer to specify code at an even higher level, using common words such as "let", "print" or "repeat". They allowed programmers to specify more complex instructions in a notation that is easier for humans to write and to read.

Since then, many hundreds of "high-level" languages have emerged, including C (and its variants C++ and C#), Java, Pascal, BASIC, Python and many more – each with their own set of commands and syntax. As these languages have become more complex, so the translation process has also evolved to fall into two main categories – **compilers** and **interpreters**.

Compilers operate by translating the entire program from the source code into (binary machine) object code before it is executed. If any errors are found in the translation (compilation) process, these are reported to the user in the form of an **error report** (or error log). The program cannot be executed until the error report is reviewed and all errors found in the source code have been corrected. Whenever changes are made to the source code to correct these errors, the compilation process must be repeated. As the compiler is aware of the complete program before code is generated, the binary code can be made as efficient as possible, resulting in a faster execution (running) time.

Interpreters operate one instruction at a time, translating the instruction and then executing it, before translating the next. As a result, errors will only be detected as they are found which may be after some of the program has already been executed. In certain situations, this can be problematic as external resources such as databases or other files may have already been modified by a program before it later terminates due to an error ('crashes'). Although interpreters generally run more slowly than compilers (as the program execution is interleaved with the translation), they are very common in languages used in web applications such as JavaScript, PHP and Python. Moreover, interpreters can also be used to help us identify errors and assist with the debugging process during program development. Once identified and corrected, we can then use a compiler to produce the appropriate object code.

9.4 Data Types and Variables

All programming languages make use of **variables**. Variables are **named locations** of computer memory that are capable of storing a single value. As their name suggests, this value can be changed. Each variable is given a **name**, sometimes called the **identifier**, so that the programmer can refer to them. Variables should be given names relevant to the data they are storing. In most programming languages there are particular rules and conventions for the naming of variables. Rules *must* be adhered to, while the conventions *should* be adhered to (as they are common, well-accepted practices that are followed by most programmers). Examples include:

- Start the variable name with a lower case letter.
- Spaces are never allowed, and often characters such as #, @ etc are not allowed.
- If you want to combine words then type the first letter of each word in upper case (apart from the first word), for example **firstName, dateOfBirth** or as separate words separated with the underscore character, for example **first_name, date_of_birth**.

Most programming languages also require you to indicate what kind of data the variable is going to be used to hold. This is known as the variable's **data type.**

A number of different data types are found in most languages, as follows (in this list, the name given to the data type in the C# language is given in brackets).

- Integers (int), for example –4, 0, 5 or 789,
- Real numbers (double), for example 6.7, 29.0 or –4.564.
- Single characters (char), for example 'A', 'g', ')', '%' or '3'.
- Multiple characters (string), for example "John", "Blue", "34 Main Street" or "077 4536 9567".
- True/false (bool), which can only hold one of two values, true or false.

The main reason that the variable's data type is required is that the named variable will occupy some of the computer's memory and this will have to be reserved. Naturally, different kinds of data have different space requirements: for example, less space is required to hold a single character than multiple characters (strings). Many programming languages require us to 'declare' a variable before we can use it within a program so that the appropriate amount of space can be reserved. How we declare a variable will vary from language to language but will typically require us to provide both a name (identifier) for the data and the data type of the variable. Optionally, we may also provide an initial value for the variable. Figure 9.3 gives some examples of data that needs to be stored in a variable. The variables have been declared using the style required by the C# language and in each case have been given an initial value:

9.5 Fundamental Programming Concepts

There are three fundamental concepts that must be understood in order to follow how algorithms, and hence programs, work. These are **sequence**, **selection** and **iteration** (**repetition**).

Sequence

As already explained, the order of instructions in an algorithm is very important. **Sequence** refers to the process of carrying out a set of instructions in the order in which they are listed. Most programming languages follow this principle, as illustrated by figure 9.4.

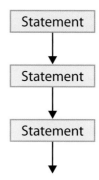

Figure 9.4: A program following a sequence will execute each statement in order.

Description of data	Suitable variable name	Data type in C#	Example in C#
Number of seats in a theatre	noOfSeats	int	int noOfSeats = 350;
Today's temperature	temperature	double	double temperature = 14.5;
Grade achieved in an exam	grade	char	char grade = 'B';
Someone's star sign	starSign	string	string starSign = "Aquarius";
Indicates if a house has a sun room	hasSunRoom	bool	bool hasSunRoom = true;

Figure 9.3: Examples of suitable variable names and data types for different types of data.

Task

A C# program always starts at the 'Main' method. In the following C# program this method contains a number of statements which are executed in sequence. Lines beginning with // are **comments**. They are included to provide the reader with more information about how the program is meant to work. They are ignored by the computer, but you should read them carefully as they often help you understand the code. Type and run this program.

```csharp
static void Main(string[] args)
  {
      //integer variable declared and initialised to 9
      int number = 9;
      //string variable declared and initialised to "Dog"
      string word = "Dog";

      //Outputting the value of the variable followed by a literal string
      Console.Write(word + " is the word");
      //Outputting a literal string followed by the value of the variable
      Console.WriteLine(" and the number is " + number);

      //Pause
      Console.ReadKey();

      //Assigning word a new value
      word = "Cat";
      //Prompting the user to enter a number
      Console.Write("Enter a number --> ");
      //Reading the value the user has entered and converting it to int
      number = Convert.ToInt16(Console.ReadLine());
      //Output the new values of the variables
      Console.WriteLine("Now " + word + " is the word and the number is " + number);
      //Pause to read output before closing Console window
      Console.ReadKey();
  }//Main
```

Your output should be similar to the following:

```
Dog is the word and the number is 9

Enter a number --> 4

Now Cat is the word and the number is 4
```

Now try to amend the program to ask the user for a new word, rather than assigning it "Cat".

Selection

Selection allows us to follow different paths through a program depending on the result of some true/false condition. As a very simple example, consider what happens at a supermarket checkout. Once the bill has been calculated and payment is due, the shopper is asked whether they are a loyalty card account holder and, if they are, points are added to their account balance (in accordance with the value of the bill) and they then pay the bill. If the user does not have a loyalty card account they will not be able to earn loyalty point so it is unnecessary to calculate their loyalty points for the purposes of updating their balance. Such users simply pay their bill. In English pseudocode, this part of the process could be written as:

```
PROMPT user as to whether they have
a loyalty card account
IF user has a loyalty card account
     CALCULATE points earned
     ADD points earned to user's
     balance
ENDIF
```

The flowchart for this logic is shown in figures 9.5 and 9.6. Note that there are two distinct paths depending on the result of the true/false condition. The IF statement(s) will only be performed if this condition evaluates to true.

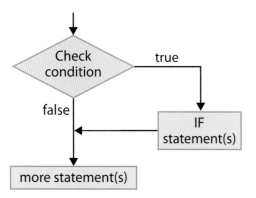

Figure 9.5: A selection flowchart using a simple IF … THEN sequence.

In the supermarket example there is a true/false condition (Is the user a card holder?). The program evaluates this condition and if it is true the IF statement(s) are performed. These calculate the points earned and use the total to update the user's balance. People who are not card holders avoid these two statements. Thereafter, regardless of the true/false condition value, ALL users proceed to pay the bill, as illustrated in Figure 9.6.

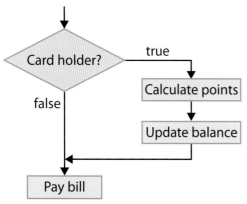

Figure 9.6: A selection flowchart for the use of a supermarket loyalty card.

As a second example, consider a program that calculates the price of pizzas in a pizza house. We assume a very simple pricing system in which the customer is charged based on the number of toppings – say, £2.50 for a maximum of three toppings and £3.50 for more than three toppings. When a customer comes to pay, the cashier counts the number of toppings on the pizza and produces the bill.

This is a more complex case but selection also allows us to deal with this situation. In this scenario, one of two sets of statements will be executed depending on a particular condition being true or false. In English pseudocode we could write the pizza shop example as:

```
GET number of toppings
IF number of toppings IS LESS THAN 4
    SET price to 2.50
OTHERWISE
    SET price to 3.50
ENDIF
```

In this example there is a true/false condition (number of toppings IS LESS THAN 4). The program evaluates this condition and comes up with either true or false. If it is true then the program executes the statement that sets the price to 2.50. If it is false then it executes the statement that sets the price to 3.50. Under no circumstances will both sets of statements be performed – it is one set of statements or the other depending on the result of the condition. This principle is illustrated by Figure 9.7.

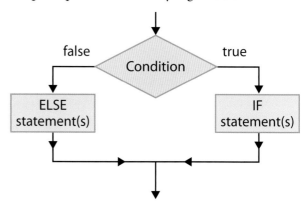

Figure 9.7: In selection, a program will execute only one of two sets of statements depending on a condition.

In the context of a computer program, a **condition** describes a relationship between two variables or values. The result of a condition is always either **true** or **false**. The **relational operators** used in most programming languages, including C#, are as follows:

Relational Operator	Meaning
==	Equal to
!=	Not equal to
<	Less than
<=	Less than or equal to
>	Greater than
>=	Greater than or equal to

When dealing with conditions, we sometimes use brackets to ensure correctness and to improve the clarity of our condition. Anything in brackets must be worked out separately.

Task

The following C# program asks the user for their age. If the number entered is greater than or equal to 18 a message "You are eligible to vote" is output. Type and run this program.

```csharp
static void Main(string[] args)
{
    int input;
    Console.WriteLine("What is your age?");
    input = Convert.ToInt16(Console.ReadLine());
    if (input >= 18)
    {
        Console.WriteLine("You are eligible to vote");
    }
    Console.ReadKey();
}//Main
```

Your output should be similar to the following:

```
What is your age?
56
You are eligible to vote
```

Amend the program so that it will output "You are eligible to vote" if the age is 18 or over, otherwise output "You are not eligible to vote".

Worked Example

Four variables in a program have the following values:

ageAlice = 30, ageBob = 40, salary = 30000, taxRate = 0.2.

What is the result of each of the following conditions?

(a) salary > 20000
(b) salary != 30000
(c) ageAlice > ageBob
(d) (salary × taxRate) < 5000

You should write out each statement again, replacing each variable name with the actual value. If there are brackets, work them out separately. Then evaluate the relational operators to find the result.

(a) 30000 > 20000 → **true**
(b) 30000 != 30000 → **false**
(c) 30 > 40 → **false**
(d) (30000 × 0.2) < 5000 → 6000 < 5000 → **false**

Combining conditions

Sometimes a programmer needs to select the correct action based on more than one condition. For example a program that records the marks obtained by students in an exam needs to make sure all marks entered are valid, i.e. in the range 0 – 100.

Conditions can be combined using one of the following **logical operators:** AND, OR, NOT.

When two conditions are combined using **AND**, the result is true only if **both** individual conditions are true (otherwise the result is false). So the mark system could check the marks obtained like this:

```
IF (mark >= 0) AND (mark <= 100)
    Mark is valid
ELSE
    Mark is invalid
ENDIF
```

In this case, both conditions must be true for the mark to be valid.

When two conditions are combined using **OR**, the result is true if **either or both** individual conditions are true – otherwise the result is false. The mark system could also check the marks obtained like this:

Task

The following C# program asks the user for a number in the range 1 – 10. If the user enters a number outside this range a message "Sorry…not within the range requested" appears. Type and run this program.

```
static void Main(string[] args)
{
    int input;
    Console.Write("Enter a number between 1 and 10: ");
    input = Convert.ToInt16(Console.ReadLine());
    if (input < 1 || input > 10)
    {
        Console.WriteLine("Sorry...not within the range requested");
    }//if
    Console.ReadKey();
}//Main
```

Your output should be similar to the following:

```
Enter a number between 1 and 10: 56

Sorry…not within the range requested
```

Amend the program so that it will also output a message, "Valid number", if the input number is within range.

```
IF (mark < 0) OR (mark > 100)
    Mark is invalid
ELSE
    Mark is valid
ENDIF
```

In this case, if either condition is true then the mark will be flagged as invalid.

When the logical operator **NOT** is placed in front of a condition, it will convert true to false and vice versa. Consider the following English example:

```
SET found to true
{Some other code which may change
the value of 'found', for example
by searching for a particular
number in a list of numbers}
IF (NOT found)
    Inform the user that the number
    has not been found
ENDIF
```

In this case, the code informing the user that the number has not been found is only executed if the condition evaluates as true. If the number has not

been found then the condition will be **NOT false**, which evaluates as **true.**

The **logical operators** used in most programming languages, including C#, are shown in the following table:

Logical Operator	Meaning
&&	AND
||	OR
!	NOT

Worked Example

Four variables in a program have been assigned values as follows:

ageAlice = 30, ageBob = 40, salary = 30000, taxRate = 0.2.

What is the result of each of the following conditions?

(a) (salary > 20000) AND (salary != 30000)
(b) (ageAlice > 50) OR (ageBob == 40)
(c) ((salary × taxRate) < 5000) OR (salary > 40000)

You should write out each statement again, replacing each variable name with the actual value. Then write them out again replacing each condition with 'true' or 'false'. If there are brackets, work them out separately. Finally, evaluate the logical operators to find the result.

(a)   (30000 > 20000) AND (30000 != 30000)
      → true AND false → **false**
(b)   (30 > 40) OR (40 == 40) → false OR true
      → **true**
(c)   ((30000 × 0.2) < 5000) OR (30000 > 40000)
      → (6000 < 5000) OR (30000 > 40000)
      → false OR false → **false**

Iteration

Repeating a set of statements is a common requirement in a computer program. Consider a program that receives a series of positive integer values entered at the keyboard and adds them up. Without going into precise details, a major component of this program is clearly going to be:

- prompting the user to input a positive integer value and
- reading in the value entered.

If the program is trying to get the total of 20 positive integers, then this activity must be repeated 20 times, once for each integer. If the program is trying to get the total of 100 integers, then this activity must be repeated 100 times. It would be extremely wasteful to have to repeat the same code 100 times to create this program.

Iteration allows a program to repeat the same sequence of instructions until or while some **condition** is met. Most programming languages provide three different kinds of repetition known as the **'for' loop**, the **'while' loop** and the **'do…while'** loop. The sequence of instructions to be repeated is known as the **body** of the loop.

The for loop

For loops are described as 'count-controlled'. They are used when we know in advance exactly how many times we wish some code to be performed. In our earlier example, if a program was trying to calculate the total value of 20 positive integers entered at the keyboard, then we would use a for loop that performs the prompt/read task exactly 20 times because we know in advance exactly how many times the loop is

to be performed. In pseudocode, the algorithm would be as follows:

```
SET total to 0
REPEAT 20 times
    READ and STORE a positive number
    ADD the number to the total
END REPEAT
OUTPUT total
```

In a programming language such as C#, a for loop uses an integer loop counter to control the number of times the body of the loop is executed. It is initialised with some value, and then altered – usually incremented by one – each time the loop is executed. It also requires the programmer to specify a condition that tells the computer whether it should loop round again. If the condition evaluates to true, then the body of the loop is repeated again. If it evaluates to false, then the program exits the loop. In the above example, the condition would be that the loop counter has not reached 20. Thus the program would keep repeating the body of the loop until the loop counter reaches 20. This principle is illustrated by figure 9.8.

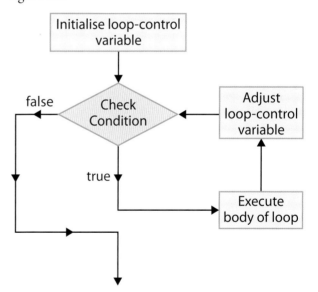

Figure 9.8: In a for loop, a loop control variable is updated with each repetition and a condition is checked each time to determine whether or not to continue repeating.

Task

The following C# program reads in three numbers, adds them up and outputs the total. Type and run this program. (The operator ++ coming after a variable name means "add 1 to the current value of the variable". In a string, the characters "\n" mean "insert a line break" which takes a new line.)

```
static void Main(string[] args)
{
    int number, total = 0;
    for (int count = 1; count <= 3; count++)
    {
        Console.Write("Enter a number: ");
        number = Convert.ToInt16(Console.ReadLine());
        total = total + number;
    }//for
    Console.WriteLine("\nThe total of the numbers is " + total);
    Console.ReadKey();
}//Main
```

Your output should be similar to the following:

```
Enter a number: 34
Enter a number: 23
Enter a number: 45
The total of the numbers is 102
```

Amend the program so that it will calculate and output the average of the three numbers.

The while loop

While loops are used when we do not know in advance exactly how many times we wish some code to be performed. These are described as 'condition-controlled' because the body of the loop keeps repeating while a specified condition is true. In our earlier example, if the program was required to calculate the total value of any sequence of positive integers entered at the keyboard then, as we do not know how many positive integers to expect, we would not use a for loop. In such circumstances we would use a while loop.

While loops are used when the loop is to be performed zero or more times – this means that the body of the loop might not even be performed at all. The condition is tested at the start of each loop. This principle is illustrated by figure 9.9.

In the earlier example, we could tell the person entering the positive integers that we will interpret a negative integer as indicating that there is no more input. The negative number is a dummy value that signifies "end of data" and is known as a **sentinel value**. A sentinel value is not part of the meaningful data.

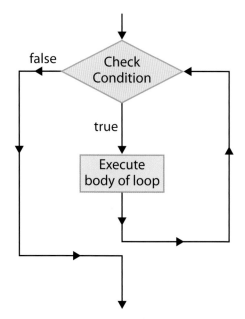

Figure 9.9: In a while loop, a condition is checked at the each of the loop. The body of the loop is repeated as long as the condition evaluates to true.

Hence, the user might enter the following values in turn:

20   30   45   15   30   −1

The first negative integer entered is –1. Because this is the sentinel value, we do not treat it as part of the meaningful data, and hence the total of the above integers is simply the sum of the meaningful values, i.e. 140. In pseudocode, the algorithm would be as follows:

```
SET total to 0
PROMPT user to enter a number
READ and STORE a number
WHILE (number is positive)
   ADD number to total
   PROMPT user to enter
   another number
   READ and STORE a number
END WHILE
OUTPUT total
```

Interestingly the following list of positive integers implies that the user has entered no meaningful values:

−1

In this case, the total of the values entered should be zero. If you work through the algorithm manually with this input you will see that, by using a while loop, the algorithm gives the correct result even in this particular case.

The do...while loop

If it is guaranteed that at least one meaningful value will be entered, then we can use a different kind of loop known as a **do...while loop** (sometimes called a **repeat...until loop**). Such loops are extremely common and are used when the loop is to be performed one or more times. Unlike a while loop, in a do...while loop the condition is tested at the **end** of each loop. This principle is illustrated by figure 9.10.

Task

The following C# program reads in a series of positive numbers terminated by any negative number, adds them up and outputs the total. Type and run this program.

```
static void Main(string[] args)
{
    int number, total = 0;
    Console.Write("Enter the first number: ");
    number = Convert.ToInt16(Console.ReadLine());
    while (number > 0)
    {
        total = total + number;
        Console.Write("Enter a number (or negative to finish): ");
        number = Convert.ToInt16(Console.ReadLine());
    }//while
    Console.WriteLine("\nThe total of the numbers is " + total);
    Console.ReadKey();
}//Main
```

Your output should be similar to the following:

```
Enter the first number: 34
Enter a number (or negative to finish): 23
Enter a number (or negative to finish): 45
The total of the numbers is 102
```

Amend the program so that it will terminate only when the value –999 is typed in.

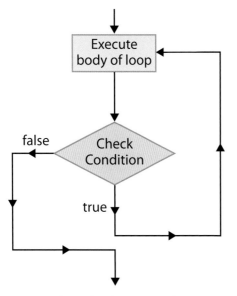

Figure 9.10: In a do…while loop, a condition is checked at the end of the loop. The body of the loop is repeated as long as the condition evaluates to true.

An example of this is using a cash machine to withdraw money from a bank. When the user inserts their card, they are prompted to enter their PIN. If they make a mistake, they will be prompted to re-renter the PIN and so on. In this case, the user will always enter their PIN at least once. Hence, the test can be performed at the end of the loop. In pseudocode, the algorithm would be as follows:

```
READ and STORE correct PIN from
card (correctPIN)
REPEAT
    PROMPT the user to enter a PIN
    READ and STORE PIN from user
    (enteredPIN)
UNTIL (correctPIN IS EQUAL TO
enteredPIN)
```

Task

The following C# program reads in a series of donations to a charity until a particular target is reached (£500). The program outputs the number of donations received. Type in and run this program. (The operator += means add the value after the operator to the variable before the operator. When the value after the operator is 1, this has the same effect as the ++ operator discussed earlier.)

```
public static void Main(String[] args)
{
    const int TARGET = 500;
    int donation, total = 0, noOfDonations = 0;
    do
    {
        Console.Write("Enter the amount of the donation £");
        donation = Convert.ToInt16(Console.ReadLine());
        total = total + donation;
        noOfDonations += 1;
    } while (total < TARGET);
    Console.WriteLine("\nThere were " + noOfDonations + " donations");
    Console.ReadKey();
}//Main
```

Your output should be similar to the following:

```
Enter the amount of the donation £150
Enter the amount of the donation £75
Enter the amount of the donation £200
Enter the amount of the donation £100
There were 4 donations
```

Amend the program so that it also prompts for the donor's name and outputs the name of the largest donor and the amount they have donated.

Case Study

Fantastic Holidays

Fantastic Holidays wants to create a computer program to calculate the total price of a family holiday. The algorithm should:

1. Read in the price of the holiday for:
   - an adult (18 years old and upwards);
   - a teenager (more than 12 years old, but less than 18 years old);
   - a child (less than or equal 12 years old).
2. Read in the total number of people travelling (there must be no more than 10 in the group) and the age of each person.
3. Display the total price of the holiday.

We will develop the algorithm step by step, i.e. sequentially. At this stage the algorithm is written in pseudocode. Any variables required, and their types, are indicated on the right.

Step 1: Read and store the price for an adult, teenager and child. In pseudocode, a suitable algorithm is as follows:

```
PROMPT the user to input the price for an adult
READ and STORE the value in adultPrice            double adultPrice
PROMPT the user to input the price for a teenager
READ and STORE the value in teenPrice             double teenPrice
PROMPT the user to input the price for a child
READ and STORE the value in childPrice            double childPrice
```

Step 2: Read and store the number of people travelling and the age of each person. We can subdivide this task into two steps:

Step 2.1: Read in the number of people, which must be in the range 1 – 10.
Step 2.2: Read in each person's age and decide if they are an adult, teenager or child.

In pseudocode, a suitable algorithm is as follows:

```
DO
   PROMPT the user to input the number of people travelling
   READ and STORE the number of people in noOfPeople    int noOfPeople
   IF (noOfPeople IS LESS THAN 1) OR (noOfPeople IS GREATER THAN 10)
      Ask user to enter a valid number in the range 1 - 10
   ENDIF
WHILE (noOfPeople IS LESS THAN 1) OR (noOfPeople IS GREATER THAN 10)
```

```
SET noOfAdults to 0                              int noOfAdults = 0
SET noOfTeens to 0                               int noOfTeens = 0
SET noOfChildren to 0                            int noOfChildren = 0
REPEAT noOfPeople times
  PROMPT the user to enter the person's age
  READ and STORE the age in age                  int age
  IF (age IS LESS THAN OR EQUAL TO 12)
    Add 1 to noOfChildren
  OTHERWISE
    IF (age IS LESS THEN 18)
      Add 1 to noOfTeens
    OTHERWISE
      Add 1 to noOfAdults
    ENDIF
  ENDIF
END REPEAT
```

Step 3: Calculate and output the total price. In pseudocode, a suitable algorithm is as follows:

```
totalPrice = (adultPrice × noOfAdults) +        double totalPrice
        (teenPrice × noOfTeens) +
        (childPrice × noOfChildren)
OUTPUT totalPrice
```

Once the algorithm has been created, Fantastic Holidays can then write the algorithm in a programming language. The following shows the algorithm written in C#. (The operator * means multiply. The {0:C} in the last Console.WriteLine statement is a way of formatting a number as a currency value.)

```csharp
static void Main(string[] args)
{
    // Declare variable for age - integer
    int age;
    // Declare variables for the number of people travelling - integers
    int noOfPeople = 0, noOfAdults = 0, noOfTeens = 0, noOfChildren = 0;
    // Declare variables for flight prices – real numbers
    double adultPrice, teenPrice, childPrice;
    // Declare a variable for the total price of the holiday – real number
    double totalPrice;
    // Enter the prices
    Console.Write("\nAdult Price:    £");
    adultPrice = Convert.ToDouble(Console.ReadLine());
    Console.Write("Teenager Price:  £");
    teenPrice = Convert.ToDouble(Console.ReadLine());
    Console.Write("Child Price:    £");
    childPrice = Convert.ToDouble(Console.ReadLine());
    Console.WriteLine();
```

```
   // Enter the number of people travelling
   do
   {
       Console.Write("How many people are in the group (1-10)? ");
       noOfPeople = Convert.ToInt16(Console.ReadLine());
       if ((noOfPeople < 1) || (noOfPeople > 10))
       {
           Console.WriteLine("  Invalid number of people, please re-enter");
       }//if
   } while ((noOfPeople < 1) || (noOfPeople > 10));
   // Enter the age of each person
   for (int count = 1; count <= noOfPeople; count++)
   {
       Console.Write("\nWhat age is person " + count + "? ");
       age = Convert.ToInt16(Console.ReadLine());
       if (age <= 12)
       {
           noOfChildren++;
       }//if
       else
       {
           if (age < 18)
           {
               noOfTeens++;
           }//if
           else
           {
               noOfAdults++;
           }//else
       }//else
   }//for
   // Calculate the total price
   totalPrice = (noOfAdults * adultPrice) + (noOfTeens * teenPrice) +
   (noOfChildren * childPrice);
   //Output total price
   Console.WriteLine(String.Format("\nTotal Price:    {0:C}", totalPrice));
   Console.ReadKey();
}//Main
```

A typical run of the program is as follows:

```
Adult Price:      £150
Teenager Price:   £120
Child Price:      £80
How many people are in the group (1-10)? 0
   Invalid number of people, please re-enter
How many people are in the group (1-10)? 4
What age is person 1? 45
What age is person 2? 43
What age is person 3? 15
What age is person 4? 8
Total Price      £500.00
```

9.6 Programming Errors

When a programmer translates an algorithm into a particular programming language, there is always a risk that they could make a mistake. Programming errors generally fall into one of four categories, and the way these errors are detected differs in each case.

Syntax errors

The **syntax** of a human language is the set of rules, principles, and processes that govern the way in which sentences are constructed. This includes word order and structure. Consider the English sentence *"I chocolate like"*. If a small child uttered this sentence most people would understand that this sentence means *"I like chocolate."* However, the sentence the child uttered is syntactically incorrect. This is because English has a syntax rule saying that sentences like this must be written in the order [subject] [verb] [object]. In a similar way, programming languages have a syntax that must be obeyed, i.e. a set of rules which define the format of each statement in the programming language. If you make a syntax error it will be flagged by the compiler and you will not be able to run your program until you correct this error.

Semantic errors

The **semantics** of a modern language relates to the meaning of sentences. Consider the sentence *"The white car is red"*. It is a syntactically correct English sentence, but it makes no sense because it contains a semantic error. In programming, an example might be to attempt to add 10 to an integer variable that has not been given an initial value. The result, therefore, is meaningless. Some semantic errors will be caught by the compiler, but others may not become apparent until the program is actually run.

Runtime errors

Sometimes a program appears to work well for a while until some set of circumstances cause it to fail due to a **runtime error.** For example, consider a program that is designed to calculate the average of a series of positive integers entered at the keyboard. The program keeps accepting numbers until a negative number is entered, at which point it calculates the average of the positive numbers. The program uses the following expression to calculate the average (where the symbol / means to divide):

average = (sum total of positive integers entered) / (number of positive integers entered)

The program appears to work well until someone decides to enter a list of zero positive integer values. Using the expression identified earlier we have a calculation:

average = (0) / (0)

The program will fail as we have attempted to divide by zero. Runtime errors are often a result of inadequate attention during the testing process. In this example, the potential for such a situation should have been anticipated and addressed during the testing stage.

Logical errors

A **logical error** occurs when the code compiles and produces an answer, but the output is incorrect because there is some flaw in its logic. For example, consider a program that accepts two integer values representing the length and breadth of a rectangle and outputs the area of the rectangle. The program might have been incorrectly written to use the following expression:

area = (length + breadth) * 2

when in fact it should have used:

area = (length * breadth)

This is a logical error. Unlike a runtime error, a logical error will often not cause the program to fail. It will simply produce the wrong result.

Questions

1. Describe three features of a good IDE.

2. (a) What is meant by the term 'translation' when referring to computer programs?
   (b) There are three types of translation program – assemblers, compilers and interpreters. Explain the difference between each of these.

3. (a) In programming, what is meant by a variable?
   (b) Suggest suitable variable names and data types to store the following data:
      (i) a person's age (in whole years),
      (ii) the first line of a person's address,
      (iii) the price of 1 kg of apples,
      (iv) an indication as to whether or not a person holds a full driver's license,
      (v) the first initial of a person's name.

4. *Extension to Chapter 8, Question 1.*
   (a) Adapt the algorithm developed for this question to ask for the amount of milk and the number of spoonfuls of sugar required.
   (b) Extend the flowchart to include the amount of milk and the number of spoonfuls of sugar required.

5. The following piece of C# code prompts the user for the ages of four people and calculates and outputs the number of people in the age range 18 to 30 (inclusive).

```
static void Main(string[] args){
    int age, total = 0;
    for (int count = 1; count <= 4;
    count++) {
        Console.Write("What is the " +
        "age of person " + count +
        ": ");
        age = Convert.ToInt16(
        Console.ReadLine());
        if (condition)
        {
            total++;
        }//if
    }//for
    Console.WriteLine("\nThe total" +
    " number of adults is " + total);
    Console.ReadKey();
}//Main
```

What code should be inserted instead of the word 'condition' to give the correct result?

Type in and run this code.

6. The quality control section of a precision engineering company must ensure that the length of a particular component is between 12 mm and 12.5 mm (inclusive). The machine for measuring this component contains the following piece of C# code (where size is the variable storing the length of the component). How could this code be changed to inform quality control whether the component is too long or too short?

```
if (size < 12 || size > 12.5)
{
    Console.WriteLine(
    "\nSize out of range");
}//if
```

7. A program reads a person's name followed by the number of overtime hours (to the nearest hour) the person has worked each day (Monday – Friday), then prints out the person's name and total overtime hours for the week.
   (a) Write an algorithm for this task.
   (b) Develop the program to carry out this task.

8. *Extension to Chapter 8, Question 2.*
   (a) Create a program for the algorithm you created to calculate the total cost of posting parcels using the Fast Delivery Company.
   (b) Extend your algorithm to perform the following validation checks:
      • The number of parcels is in the range 1 – 10.
      • The weight (to the nearest kg) of each parcel is in the range 1 kg – 5 kg.

   The algorithm should then calculate the total weight of all the parcels and work out the postage as follows:

Total Weight	Cost
Less than or equal to 8 kg	£5
More than 8 kg, but less than 20 kg	£10
20 kg or more	£20

   The algorithm should then print out the number of parcels, total weight and total cost.

(c) Explain the difference between a count-controlled loop and a condition-controlled loop. Identify an example of each in the algorithm you developed in part (b).

(d) Extend your program created in part (a) to include the additions in part (b).

9. Fresh Fruits is a fruit wholesale company which sells fruit to independent retailers in Northern Ireland. The algorithm to calculate the total cost of an order is as follows:

```
SET Total Cost to zero
READ and STORE Number of Items
REPEAT for each item
        READ and STORE Cost of Item
        ADD Cost of Item to Total Cost
END REPEAT
IF (Total Cost >= 500)
        Apply 20% discount
ENDIF
PRINT Total Cost
```

(a) By referring to the algorithm above, explain the following concepts:
    (i) sequence,
    (ii) selection,
    (iii) iteration.

(b) Draw a flowchart for this algorithm.

(c) Create a program for this algorithm in a language of your choice.

10. (a) Explain the difference between a syntax error, a runtime error and a logical error.

(b) The following section of code prompts for a person's gross pay and calculates the income tax they need to pay (tax-free allowance of £10 000; 20% tax is paid on any additional pay above £10 000). The person's gross pay, tax and net pay are then printed out.

```csharp
static void Main(string[] args)
{
    double grossPay, tax;
    // Prompt for and read in the gross pay
    Console.Write("\nPlease enter your Gross Pay: £")
    grossPay = Convert.ToDouble(Console.ReadLine());
    // Calculate tax and net pay
    if (grossPay == 10000)
        tax = (grossPay - 10000) * 0.2;
    }//if
    else
    {
        tax = 0;
    }//else
    netPay = grossPay - tax;
    // Output gross pay, tax and net pay
    Console.WriteLine("Gross Pay:\t£" + grossPay);
    Console.WriteLine("Tax:\t\t£" + tax);
    Console.WriteLine("Net Pay:\t£" + netPay);
    Console.ReadKey();
}//Main
```

    (i) The code contains three syntax errors. Identify these errors.
    (ii) Assuming the syntax errors in the above code have been corrected, the program is tested.

Part of the test plan is shown below. There is a discrepancy between the expected and actual results for Test 2. Identify and correct the programming statement which has caused this logical error.

Test	What part of system being tested	What is being tested	Data to be used for the test	Expected Outcome	Actual Outcome	PASS/ FAIL
1	Initial Data Input	Valid data in the range 0 – £10 000	5000	Gross Pay £5000 Tax: £0 Net Pay: £5000	Gross Pay £5000 Tax: £0 Net Pay: £5000	PASS
2	Initial Data Input	Valid data above £10 000	15000	Gross Pay £15000 Tax: £1000 Net Pay: £14000	Gross Pay £15000 Tax: £0 Net Pay: £15000	FAIL
3	Initial Data Input	Boundary data – lower limit	0	Gross Pay £0 Tax: £0 Net Pay: £0	Gross Pay £0 Tax: £0 Net Pay: £0	PASS
4	Initial Data Input	Boundary data – between tax-free and taxable data	10000	Gross Pay £10000 Tax: £0 Net Pay: £10000	Gross Pay £10000 Tax: £0 Net Pay: £10000	PASS

(c) The government has introduced a higher rate of tax. Everything earned above £40 000 is now taxed at 40%.
(i) Amend the program to deal with this higher rate of tax.
(ii) Complete columns 4 and 5 in the following test plan with two values of input data which would test the new higher tax rate and boundary between low and high taxable rates.

Test	What part of system being tested	What is being tested	Data to be used for the test	Expected Outcome	Actual Outcome	PASS/ FAIL
5	Initial Data Input	Valid data – high taxable rate				
6	Initial Data Input	Boundary data – between low and high taxable rates				

CHAPTER 10
Object-Oriented Programming

By the end of this chapter students should be able to:

- explain object-oriented programming terminology: objects, classes, methods and inheritance; and
- evaluate the use of the object-oriented approach.

10.1 Introduction

Object-oriented programming (commonly abbreviated to OOP) is a style of programming that became increasingly popular in the early 2000s. The basic concepts of object-oriented programming are **classes** and **objects**, which are analogous to real-life entities.

10.2 Classes and Objects

A **class** is the basic building block of object-oriented programming. It specifies attributes (properties) together with behaviours (methods) which can be thought of as a general *type* of something. Examples of classes are "Car", "Bridge", "Film" and "Person". By convention, and to make programs easier to read, the first letter of a class name is usually written in upper case.

An **object** is a specific member of a **class**. It can be thought of as an *entity*. For example, if there was a class called "Person", then an example of an object would be "Declan O'Neill".

An object-oriented programming language allows the programmer to define their own classes. Whenever the programmer then creates an object, it is built according to the pattern defined by whatever class it belongs to. The definition of a class will specify:

- the **attributes** (or properties) for each member of the class;
- the **behaviours** (or methods) that are allowed on each member of the class.

Class attributes

Let us consider a class called "Car". For such a class, we might wish to identify six attributes (properties) that we would associate with cars in general. Each attribute is defined as a variable of an appropriate type. Some of these are listed in the following table.

Attribute (Property)	Nature of Information
carRegistrationNumber	string
year	integer
colour	string
numberOfDoors	integer
engineSize	real number
petrol	true/false

Figure 10.1: Attributes defined by the class "Car".

We can now create "Car" objects, each of which will have its own personal set of attributes based on the pattern defined in the class. Thus, the set of attributes related to two car objects might be as shown in the following tables.

My best friend's car	My sister's car
"YNZ 1234"	"VIG 9102"
2016	2015
"red"	"silver"
5	4
2.2	1.6
false	true

Figure 10.2: Data stored in two objects that belong to the class "Car".

Class behaviours

Behaviours are the actions we are able to perform on the objects of a class. In the C# programming language these actions are referred to as **methods**. For example, in the Car class we might have an action (method) that allows us to inspect (or retrieve) the engine size of a particular Car object. We might also have an action (method) that allows us to change the colour of a particular Car object. These methods are very flexible and can be used by any of the class objects.

When dealing with methods it is important to understand the concept of **parameter lists**. Parameter lists describe what additional information, if any, a method needs in order to work properly. Some methods require us to supply some additional information: for example, if we wish to change the colour of a particular Car object it is important that we are able to say what its new colour will be. To achieve this, we change the method description to include details of any required additional information, for example to:

setColour(string newColour)

The information in brackets is referred to as the method's parameter list and, whenever we use this method, we are now required to supply some string information. In the case of the setColour(string newColour) method, we are required to supply a string such as "blue" or "metallic-grey".

Some methods do not require any additional information to work: these methods have an empty parameter list. An empty parameter list is indicated by two brackets, i.e. (). For example, we could describe our method to inspect the engine size of a particular Car object as getEngineSize().

10.3 Encapsulation

Another key concept in object-oriented programming is that of **encapsulation.** This is where the technical details of attributes and behaviours are hidden within the object so that data can only be changed by using an appropriate method. To enforce this, we usually define the attributes of an object as **private.** Then, we define a method that allows us to inspect the current value of a specific attribute of an object (we call this a

get method) and a method that allows us to amend the value of the attribute (we call this a **set** method).

Many attributes are likely to have both a get and a set method. If no set method is provided, then it is not possible to alter the value of that attribute. For example, attributes such as National Insurance number may not have a set method because once this number is allocated to a person it should not be possible to change it.

Although it may seem like more effort to write, encapsulation encourages better quality programs because it allows the programmer to keep related code together in one place. Suppose that, in the "Car" example, the system needs to inform the tax office of any car which has been re-sprayed in a different colour, so they can update their records. Simply changing the attribute "colour" to a different value would not accomplish this – it would require the programmer to write some code at that point in the program to explicitly notify the tax office. However, if the class had been defined with a setColour(string newColour) method, then this method could initiate a message to the tax office as well as changing the attribute "colour". The program using the method to note a change of colour does not need to worry about this complication because it is taken care of within the setColour(string newColour) method of the class. This allows the programmer to focus on the task at hand, rather than being distracted by its side effects.

Worked Example

Define a class, **House,** in C# with appropriate attributes and behaviours suitable for holding and processing information about the specific houses on a street. Every house on the street will be a separate object, and each object will have a number of attributes:

- street name of the house (string),
- house number (integer),
- number of rooms (integer),
- has a garden (true/false),
- category for establishing the rateable value (character – for example, category 'A').

The class will also need to define the following behaviours:

- get methods to retrieve the value of each of the five attributes;
- a set method to amend the number of rooms (to allow for extension);
- a set method to amend the "has a garden" attribute (for example a garden may disappear with the construction of an extension);
- a method to print out all the attributes of a house object.

The C# code for this class is defined on the next page.

```
class House
{
    private string streetName;
    private int houseNumber;
    private int noOfRooms;
    private bool hasGarden;
    private char rateCategory;
    //Constructor to create a house
    public House(string newStreetName, int newHouseNumber,
        int newNoOfRooms, bool newHasGarden,
        char newRateCategory)
    {
        streetName = newStreetName;
        houseNumber = newHouseNumber;
        noOfRooms = newNoOfRooms;
        hasGarden = newHasGarden;
        rateCategory = newRateCategory;
    }
    public string getStreetName() { return streetName; }
    public int getHouseNumber() { return houseNumber; }
    public int getNoOfRooms() { return noOfRooms; }
    public bool getHasGarden() { return hasGarden; }
    public char getRateCategory() { return rateCategory; }
    public void setNoOfRooms(int newNoOfRooms)
    {
        noOfRooms = newNoOfRooms;
    }
    public void setHasGarden(bool newHasGarden)
    {
        hasGarden = newHasGarden;
    }
    public void printAllDetails()
    {
        Console.WriteLine("\nHouse Details");
        Console.WriteLine("*************");
        Console.WriteLine("Address: " + houseNumber + " " + streetName);
        Console.WriteLine("It has " + noOfRooms + " rooms");
        if (hasGarden)
        {
            Console.WriteLine("There is a garden");
        }
        Console.WriteLine("It is in rateable category " + rateCategory);
    }
}//House
```

Below is the C# code for the Main method to create three houses and output the details of each house.

```
static void Main(string[] args)
{
    //Create myHouse, sistersHouse, friendsHouse
    House myHouse = new House("Church Road", 6, 6, true, 'A');
    House sistersHouse = new House("Green Street", 23, 5, false, 'C');
    House friendsHouse = new House("McAuley Gardens", 18, 7, true, 'A');
    //Print out the attributes of each house
    myHouse.printAllDetails();
    sistersHouse.printAllDetails();
    friendsHouse.printAllDetails();
    Console.ReadKey();
}//Main
```

Typical output for the program should be as follows:

```
House Details
*************
Address: 6 Church Road
It has 6 rooms
There is a garden
It is in rateable category A


House Details
*************
```

```
Address: 23 Green Street
It has 5 rooms
It is in rateable category C

House Details
*************
Address: 18 McAuley Gardens
It has 7 rooms
There is a garden
It is in rateable category A
```

Task

Looking at the previous worked example, write some C# code to add another house and print out all of its attributes.

10.4 Inheritance

Inheritance is the mechanism whereby the attributes and behaviours of one class can be shared or inherited by a new, more specialised, class derived from it. The original, general, class is referred to as the **superclass** (or base class). We can then create new **subclasses** (or derived classes) based on this one but more specialised.

For example, consider a superclass called "Vehicle". This would be quite a general class defining attributes that are common to all vehicles. However, we might then choose to define several subclasses from this superclass, such as "Car", "Van" and "Bus". As subclasses, these three classes will inherit all of the attributes and behaviours of the "Vehicle" class, but they also have other attributes and behaviours.

Suppose the "Vehicle" superclass has three attributes: "yearBuilt", "colour" and "engineSize". All of the subclasses also have these three attributes. However, they will also have their own additional attributes. So the "Van" class might have an attribute "cargoCapacity" and this would give it four attributes in total (three inherited and one specific to the subclass).

Similarly, the "Bus" subclass might have two extra attributes: "numberOfSeats" and "numberOfDecks". This would give "Bus" objects five attributes in total (three inherited and two specific to the subclass). Note that it is not essential for a subclass to have any additional attributes, but it is usually the case.

In a similar way, the subclasses can define their own additional behaviours as well as those they inherit from the superclass.

Case Study

Fantastic Holidays

Fantastic Holidays wishes to create a program for managing the employees of the company. They are using the object-oriented approach and at this stage they want to define the classes needed.

An object will be created for each of the company's employees. First, they create the superclass "Employee" which covers all the employees of the company in a general sense. It will have attributes, such as:

- employee number,
- name,
- address.

There will also be a number of methods in the Employee class, such as:

- get the employee number,
- get and set the name,
- get and set the address.

The company has two different types of employees – full time employees and part time employees, so next two different subclasses are created:

- "FullTimeEmployee" – which needs to store the employee's annual salary;
- "PartTimeEmployee" – which stores the number of hours worked per week and their hourly rate of pay.

Each of these subclasses has different methods such as:

- for "FullTimeEmployee", methods to get and set the annual salary and calculate their monthly pay;
- for "PartTimeEmployee", methods to get and set the number of hours worked, the hourly rate and to calculate their weekly pay.

Visually, this hierarchical class structure is represented as shown in figure 10.1. The superclass ("Employee") is at the highest level. As we move to the next level down the hierarchy, we accumulate attributes, so a "FullTimeEmployee" object has four attributes (three inherited and one of its own) while a "PartTimeEmployee" attribute has five attributes (three inherited and two of its own).

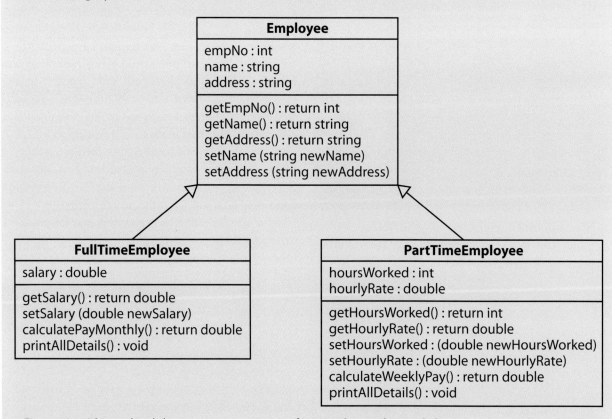

Figure 10.1: A hierarchical class structure, consisting of a superclass and two subclasses, represented graphically.

Note the following points:
- All the methods in the "Employee" class can be used by both "FullTimeEmployee" and "PartTimeEmployee" objects.
- You cannot record a monthly salary for a part-time employee.
- You cannot record the hours worked and hourly rate for a full-time employee.
- The calculateMonthlyPay() method can only be used by full-time employees.
- The calculateWeeklyPay() method can only be used by part-time employees.
- printAllDetails() is defined in both the FullTimeEmployee and PartTimeEmployee classes. The appropriate method will be executed depending on which class of object is created.

Type in the following C# code and run the program. Note that the "Employee" class is defined as abstract so that any object created must be either "FullTimeEmployee" or "PartTimeEmployee".

```csharp
//Base Class
abstract class Employee
{
    private int empNo;
    private string name;
    private string address;
    public Employee(int newEmpNo) //Constructor to create an Employee
    {
        empNo = newEmpNo;
    }
    public int getEmpNo() { return empNo; }
    public string getName() { return name; }
    public string getAddress() { return address; }
    public void setName (string newName)
    {
        name = newName;
    }
    public void setAddress(string newAddress)
    {
        address = newAddress;
    }
}//Employee

//Define FullTimeEmployee - Subclass of Employee class
class FullTimeEmployee : Employee
{

    public FullTimeEmployee(int newEmpNo)
    //Constructor to create a FullTimeEmployee
    : base (newEmpNo)
    {
    }

    private double salary;
    public double getSalary() { return salary; }

    public void setSalary(double newSalary)
    {
        salary = newSalary;
    }
```

```
        //Method to calculate and return the monthly salary
        public double calculateMonthlyPay()
        {
            return salary / 12;
        }
        //Print all details of a FullTimeEmployee
        public void printAllDetails()
        {
            Console.WriteLine("Employee No:    " + getEmpNo());
            Console.WriteLine("Name:           " + getName());
            Console.WriteLine("Address:        " + getAddress());
            Console.WriteLine("Monthly Salary: {0:C}", calculateMonthlyPay());
        }
}//FullTimeEmployee

//Define PartTimeEmployee - Subclass of Employee class
class PartTimeEmployee : Employee
{
        public PartTimeEmployee(int newEmpNo)
        //Constructor to create a PartTimeEmployee
        : base(newEmpNo)
        {
        }

        private int hoursWorked;
        private double hourlyRate;

        public int getHoursWorked() { return hoursWorked; }
        public double getHourlyRate() { return hourlyRate; }

        public void setHoursWorked(int newHoursWorked)
        {
            hoursWorked = newHoursWorked;
        }
        public void setHourlyRate(double newHourlyRate)
        {
            hourlyRate = newHourlyRate;
        }

        //Method to calculate and reutrn the weekly pay
        public double calculateWeeklyPay()
        {
            return hoursWorked * hourlyRate;
        }

        //Print all details of a PartTimeEmployee
        public void printAllDetails()
        {
            Console.WriteLine("Employee No:    " + getEmpNo());
            Console.WriteLine("Name:           " + getName());
            Console.WriteLine("Address:        " + getAddress());
            Console.WriteLine("Weekly Pay:     {0:C}", calculateWeeklyPay());
        }
}//PartTimeEmployee
```

```csharp
    static void Main(string[] args)
    {
        string newName, newAddress;
        int newSalary;
        //Create a FullTimeEmployee object called employee1 and assign values
        FullTimeEmployee employee1 = new FullTimeEmployee(1001);
        employee1.setName("James Smith");
        employee1.setAddress("45 Grange Road, Belfast BT3 2EF");
        employee1.setSalary(40000);

        //Create a PartTimeEmployee object called employee2 and assign values
        PartTimeEmployee employee2 = new PartTimeEmployee(3001);
        employee2.setName("Sarah Jones");
        employee2.setAddress("2 Hillside, Belfast BT4 5GG");
        employee2.setHourlyRate(12.50);
        employee2.setHoursWorked(30);

        //Create a FullTimeEmployee object called employee3
        //and prompt the user for values
        FullTimeEmployee employee3 = new FullTimeEmployee(1002);
        Console.Write("Name:            ");
        newName = Console.ReadLine();
        Console.Write("Address:            ");
        newAddress = Console.ReadLine();
        Console.Write("Yearly Salary (£): ");
        newSalary = Convert.ToInt32(Console.ReadLine());
        employee3.setName(newName);
        employee3.setAddress(newAddress);
        employee3.setSalary(newSalary);
        //Print details of employee1 to the console
        Console.WriteLine("\nDetails for employee1");
        Console.WriteLine("====================");
        employee1.printAllDetails();
        //Print details of employee2 to the console
        Console.WriteLine("\nDetails for employee2");
        Console.WriteLine("====================");
        employee2.printAllDetails();
        //Print details of employee3 to the console
        Console.WriteLine("\nDetails for employee3");
        Console.WriteLine("====================");
        employee3.printAllDetails();
        Console.ReadKey();
    }//Main
```

Typical output for the program should be as follows:

```
Name:            Hazel Hamilton
Address:            4 Compton Road, BT55 1SA
Yearly Salary (£): 36000

Details for employee1
====================
Employee No:    1001
Name:           James Smith
```

```
Address:        45 Grange Road, Belfast BT3 2EF
Monthly Salary: £3,333.33

Details for employee2
=====================
Employee No:    3001
Name:           Sarah Jones
Address:        2 Hillside, Belfast BT4 5GG
Weekly Pay:     £375.00

Details for employee3
=====================
Employee No:    1002
Name:           Hazel Hamilton
Address:        4 Compton Road, BT55 1SA
Monthly Salary: £3,000.00
```

Task

Write some code that could be added to the Main() method of the program in the previous case study to create and print out the details of a fourth part-time employee with the following attributes:

Employee No: 3002
Name: Kevin Gaston
Address: 34A Comber Road, BT21 H66
Hours Worked: 20
Hourly Rate: £12.50

10.5 Evaluation of the Object-Oriented Approach

The main advantages of the object-oriented approach to programming are as follows.

- More accurate modelling – the object-oriented approach models the real world more realistically than traditional methods which focus on data and processing.
- Improved productivity due to code reusability – when a new object is created, it will automatically inherit the attributes and behaviours of the superclass from which it is derived.
- Improved productivity due to less testing required – only the new methods developed for the derived class need to be tested.

The main disadvantages of the object-oriented approach to programming are as follows.

- The object-oriented approach is not suitable for all applications. Some programs are very abstract and do not readily correspond to real world 'objects'.
- It has been widely adopted in computer-aided design (CAD), computer-aided manufacturing (CAM) and engineering design systems. However, it has not been as successful for either corporate systems or many 'run of the mill' information systems applications such as payroll and accounting.

Questions

1. (a) By referring to the program code shown on the next page, explain each of the following terms which are used in object-oriented programming:
   (i) class,
   (ii) object,
   (iii) attribute,
   (iv) behaviour.
   (b) What output would be produced by the code shown on the next page?

```
class Square
{
    private string description;
    private double lengthOfSide;

    public Square(string newDescription, double newLengthOfSide)
    {
        this.description = newDescription;
        this.lengthOfSide = newLengthOfSide;
    }

    public void setDescription(string newDescription)
    {
        this.description = newDescription;
    }

    public void setLengthOfSide(double newLengthOfSide)
    {
        this.lengthOfSide = newLengthOfSide;
    }

    public string getDescription()
    {
        return this.description;
    }

    public double getLengthOfSide()
    {
        return this.lengthOfSide;
    }

    public virtual double calculateArea()
    {
        return Math.Pow(lengthOfSide, 2);
    }

}//Square

static void Main(string[] args)
{
    Square square1 = new Square("Small Square", 3);
    Square square2 = new Square("Large Square", 25);

    Console.WriteLine("\nThe area of " + square1.getDescription() + " is " +
        square1.calculateArea() + " units squared");
    Console.WriteLine("The area of " + square2.getDescription() + " is " +
        square2.calculateArea() + " units squared");
    Console.ReadKey();
}//Main
```

2. Describe (using an example) the relationship between classes and objects.

3. What is meant by 'encapsulation' in object-oriented programming?

4. Define the term 'inheritance' in object-oriented programming.

5. Evaluate the usefulness of object-oriented programming, referring to both advantages and disadvantages of the methodology.

6. A sixth form college wishes to store details of their students electronically.
   (a) Create a class (called Student) which has the following attributes for each student:
       • Student number (three letters followed by six digits)
       • Surname
       • First name(s)
       • Course enrolled on
       • Year of course
   (b) Write appropriate methods for this class. Remember that you should not be able to change the student number. Include a method to print all student details.
   (c) Write a Main method to create three students and print out their details.
   (d) What output would be produced by the code you wrote in part (c)?

UNIT AS 2
Fundamentals of
Digital Technology

CHAPTER 11
Data Representation

By the end of this chapter students should be able to:

- explain the terms bit, byte, kilobyte, megabyte, gigabyte and terabyte;

- demonstrate that 2^n different values can be represented with n bits (maximum n = 8);

- perform conversions from decimal to binary and from binary to decimal for a maximum of 8 bits;

- demonstrate how the two's complement system can represent positive and negative numbers in binary using 8 bits; and

- demonstrate how American Standard Code for Information Interchange (ASCII) and Unicode are used to represent characters.

11.1 Bits and Bytes

Computers use the **binary** number system to store data. We will look at the number system itself in section 11.2. At this point it is sufficient to understand that the smallest unit of data storage in any computer system is a **bit** (derived from the words **b**inary dig**it**). A bit can store a 0 or a 1 only.

In computers, bits are rarely treated in isolation; they are almost always grouped together into 8-bit collections to make them easier to work with. A group of 8 bits is called a **byte**. One byte is sufficient to store a value that represents a single character such as 'A', 'g', '6' or '£'.

Computer memory (RAM), hard disk capacity and file sizes are all measured in bytes. Increasingly computers have more memory and larger hard disks capable of storing millions of bytes. For convenience we use terms for larger groups of bytes, as shown in figure 11.1.

From Figure 11.1 it can be seen that:
- one **kilobyte** is *approximately* one thousand bytes
- one **megabyte** is *approximately* one million bytes
- one **gigabyte** is *approximately* one billion bytes
- one **terabyte** is *approximately* one trillion bytes.

Hence, a computer with 4 GB of RAM can store 4 gigabytes, or approximately 4 billion bytes, or exactly 4 294 967 296 bytes of data. A 2 TB hard disk drive can store 2 terabytes, or approximately 2 trillion bytes, or exactly 2 199 023 255 552 bytes of data.

Term (abbreviation)	Number of Bytes	Binary Multiplier
Kilobyte (KB)	1024 bytes	2^{10} bytes
Megabyte (MB)	1 048 576 bytes = 1024 kilobytes	$2^{20} = 2^{10} \times 2^{10}$ bytes
Gigabytes (GB)	1 073 741 824 bytes = 1024 megabytes	$2^{30} = 2^{10} \times 2^{10} \times 2^{10}$ bytes
Terabyte (TB)	1 099 511 627 776 bytes = 1024 gigabytes	$2^{40} = 2^{10} \times 2^{10} \times 2^{10} \times 2^{10}$ bytes

Figure 11.1: Groups of bytes.

Different types of data require different amounts of storage space. Figure 11.2 shows the approximate amount of storage space required for text, graphics, music and video. It can be seen from this table that text uses relatively little space compared to graphics and video.

Data	Storage
A character in a text file (for example 'T', '+' or '7')	1 byte
The word "Computer" in a text file	8 bytes (one for each character)
A 64 pixel × 64 pixel jpeg file	12 KB
A 10-megapixel photo	11 MB
A five-minute MP3 audio file	5 MB
One hour of video data	2 GB

Figure 11.2: Space requirements for different types of data.

A 2 TB hard drive may sound like a lot of storage space, but consider a recorded video. Each hour of video needs approximately 2 GB of space. Hence a typical two-hour film can be stored on one 4.38 GB DVD. Therefore, a 2 TB hard drive is capable of holding approximately 1000 hours of video data.

11.2 Binary and Decimal Systems

In everyday life we use numbers based on a combination of the digits 0 to 9 inclusive. This counting system is known as decimal, denary or base 10. The base indicates how many digits are available within the numerical system. Decimal is known as **base 10** because there are 10 choices of digit. The binary system is **base 2** because there are two choices

of digit (0 and 1). All decimal numbers have a binary equivalent, and vice versa, and numbers can be converted between the two formats. Let us consider the two systems in more detail.

The decimal number system

As in any number system, the ten possible digits in the decimal system can be combined to create larger numbers. For example, 4652 reads as "four thousand, six hundred and fifty-two". It is understood that the 2 is filling the 'units' (or 1s) place, the 5 is filling the 10s place, the 6 is filling the 100s place and the 4 is filling the 1000s place.

This could be more explicitly expressed as:

$$(4 \times 1000) + (6 \times 100) + (5 \times 10) + 2$$
$$= \quad 4000 + 600 + 50 + 2$$
$$= \quad 4652$$

Another way of expressing it would be to use powers of 10, in which case 4652 would be represented as:

$$(4 \times 10^3) + (6 \times 10^2) + (5 \times 10^1) + (2 \times 10^0)$$
$$= \quad (4 \times 1000) + (6 \times 100) + (5 \times 10) + (2 \times 1)$$
$$= \quad 4000 + 600 + 50 + 2$$
$$= \quad 4652$$

Starting from the right-hand side (known as the least significant digit), each digit has a **place value** for successively higher powers of 10. The place value of the least significant digit is 10 raised to the power of 0, as shown in Figure 11.3. The place value of the next digit is 10 raised to the power of 1, and so on.

Note: Any number to the power of 0 has the value 1, i.e. $10^0 = 5^0 = 2^0 = 1$.

Place value	Thousands (1000s)	Hundreds (100s)	Tens (10s)	Units (1s)
Place value (power of 10)	10^3	10^2	10^1	10^0
Example number	4	6	5	2

Figure 11.3: Place values for the decimal number 4652.

The binary number system

A binary number can be broken down in the same way as decimal numbers, but each column is a power of 2 instead of a power of 10. Starting from the right-hand side (the least significant digit), each digit has a **place value** for successively higher powers of 2. The place value of the least significant digit is 2 raised to the power of 0, as shown in figure 11.4. The place value of the next digit is 2 raised to the power of 1, and so on.

Note: When reading out binary numbers, the number 1010 is spoken as "one zero one zero" and not "one thousand and ten". Can you explain why?

Place value	Eights (8s)	Fours (4s)	Twos (2s)	Units (1s)
Place value (power of 2)	2^3	2^2	2^1	2^0
Example number	1	0	1	0

Figure 11.4: Place values for the binary number 1010.

Binary and decimal equivalents

The integers 0 to 20 are shown in figure 11.5, expressed in both decimal and binary.

Looking at the sequence of numbers in figure 11.5 it can be seen that 0 and 1 are written the same in both number systems. Once we reach the number 2, 'carrying' takes place in the binary system.

To illustrate 'carrying' let us review how we add two numbers together. Binary addition works in exactly the same way as decimal addition.

To add 964 and 75 in the decimal system, we proceed as follows:

$$\begin{array}{r} 964 \\ +75 \\ \hline 1039 \end{array}$$

Starting at the least significant digit (on the right), 4 + 5 = 9. Next, 6 + 7 = 13. Since 13 is greater than 9 (the largest decimal digit), we save the 3 and carry the 1 over to the next place. Next, 9 + 0 + 1 (because of the carry) = 10, so we save the 0 and carry the 1 over to the next place. Finally, 0 + 0 + 1 = 1. So the answer is 1039.

In a similar way, in the binary system, if a bit is 1 and 1 is added to it, the bit becomes 0 and 1 is carried over to the next place. So 1 + 1 = 10. Similarly, when adding 1 to 11 the 'carry' rolls over through 2 bits turning 11 into 100. Adding 1 to 111 the 'carry' rolls over through 3 bits turning 111 into 1000 and when adding 1 to 1111 the 'carry' rolls over through 4 bits turning 1111 into 10000.

Adding a number greater than 1 in the binary system is performed in a similar manner. For example, to add 111 and 11 we proceed as follows:

$$\begin{array}{r} 111 \\ +11 \\ \hline 1010 \end{array}$$

Starting at the right, 1 + 1 = 10, so we save the 0 and carry the 1 over to the next place. Next, 1 + 1 + 1 (because of the carry) = 11, so we save the 1 and carry the 1 over to the next place. Next, 1 + 0 + 1 = 10, so we save the 0 and carry the 1 over to the next place. Finally, 0 + 0 + 1 = 1. So the answer is 1010.

Decimal number	Binary number	Decimal number	Binary number	Decimal number	Binary number
0	0	7	111	14	1110
1	1	8	1000	15	1111
2	10	9	1001	16	10000
3	11	10	1010	17	10001
4	100	11	1011	18	10010
5	101	12	1100	19	10011
6	110	13	1101	20	10100

Figure 11.5: Equivalent binary and decimal numbers.

Writing binary and decimal numbers

As we have seen, in the decimal number system values are expressed in terms of ones, tens, hundreds, thousands etc (powers of 10). In the binary number system values are expressed in terms of ones, twos, fours, eights etc (powers of 2).

In the decimal number system, zeros to the left of a whole number (**leading zeroes**) are usually omitted, i.e. we would write 34 rather than 0034. In the binary number system, leading zeros are sometimes omitted, i.e. we would write 1101 rather than 001101. However, when transmitting data in bytes the zeros are included, because each byte is made up of 8 bits and the computer must know where one byte finishes and the next one starts. So 1101 is transmitted as 00001101.

Binary combinations

The number of different values that can be represented in binary depends on how many bits are available. If there is only one bit, there is only one place value to consider (the units) so there are only two (2^1) possible options – clearly these are 0 and 1. In a 2-bit system

two place values need to be considered (twos and units), so there are four (2^2) possible options – 00, 01, 10 and 11. In a 3-bit system three place values need to be considered (fours, twos and units), so there are eight (2^3) possible options – 000, 001, 010, 011, 100, 101, 110 and 111.

Hence, if there are **n bits** then there are **2^n different values**. This idea is summarised in figure 11.6.

As we know, computer systems usually work with bytes (8-bit collections). With 8 bits, 256 (2^8) different values (the integers 0 to 255) can be represented (0 = 00000000, 1 = 00000001, ... 254 = 11111110, 255 = 11111111). By contrast, a computer that is equipped with a 64-bit processor can have 2^{64} different values – over 18 quintillion different values.

> **Note:** When using a mixture of values from different number systems we sometimes use subscript notation to avoid confusion, where the subscript gives the base. For example, decimal number 34 would be written as 34_{10} and the binary number 1101 would be written as 1101_2.

Number of Bits	Number of Different Values	Values
1	$2^1 = 2$	0 and 1
2	$2^2 = 4$	00, 01, 10 and 11
3	$2^3 = 8$	000, 001, 010, 011, 100, 101, 110, 111
4	$2^4 = 16$	0000, 0001, 0010, 0011, 0100, 0101, 0110, 0111, 1000, 1001, 1010, 1011, 1100, 1101, 1110, 1111
5	$2^5 = 32$	00000, 00001, 00010, 00011, 00100, ... 11011, 11100, 11101, 11110, 11111
6	$2^6 = 64$	000000, 000001, 000010, 000011, 000100, ... 111011, 111100, 111101, 111110, 111111
7	$2^7 = 128$	0000000, 0000001, 0000010, 0000011, 0000100, ... 1111011, 1111100, 1111101, 1111110, 1111111
8	$2^8 = 256$	00000000, 00000001, 00000010, 00000011, 00000100, ... 11111011, 11111100, 11111101, 11111110, 11111111

Figure 11.6: Binary combinations.

Converting binary to decimal

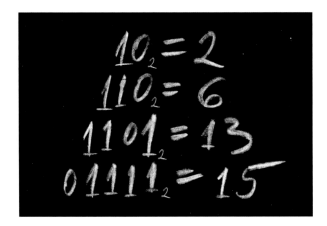

To convert a binary number to the equivalent decimal number we use the place values of multiples of 2, starting from the least significant bit, giving each number a place value for the next higher power of 2, with the first bit raised to the power of zero. So the binary number 10111 would have the following decimal equivalent:

$$(1 \times 2^4) + (0 \times 2^3) + (1 \times 2^2) + (1 \times 2^1) + (1 \times 2^0)$$
$$= (1 \times 16) + (0 \times 8) + (1 \times 4) + (1 \times 2) + (1 \times 1)$$
$$= 16 + 0 + 4 + 2 + 1$$
$$= 23$$

So we can write that $10101_2 = 23_{10}$

Worked Example

Covert the binary number 10110011 to a decimal number.

First write out the binary number and the place values in each case. Then multiply each pair together to give the weightings. Finally, add up the weightings to give the decimal number.

Binary number	1	0	1	1	0	0	1	1
	×	×	×	×	×	×	×	×
Place values	2^7	2^6	2^5	2^4	2^3	2^2	2^1	2^0
	=	=	=	=	=	=	=	=
Weightings	128	0	32	16	0	0	2	1

Sum of weightings = 179

So we can write that $10110011_2 = 179_{10}$

Converting decimal to binary

There are two methods for converting a decimal number to a binary number.

Method 1 – using division

One way to convert a decimal number to a binary number is to keep dividing by two and noting the remainders until there is nothing left, then reverse the remainders.

> **Note:** in binary, an even number always ends with a 0 and an odd number always ends with a 1.

Worked Example

Convert the decimal number 175 to binary notation.

$175 \div 2 =$	87	remainder	1
$87 \div 2 =$	43	remainder	1
$43 \div 2 =$	21	remainder	1
$21 \div 2 =$	10	remainder	1
$10 \div 2 =$	5	remainder	0
$5 \div 2 =$	2	remainder	1
$2 \div 2 =$	1	remainder	0
$1 \div 2 =$	0	remainder	1

Reversing the remainders (i.e. reading from bottom to top) gives 10101111.

So the answer is $175_{10} = 10101111_2$

We can check whether this is correct by converting back to decimal:

$$(1 \times 2^7) + (0 \times 2^6) + (1 \times 2^5) + (0 \times 2^4) +$$
$$(1 \times 2^3) + (1 \times 2^2) + (1 \times 2^1) + (1 \times 2^0)$$
$$= (1 \times 128) + (0 \times 64) + (1 \times 32) + (0 \times 16) +$$
$$(1 \times 8) + (1 \times 4) + (1 \times 2) + (1 \times 1)$$
$$= 128 + 0 + 32 + 0 + 8 + 4 + 2 + 1$$
$$= 175, \text{ which is correct.}$$

Worked Example

Convert the decimal number 199 to binary notation.

Start by setting up columns for each place value, as shown below. Then:

- Enter 1 under 128
- $199 - 128 = 71$
- Enter 1 under 64
- $71 - 64 = 7$
- Enter 1 under 4
- $7 - 4 = 3$
- Enter 1 under 2
- $3 - 2 = 1$
- Enter 1 under 1
- $1 - 1 = 0$
- Fill all other columns with 0

$2^7 = 128$	$2^6 = 64$	$2^5 = 32$	$2^4 = 16$	$2^3 = 8$	$2^2 = 4$	$2^1 = 2$	$2^0 = 1$
1	1	0	0	0	1	1	1

So the answer is $199_{10} = 11000111_2$

We can check whether this is correct by adding up all the binary place values that have a 1 against them:

$$128 + 64 + 4 + 2 + 1$$
$$= 199$$

Method 2 – using place values

A second method for converting a decimal number to a binary number is to use the binary place values. The process is as follows:

1. Set up columns for each binary place value.
2. Enter 1 against the highest binary place value which is less than or equal to the number being converted. So, for example, if the number to be converted is 88, then enter a 1 against the place value 64.
3. Subtract the highest place value number from the number being converted to create a new number to be converted.
4. Repeat steps 2 and 3 until the new number to be converted is 0.
5. Fill in all the remaining columns with zeros.

11.3 Negative Numbers

Sometimes we need to work with negative numbers. In the decimal number system, we indicate this by inserting a minus sign (–) in front of the number. However, for many reasons, trying to precede a binary number with a minus sign causes problems in computers. So how does a computer store a negative number?

You Are At
-415.⁷⁵ M
Below Sea Level

CHAPTER 11 – DATA REPRESENTATION

Sign-magnitude representation

At first glance, the simplest way would be to use the left-most bit (the most significant bit) to indicate whether the number is positive or negative (0 meaning a positive number, 1 meaning a negative number) and then using the remaining bits to store the magnitude of the number. This is known as the sign-magnitude representation. In a 4-bit system you would have:

```
0000 =    +0
0001 =    +1
0010 =    +2
...
1000 =    −0
1001 =    −1
...
1111 =    −7
```

The first problem with this approach is that the number 0 appears twice, i.e. there is both a positive 0 and a negative 0, which does not make mathematical sense.

A more significant problem occurs when we are adding and subtracting binary numbers using this representation. Consider the sum 3 + (−2). Obviously, the correct answer is 1. However, in sign-magnitude representation this would be calculated as:

```
      0011
 +    1010
      1101
```

1101 means −5 which is incorrect. So basic addition involving negative numbers does not work under sign-magnitude representation.

Two's complement representation

A better solution for storing negative numbers is to use a **complement** representation. As computers work with the binary number system, they use **two's complement** to represent negative numbers. Two's complement involves inverting the digits of the number (changing every 1 into a 0, and vice versa). This includes the (implied) leading zeros which come before a normal positive number. Because the numbers in a computer are constrained to a particular length (say, 8 bits) we always know how many leading zeros there need to be.

Beginning with a positive binary number, we can find the negative equivalent by finding the two's complement (8-bit notation) of the binary number.

The process is as follows:

1. Add leading zeros so there are 8 digits.
2. Invert (i.e. find the complement of) each digit.
3. Add 1 to this number.

Effectively, the meaning of the highest-order bit is changed. It now represents −1, rather than 1, and is multiplied by 2^7.

Find the two's complement (8-bit notation) of 10110.

1. Add leading zeros: 00010110
2. Invert: 11101001
3. Add 1: 11101010

So the answer is 11101010. We can check that this is correct by adding the original number to its two's complement representation. Ignoring the final 'carry', which goes outside the bounds of 8 bits, the answer should be zero (because adding any positive number to its negative equivalent should give a total of zero):

```
      00010110
 +    11101010
     100000000
```

Converting binary number to decimal (two's complement representation)

The key point to remember is that if the first digit in the two's complement notation is 1, it represents $(−1 \times 2^7)$ rather than (1×2^7). Other than this, the process is the same as before. Therefore, converting a binary number in two's complement notation to decimal is simply a matter of multiplying each digit by the appropriate power of 2.

Worked Example

Convert the binary number 10010111 (two's complement representation) to decimal.

$$
\begin{aligned}
& 10010111 \\
= \quad & (−1 \times 2^7) + (0 \times 2^6) + (0 \times 2^5) + (1 \times 2^4) + \\
& (0 \times 2^3) + (1 \times 2^2) + (1 \times 2^1) + (1 \times 2^0) \\
= \quad & −128 + 16 + 4 + 2 + 1 \\
= \quad & −105
\end{aligned}
$$

So the answer is $10010111_2 = −105_{10}$

Converting decimal numbers to binary (two's complement representation)

To convert a negative decimal number to binary, the process is as follows:

1. Convert the number to binary (ignoring the sign).
2. Add leading zeros so there are 8 digits.
3. Invert (or find the complement of) each digit.
4. Add 1 to this number.

Worked Example

Convert the decimal number –76 to binary notation using the two's complement system.

1. Convert 76 to binary: 1001100
2. Add leading zeros: 01001100
3. Invert: 10110011
4. Add 1:   10110100

So the answer is 10110100.
We can check whether this is correct by converting back to decimal:

$$10110100$$
$$= (-1 \times 2^7) + (0 \times 2^6) + (1 \times 2^5) + (1 \times 2^4) + (0 \times 2^3) + (1 \times 2^2) + (0 \times 2^1) + (0 \times 2^0)$$
$$= -128 + 0 + 32 + 16 + 0 + 4 + 0 + 0$$
$$= -76, \text{ which is correct.}$$

Another way to check our answer is to add the binary equivalents of the positive and negative numbers. The result should be zero (ignore the final 'carry').

```
    01001100
+   10110100
 ↑00000000
```

Addition with two's complement

Using two's complement representation, a computer can correctly perform arithmetic addition. This is shown in the following worked examples.

Worked Example

Work out –3 + 7 (i.e. 11111101 + 00000111) in two's complement representation.

Add the two binary numbers together. As always, the final 'carry' is ignored.

```
  11111101
+ 00000111
 ↑00000100
```

So the answer is 00000100_2

We can check this result by converting the number back to decimal:

$$(0 \times 2^7) + (0 \times 2^6) + (0 \times 2^5) + (0 \times 2^4) + (0 \times 2^3) + (1 \times 2^2) + (0 \times 2^1) + (0 \times 2^0)$$
$$= (0 \times 128) + (0 \times 64) + (0 \times 32) + (0 \times 16) + (0 \times 8) + (1 \times 4) + (0 \times 2) + (0 \times 1)$$
$$= 0 + 0 + 0 + 0 + 0 + 4 + 0 + 0$$
$$= 4, \text{ which is correct.}$$

Worked Example

Work out –7 + 3 (i.e. 11111001 + 00000011) in two's complement representation.

Add the two binary numbers together. In this case there is no final 'carry'.

```
  11111001
+ 00000011
  11111100
```

So the answer is 11111100_2

We can check this result by converting the number back to decimal:

$$(-1 \times 2^7) + (1 \times 2^6) + (1 \times 2^5) + (1 \times 2^4) + (1 \times 2^3) + (1 \times 2^2) + (0 \times 2^1) + (0 \times 2^0)$$
$$= (-1 \times 128) + (1 \times 64) + (1 \times 32) + (1 \times 16) + (1 \times 8) + (1 \times 4) + (0 \times 2) + (0 \times 1)$$
$$= -128 + 64 + 32 + 16 + 8 + 4 + 0 + 0$$
$$= -4, \text{ which is correct.}$$

Worked Example

Work out –3 + (–2) (i.e. 11111101 + 00000111) in two's complement representation.

Add the two binary numbers together. As before, the final 'carry' is ignored.

```
  11111101
+ 11111110
 +11111011
```

So the answer is 11111011_2

We can check this result by converting the number back to decimal:

$$(-1 \times 2^7) + (1 \times 2^6) + (1 \times 2^5) + (1 \times 2^4) + (1 \times 2^3) + (0 \times 2^2) + (1 \times 2^1) + (1 \times 2^0)$$

$$= \quad (-1 \times 128) + (1 \times 64) + (1 \times 32) + (1 \times 16) + (1 \times 8) + (0 \times 4) + (1 \times 2) + (1 \times 1)$$

$$= \quad -128 + 64 + 32 + 16 + 8 + 0 + 2 + 1$$

$$= \quad -5, \text{ which is correct.}$$

11.4 ASCII and Unicode

Computers store each individual character of a text document as a binary number in a byte. To make sure that documents created on one computer can be read on a different computer a standard coding system is needed, so that the same number represents the same character on different computers. The system used by virtually all computer systems is the **ASCII** (American Standard Code for Information Interchange) **character set**. A character set is a defined list of characters that can be represented by a particular system. The ASCII character set includes all English characters as well as a number of control characters such as the Escape and Delete keys. Other character sets include the Unicode character set, which represents a wider range of characters – for example, accented characters, like á, è and ç, from languages such as French, German and Irish.

In ASCII, every character on a computer keyboard is represented by a number from 0 to 127 (2^7 different values or 0000000_2 to 1111111_2). The first 32 values (0 to 31) are reserved for special purposes, such as line feeds or carriage returns. ASCII character 32 represents the space character, followed by the digits 0 to 9, punctuation, uppercase letters and then lowercase letters.

The ASCII character set only uses seven of the eight bits in a byte. The eighth bit can used to either

have a parity check (see below) or to handle special circumstances such as accented characters like é or ç used in non-English languages (extended ASCII).

If the user types a letter 'A' on the keyboard an electronic signal for capital letter A (ASCII code 65) is sent to the computer. This signal is converted to its ASCII binary code (1000001) and stored in memory for processing. After processing, the binary code for capital letter A is converted into an appropriate image and displayed on the output device.

ASCII with parity check

Parity checking is a form of error checking that involves adding an additional bit (called a **parity bit**) to the end of the 7 bits which hold the data, to form a byte. The value of this bit is calculated from the other 7 bits. In **even parity** the value of the parity bit is such that the total number of 1s in the byte is even. Similarly, in **odd parity** the value of the parity bit is such that the total number of 1s in the byte is odd. Following transmission of data, say along a cable, the parity check for each byte can be re-calculated at the receiving end. If the calculated parity bit does not match the received parity bit, then the computer knows that the byte must have been corrupted during transmission. It does not tell the receiving computer which bit is incorrect, but it is enough that it can request the data to be re-transmitted.

While either odd parity or even parity may be used in any particular transmission system, it is imperative that agreement is reached in advance as to which protocol is actually to be employed. In the absence of an agreement, checking the parity bits for correct transmission becomes a meaningless exercise.

Case Study

Parity Bits

A particular data communications system represents characters using ASCII with odd parity, i.e. each 7-bit ASCII character is followed by a parity bit. The system is used to transmit the letter 'J'. The ASCII code for 'J' is 74, which is represented in binary as 1001010. Because the system uses odd parity, and there are three 1s in the number, the digit 0 will be added to the end, giving 10010100. Thus, the number 10010100 is transmitted.

However, during the transmission, interference corrupts one of the bits, switching it from a 0 to a 1. The computer at the other end of the communications system receives the binary

number 10010110. It re-calculates the parity bit, and determines that it should be 1. However, the number received has a parity bit of 0, so the receiving computer knows that the data has been corrupted. It cannot tell which bit has been corrupted, but it can request that the data be re-transmitted.

Extended ASCII

Instead of adding the parity check, the eighth bit can be used to double the number of available characters (from 2^7 to 2^8). In Extended ASCII the first 128 characters (0 to 127) are the same as the standard ASCII codes and the upper 128 characters (128 to 255) handle additional characters such as accented letters. The first 128 characters have a leading 0 added to them to distinguish them from the extended character set. Hence, the letter 'J' (ASCII code 74 or 1001010 in binary) would be stored as 01001010 under Extended ASCII.

ASCII in text documents

A text document encoded using the ASCII character set uses one byte to store each character. For example, suppose a text document is to store the word "Hello". Each character is first converted into its ASCII code which, in this example, gives:

72   101   108   108   111

Converting these ASCII codes into binary numbers gives:

01001000   01100101   01101100
01101100   01101111

Note that leading zeros have been inserted so that each character consists of 8 bits (1 byte). This means that the computer knows where one code finishes and the next one begins.

Task

1. Open a simple word processor, such as Notepad, and type the word 'Hello'.
2. Save the file as a plain text file.
3. Check the size of the file. You should find that the size of the file is 5 bytes (1 byte of memory per character).
4. Add a space followed by your name and save your document again.
5. Check the size of the file. The file size should increase to the appropriate number of bytes. For example, if your name has six characters, then the file size should now be 12 bytes.

Note: In this example, only the text is being saved. If you were using a word processor (such as Word) where formatting information was also being saved, then the size of the file would be much larger.

Unicode

Even the extended ASCII coding system does not have enough characters to cover some languages in the world. To deal with this problem, **Unicode** specifications have been developed to include characters from almost all of the languages in the world and are now part of all major operating systems, search engines, email systems, application programs and the World Wide Web. There are different ways to encode Unicode but the most common is called **UTF-8** which uses two bytes per character (16 bits) and keeps compatibility with ASCII i.e. 2^{16} (65 536) different values. Unicode is being continually updated and now includes emoji characters.

Questions

1. Explain what is meant by each of the following terms:
   (a) bit,
   (b) byte,
   (c) kilobyte,
   (d) megabyte,
   (e) gigabyte,
   (f) terabyte.

2. State the minimum number of bits required to represent the range of positive numbers from 0 to 16 777 215.

3. Convert each of the following binary numbers to decimal:
   (a) 1011
   (b) 100111
   (c) 10001000

4. Convert each of the following decimal numbers to binary:
   (a) 45
   (b) 99
   (c) 120

5. What is the two's complement (8-bit system) of each of the following numbers?
   (a) 01011010_2
   (b) 100111_2
   (c) 10001000_2

6. Show how each of the following decimal numbers can be represented as a two's complement binary number using 8 bits:
   (a) –30
   (b) –88
   (c) –121

7. Using the two's complement system, convert each of the following binary numbers to decimal:
   (a) 00101010_2
   (b) 10000010_2
   (c) 11101010_2

8. A linguistics expert is using a data file containing 2000 different ancient Chinese characters. Is the file an ASCII file or a Unicode file? Explain your answer.

CHAPTER 12
Data and Information

12.1 Data, Information and Knowledge

In computing, the terms **data**, **information** and **knowledge** mean different things and it is important to be able to distinguish between them. In basic terms, **data** is processed by computers and the resulting **information** is used to make decisions to gain some **knowledge**.

Data

Data can be thought of as raw facts and figures which cannot be understood without being set in some kind of context. Some examples of data are:

- numbers, for example 2, 55, 3.4, 07743564722 and 22101990;
- words, for example "computer", "cat" and "building";
- alphanumeric combinations, for example ACD1324, 13:00, 20/10/2020 and £25.34.

The examples above appear to be a random set of numbers, letters and words which do not mean much because they are not set in context. We don't know what the numbers, words or alphanumeric combinations refer to. While data very often consists of raw facts and figures (usually alphanumeric), it can consist of anything that can be stored, including images and sound.

Information

Information is data which has been put into a context (processed) which gives it some meaning that is relevant to the person using it. Thus, we can write that:

information = data + context + meaning

Figure 12.1 gives some examples of data, and how it can be converted into information by adding context and meaning. The first row shows a list of numbers which makes no sense until you know that these numbers represent the sales of bags of apples from Monday to Saturday. Further information can be obtained by analysing the data. For example, from the context and meaning we can calculate the average weekly sales.

Knowledge

If we provide our raw data with a context we produce information. We can then apply some rules to this information and this in turn will provide us with additional knowledge. We can use this knowledge to make informed (and better) decisions. Hence **knowledge** is the application of a rule (or set of rules) to information in order that informed decisions can be made.

In the first row in figure 12.1 the meaning is that the number 10 represents the sales of bags of apples on a Monday, so by applying the rule "if no more than 12 bags of apples are sold on a particular day, the item does not need restocked" the greengrocer can work out if the bags of apples need restocked each day.

Data	Context	Meaning
10 40 20 22 36 45	Sales of bags of apples	Number of bags of apples sold each day from Monday to Saturday
22081999	Date represented in the format DDMMYYYY	Date of birth
£2.99	Price of an item	Cost of a bag of oranges
ACD132477	Part Code: First 3 letters – Supplier ID First 2 digits – Car Make Middle 2 digits – Car Model Last 2 digits – Part ID	Oil Filter for a Ford Fiesta 1.2XL from Parts Direct
133 141	Distances in kilometres	Distance from Belfast to Enniskillen and Belfast to Strabane

Figure 12.1: Adding context to convert data to information.

In the second row in figure 12.1 the number 22081999 represents someone's date of birth (22 August 1999), so by applying the rule "if someone is over 17 they can apply for a driving license", we can work out if this particular person is entitled to apply for a driving license.

In the last row in figure 12.1 the information gives us the distance between Belfast and two different towns. By applying the rule "the destination of the company van is the town that is closest to Belfast" we can work out where the van should go.

Case Study

Figure 12.2 shows a table of **data**. Columns 2 to 4 have no meaning.

Oranges	2.5	1.53	2.99
Apples	2.0	1.33	2.50
Pears	2.0	1.76	2.99

Figure 12.2: A table of data.

If we add headings to the data in figure 12.2, we have some **information**, as shown in figure 12.3. For example, we now have the information that 2.5 kg of oranges are bought for £1.53 and sold for £2.99.

Fruit	Weight (kg)	Cost Price (£)	Selling Price (£)
Oranges	2.5	1.53	2.99
Apples	2.0	1.33	1.75
Pears	2.0	1.76	2.99

Figure 12.3: A table of sales information.

We can take the information in figure 12.3 and derive **knowledge** from it. For example, we can apply the rule "profit must be at least 50% of cost price", by calculating the profit margin for each fruit and seeing if each fruit makes the required profit. We will then obtain knowledge, in this case that we need to reconsider the price at which we are selling apples.

Worked Example

With reference to the table below, explain the difference between data, information and knowledge.

Student ID	Module Code	Mark (%)
HF4539	COM312	86

Tip: If you are told in a question to make "reference" to something, then you must refer to it in your answer or you will lose marks.

Data is the raw figures, without context, for example HF4539.

Information is the processed data with context and meaning. For example, student HF4539 achieved a mark of 86% in module COM312.

Knowledge is the application of a rule to the information. For example, if the rule "a student is awarded a grade A if they achieve at least 80%" is applied to this information then we know that student HF4539 has achieved a grade A.

12.2 Quality of Information

Data and information are very important to every business, but good quality information depends upon the quality of the underlying data. If data of poor quality is put into a system, then no matter how good the system is, the information output will also be of poor quality. Using bad information can be worse than having no information, as it can lead to businesses making poor business decisions based on inaccurate information.

Note: We sometimes refer to this idea by the acronym **GIGO**, meaning "garbage in, garbage out".

We can ensure that we are using good quality information by making sure it is accurate, relevant, up-to-date, complete, well-presented and reliable. We shall consider each of these factors in turn.

Accurate

Steps must be taken to ensure that data is **accurate** so that, as far as possible, it is recorded exactly as it is and be free from errors. It should also be protected from being changed accidentally or maliciously. Users of information need to be informed where any assumptions or estimates have been made in recording the underlying data. Some examples of how inaccuracies can be introduced into information are as follows.

- **Transcription errors** occur when data is mis-typed as it is being entered into a system, for example in a stock control system where someone enters 1000 instead of 100.
- **Transposition errors** occur when the positions of two characters are interchanged. For example, if our credit card PIN was 27963 but we entered 23967, we have mistakenly interchanged the characters (digits) 7 and 3. In such circumstances our transaction would fail as the PIN entered was incorrect.
- Use of **incorrect formulae,** for example in spreadsheets. Checks should be put in place to ensure correct formulae have been entered into the appropriate cells. For example, if a spreadsheet calculates total yearly sales based on figures for monthly sales, where the monthly sales are themselves calculated from weekly sales data, then there should be a formula to add up the 52 weekly sales totals and the 12 monthly totals and check that the totals are the same. If they are not, then this suggests there is an error in one of the formulae.
- **Biased or meaningless information** can result from badly worded questions in questionnaires and surveys. Users may misunderstand the question, or poor wording may encourage biased answers. For example, if a radio presenter wants to find out how much his listeners like his show, he decides to send a questionnaire to the next 500 listeners who send him fan mail. The results of this survey will be biased as only those who send him fan mail are surveyed.

Inaccurate information can result in very serious mistakes. For example, if the accountants in a business provided the directors with the wrong profit figures it could affect decisions about expansion, redundancies etc. In a worst-case scenario, the business could fail.

Relevance

Information needs to be **relevant** to the person who wants to use it. It is very easy to produce too much information, but often providing a smaller quantity of more relevant information is more useful. Examples of irrelevant information are as follows.

- An employee produces a ten-page report on a question when all their boss requires is a one paragraph summary outlining the bottom line.
- A person goes to a travel agent to book a holiday to Spain and the travel agent provides him with details of all holiday packages that are available anywhere in Europe.
- A student is studying for the AS exam in Digital Technology. Her teacher loves Java programming and spends six weeks teaching her this topic. However, it is not part of the AS Digital Technology syllabus so, while the information may be highly accurate, it is irrelevant to the student's needs.

Up-to-date

Information needs to be **up-to-date** if it is to be useful. Sometimes information changes over time, so using old or out-of-date information can mean that wrong decisions are made. Examples of how out-of-date information can cause problems are as follows.

- The manager of a supermarket needs up-to-date information on the sales of all products to know what needs to be re-ordered. If she only has sales from last month, rather than current sales, she may order the wrong quantities of items.
- A person goes into a garage to buy a new car and the salesperson gives them performance data for an older model than the one he is trying to sell you.

- DFI Roads is considering whether to upgrade a busy road junction. However, their most recent traffic surveys are eight years old and, since they were made, a new housing development and a supermarket have been built nearby.

Complete

Information must be **complete** for the purpose it is intended for. As we have seen, too much irrelevant detail can make the information overwhelming, but it is nevertheless vital to have enough detail to properly understand the full picture. Examples of incomplete information causing problems are as follows.

- A supermarket system informs the re-order clerk that stock of McVitie's Chocolate biscuits has reached the re-order point, but does not include information on whether it is the 300g or 400g packets.
- A recipe gives the length of time to bake a cake, but does not specify the temperature.
- A passenger wanting to fly from Belfast to Sydney is given two different airline routes (Belfast – London – Dubai – Sydney, and Belfast – Amsterdam – Singapore – Sydney) but no indication of the connection times, which in one case turns out to be over 24 hours.
- A questionnaire only surveys people over the age of 60, but the results are published as if the questionnaire has surveyed all age groups. It thus gives an incomplete picture of the views of the general public.

Well-presented

The **presentation** of information should be such that it is easy to understand. In some cases, this means that information should be available in different formats, for example audio or braille for visually impaired, in addition to text. Different methods of presentation, for example, text, graphics, sound and video are better placed to convey information in different situations. Examples of situations where the correct method of presentation of information is important are as follows.

- A road sign whose intention is to warn users that there is a bend ahead could present the driver with a picture of a bend, or it could display the words "BEND AHEAD". However, the picture is much better than the words because it can be understood at a glance and because not all road users may speak English.

- A loud sound is the most appropriate way to indicate that a building needs to be evacuated in the event of a fire. Any other form of presentation, such as placing a flashing light above each fire exit, may not get the information to everyone rapidly enough.
- A customer wants to know the destinations of all flights in a particular airline that depart from Belfast. This could be presented either as a text list or as a map but the latter is probably more intuitive for the customer to use.

Reliable

Information needs to be **reliable**. This means that it should be from authoritative sources that can be trusted. It is good practice to quote the source of the information and ensure that it has been verified upon entry. Examples of how unreliable information can cause problems are as follows.

- A customer comes into an ice-cream shop and comments that it is going to be an exceptionally warm day the next day. The owner orders more ice-cream than normal without checking a reliable source, such as the Met Office web site.
- A person tells their doctor that they weigh 60 kg. The doctor records this weight without actually weighing them, even though the amount of medication they prescribe is dependent on this figure.
- A news reporter files a story about a celebrity misdemeanour as fact, despite it being based on a single comment by an unknown social media user that the reporter has not verified.

12.3 Data Validation

In section 12.2 we saw how important it is for any organisation to have good quality data. Whenever data is entered into any computer system, two independent procedures should take place to ensure data integrity – **validation** and **verification**. In this section we will consider validation, and in section 12.4 we will look at verification.

Validation is a check or checks that take place to ensure that the data entered is **sensible and reasonable** within acceptable boundaries. For example, if a database field is intended to hold a person's age, acceptable boundaries might be 0 to 120. An attempt to enter a value of –13 or 478 would fail a validation check.

Validation does **not** check the accuracy of data which means that, while it helps to reduce the number of errors, it cannot stop them occurring completely. For example, someone may enter an age of 34 when it should have been 43 (a transposition error). Both are valid numbers for representing someone's age but no amount of validation can pick up the fact that the user has entered the value incorrectly.

The simplest form of validation is checking the input to make sure it is made up of characters from a 'valid' set. For example, in a text document a spell checker looks up each word in a dictionary to see if it is present. Other validation checks are range, type, length, format, presence, lookup and the use of Modulus 11 check digits. We will briefly consider each below.

Range check

A **range check** is used to make sure that a value falls within a specified range, defined by a lower limit (or boundary) and an upper limit within which the value must lie. Examples of situations when a range check can be used are shown in figure 12.4.

Type check

A **type check** is used to ensure the correct type of data is entered into a particular field. Examples are shown in figure 12.5.

Length check

A **length check** is used to ensure that the correct number of characters has been entered into a particular field. Examples are shown in figure 12.6.

Description	Validation range check	Example of valid data	Example of invalid data
On-line airline booking system where a user can book up to 10 seats	>=1 AND <=10	6	12
Day of the month	>=1 AND <=31	24	32
Mark to achieve a grade 'C' in an AS Level exam	>= 60 AND <70	64	57
An uppercase letter of the alphabet	>='A' AND <='Z'	'G'	'g'

Figure 12.4: Validating data using range checks.

Description	Validation type check	Example of valid data	Example of invalid data
Adult age	Is an integer	70	seventy
Date	Routine to check that the date actually exists	29/02/16	30/02/17
Grade achieved in an AS Level exam	Is a character	'D'	45
Block numbering in a building	Is a character	'A'	'('

Figure 12.5: Validating data using type checks.

Description	Validation length check	Example of valid data	Example of invalid data
Alphanumeric password	8 characters	a5G4jf6H	G6h4jD
Telephone number	11 characters	02884556477	84556477 028-8455-6477
Postcode (without spaces)	5, 6 or 7 characters	BT321FG T51DD	BT2319GG
Block numbering in a building	1 character	'A'	"BB"

Figure 12.6: Validating data using length checks.

Description	Validation format check	Example of valid data	Example of invalid data
Date (DD/MM/YY)	DD, MM and YY are digits (00–99)	03/02/45 45/33/87	3/3/45 23-07-90
National Insurance Number	XX 99 99 99 X (where X is a letter and 9 is a digit)	FM 74 34 64 T	67 FM 46 GG 7
Postcode (without space)	X99XX OR X999XX OR XX99XX OR XX999XX (where X is a letter and 9 is a digit)	T51DD B545FG SW14DD BT563DF	8HYF66 B5768HJ GS43HFM

Figure 12.7: Validating data using format checks.

Format check

A **format check** is used to check that the data entered conforms to a certain pattern. Examples are shown in figure 12.7. Note that a format check does not determine whether the data is sensible. In the first row in figure 12.7, the date 45/33/87 conforms to the DD/MM/YY format, so would pass a format check. However, further checks (range and/or type check) would be needed to fully validate the date.

Presence check

A **presence check** is used to ensure that some data has actually been entered into a field. When completing forms on the internet there will often be mandatory fields (usually shown with an asterisk * beside the field name) to complete. For example, when booking a flight a contact email address must be provided, and a date of birth must be entered when applying for a driving license or passport. A presence check makes sure that the user cannot progress if a critical field has been left blank.

Lookup check

A **lookup check** is automatically made against a file of valid values. Consider a golf club that maintains two files – one for its playing members and one for all other members (e.g. social members). Each file consists of member details, including their unique membership number.

Suppose that only playing members may make an advance booking of a round of golf. To do this, they must use the club's online booking system, access to which is controlled by entering a valid playing membership number. When a member enters their number, an automatic lookup check (a search) takes place within the playing member file to ensure that the number entered is that of a playing member. If this lookup check is successful, the member is permitted to make a booking. If the lookup check is unsuccessful and the number provided is not recognised as a number of a playing member, the member has either entered their membership number incorrectly or they are not recorded as a playing member of the club.

Modulus 11 check digit

It is easy to make mistakes when entering lots of numbers. A **check digit** is a number that is used to ensure the accuracy of a series of digits. It will detect most transposition errors. In this methodology, the last digit of a number is an extra 'check digit' calculated from the preceding series of digits. The numbers can then be checked for validity at any time by recalculating the check digit and comparing it to the check digit actually being stored.

In most 16-digit credit card numbers the first 15 digits determine the issuing bank and the last digit is a check digit. Similarly, a barcode incorporates codes identifying the manufacturer and product, with a final number to serve as a check digit. When a barcode is scanned, a formula is applied to the digits of the barcode and the result compared to the check digit scanned. Any difference between the computer-generated number and the last number on the barcode tells the computer system that the barcode has not been read correctly.

One of the most common methods of generating a check digit is the **Modulus 11** method. This method works for base numbers of up to nine digits in length.

The process is as follows.

1. Set up **weightings** for each digit of the input number (n digits), starting with 2 for the least significant figure (on the right) up to (n + 1) for the most significant figure (on the left).
2. Enter each digit of the base number in the appropriate column.
3. Multiply each digit by its weighting.
4. Calculate the **checksum** by adding all the (digit × weightings) together.
5. Calculate the remainder when the checksum is divided by the prime number 11 (this is what 'modulus 11' means).
6. The check digit is then calculated as follows:
   - If the remainder is zero, then the check digit is 0.
   - If the remainder is 1, then the check digit is X.
   - Otherwise, the check digit is the value of 11 minus the remainder.
7. The check digit is appended to the base number.

Note: The Modulus 11 system can detect all single-digit transcription and transposition errors.

Note: A number stored with a Modulus 11 check digit needs to be stored as a string because the check digit could be the letter X.

Worked Example

Calculate the Modulus 11 check digit for the number 8803.

1. Set up the weightings (5, 4, 3, 2) as shown in the table below.
2. Enter 8803 under each of the weightings 5, 4, 3, 2.
3. Multiply each digit by its weighting.

Weighting	5	4	3	2
Digit	8	8	0	3
Weighting × Digit	40	32	0	6

4. Calculate the checksum: 40 + 32 + 0 + 6 = 78
5. Calculate the remainder: 78 ÷ 11 = 7 remainder 1
6. Remainder = 1, so the check digit is X.
7. Therefore, the number with the check digit is 8803X.

We can check that this is correct by using the same method as above, but using a weighting of 1 for the check digit. The remainder should be 0 if there is no error. Note that the digit 'X' is given a value of 10 when calculating the (weighting × digit).

1. Calculate the (weighting × digit) and add them together to get the checksum:

$$= (8 \times 5) + (8 \times 4) + (0 \times 3) + (3 \times 2) + (10 \times 1)$$
$$= 40 + 32 + 0 + 6 + 10$$
$$= 88$$

2. Calculate the remainder: 88 ÷ 11 = 8 remainder 0. Therefore, the number is correct.

If the user transposed two digits and entered the number 8083X, the Modulus 11 check digit for 8083 would be calculated as follows:

Checksum: $(5 \times 8) + (4 \times 0) + (3 \times 8) + (2 \times 3)$
$= 40 + 0 + 24 + 6$
$= 70$
Remainder: 70 ÷ 11 = 6 remainder 4
Check digit: 11 – 4 = 7

However, the check digit actually entered was X, so the computer knows that an error has been made when entering this number. In this example it is a transposition error (0 and 8 entered in the wrong order), but it could be the entry of an incorrect digit. The positions of the two digits which have been transposed results in the product of (weighting × digit) being changed and therefore the checksum changes.

The ISBN-10 numbering system for books, which was in use until 2007, makes use of a Modulus 11 check digit. An ISBN-10 is usually in a format such as 0-85312-249-0. The first nine digits of an ISBN-10 hold information on the publisher and title. A check digit is then calculated and added to the end to make up the tenth character. When the ISBN barcode is scanned, or the number is entered from the keyboard, the computer uses the check digit to ensure that the number has been input correctly.

12.4 Data Verification

In section 12.3 we looked at **validation**, which is a check to ensure that the data entered is **sensible** and **reasonable.** In this section we shall consider **verification,** which is a check to ensure that all copies of the **data exactly match the original source.** Verification checks are used to ensure the data contains as few mistakes as possible.

For example, most people have had the experience being asked to verify the details of the data displayed on the screen by answering a simple "Is this correct (Y/N)?" message. When checking-in at an airport, passengers need to bring some form of identification to verify that the data they have entered when booking the flight is correct.

Data verification is also used when making a backup, because we need to be confident that the data on the backup has been copied correctly and can be used if the original data is lost or corrupted. Most software systems that perform backups have some inbuilt verification functionality. Software that burns DVDs usually allows the user to perform a verification check at the end of the burning process.

Examples of data verification checks are double entry and proofreading. We will briefly consider each below.

Double entry

Double entry is a common method of checking that the data entered matches the original source. For example, when a computer system asks for a new password the user is often asked to type it twice. The computer will check if the same string of characters has been typed each time and notify the user if there is a difference. The main advantage of this approach is that having to enter the data twice will identify the majority of mistakes. However, it doubles the workload and therefore can be very costly if large amounts of data are being entered. In these cases, it is best to use it only to verify the most important information (figure 12.8).

Proofreading

Proofreading is a method of verification that is suitable when both copies of the data are available. The original data is visually checked against the data entered into the computer, either on screen or from a printout. Ideally the proofreading should be done by a different person from the one who typed in the data. This method is often used in pharmacies to check that prescriptions have been made up correctly. One pharmacist will typically proofread the label generated

Figure 12.8: "The Important Field" (XKCD.com). Developers should consider what data most needs a verification check.

by a second pharmacist against the doctor's original prescription, to ensure that no errors have been made. The main disadvantage is that proofreading can be time consuming and expensive if there is a lot of data, and mistakes can be overlooked if the proofreading is performed too quickly.

For example, a teacher uses a spreadsheet to calculate the final marks for each of her students, and then enters the final marks into a central computer system. She then gives a printout of the spreadsheet marks to the secretary who then logs into the central system and checks that the mark entered against each pupil corresponds to what is on the printout.

12.5 Further Validation Checks – Batch and Hash Totals

Sometimes data is entered into a computer system and processed in **batches** of documents. Standard validation and verification checks are, of course, performed during data entry on each individual document. However, when multiple documents are entered in batches a further validation check is needed to verify that the data in all the documents in a batch have been entered exactly once, for example to ensure that data from a document has not been accidentally missed out and no document has been entered twice. **Batch and hash totals** are two types of validation check designed to address this problem. They are used as a control precaution to ensure that data from each document in a batch is entered exactly once.

A **batch total** is a fairly basic check. Before any data is entered the user manually counts how many documents there are – this is the 'batch total'. As the data from each document is typed in, the computer maintains a count of how many documents have been entered. After all the data is entered, the computer-generated total is compared to the manual total. If there is a discrepancy then it means that either data from one document has been missed or that some data has been entered twice. The main disadvantage of this approach is that a batch total would not give an error if the data from one document had been left out and data from another document had been entered twice.

A **control** or **hash** total is intended to identify this type of error. The user chooses a data field which is entered for each document (for example, in a hospital where nurses submit a form containing the number of hours they have worked in a particular week, the chosen data field could be the number of hours worked or even their staff ID number). The values for the chosen field on each document in the batch are then totalled manually. A batch total which is meaningful (for example, the total number of hours worked by all nurses) is known as a 'control total', whereas a batch total which has no clear meaning (for example, the total of all staff IDs) is known as a 'hash total'. Next, all the documents in the batch are entered into the computer. The computer will sum up the chosen data field automatically. If the manually-calculated total and the computer-calculated total differ, then it means that a mistake has been made at some point during data entry.

Note: The data field chosen for the control or hash total should not have the same value in each document, otherwise this total would not give any more information than a batch total.

Case Study

Results of a Digital Technology Exam

The teacher of an AS Digital Technology class wishes to store the marks achieved by each student in each question of an exam in a spreadsheet. The front page of each exam script contains a table giving the student ID and marks in each of four questions. The front pages of four of the student scripts are shown in figure 12.9.

Student ID	6502
Q1 (25)	19
Q2 (25)	13
Q3 (25)	14
Q4 (25)	14
TOTAL	60

Student ID	3885
Q1 (25)	20
Q2 (25)	18
Q3 (25)	12
Q4 (25)	22
TOTAL	72

Student ID	4550
Q1 (25)	20
Q2 (25)	13
Q3 (25)	10
Q4 (25)	12
TOTAL	55

Student ID	9364
Q1 (25)	22
Q2 (25)	19
Q3 (25)	21
Q4 (25)	22
TOTAL	84

Figure 12.9: Marks on four student scripts.

A spreadsheet with six columns (Student ID, Q1, Q2, Q3, Q4 and Total) is constructed. The teacher wants to use data validation to ensure all the scripts have been entered into the spreadsheet.

The teacher could use a batch total. In this case, a cell in the spreadsheet is used for the batch total, i.e. to provide a count of the number of Q1 marks entered or the number of Student IDs entered. When the teacher finishes entering the data, she counts the number of scripts and checks this against the batch total in the spreadsheet. If they are not the same she may have missed a script or entered a student's details twice.

Alternatively, the teacher could use a control or hash total. She could choose the mark for Q1 for the control, and add the Q1 marks from each paper together to give the control total. When the teacher finishes entering the data, she would add up the marks achieved by all students for Q1. If the total for the column is the same as the manually calculated total, then it is likely that data from all documents have been entered.

However, the student ID would be a better data item for the total because the student ID is unique for each candidate. This is a hash total. The teacher first calculates the manual total of student IDs. When the teacher finishes entering the data, she would check that the manual total matches the computer-generated hash total.

Suppose that the teacher misses out one of the exam scripts. The manually-calculated batch and hash totals for the above methods are as follows:

Manual Totals: Batch Total = 4
Control Total (Q1) = 19 + 20 + 20 + 22 = 81
Hash Total (Student ID) = 6502 + 3885 + 4550 + 9364 = 24301

However, the computer totals from the spreadsheet are as follows:

Computer Totals: Batch Total = 3
Control Total (Q1) = 19 + 20 + 22 = 61
Hash Total (Student ID) = 6502 + 3885 + 9364 = 19751

The differing manual and computer totals for both the batch and control totals indicate an error. As the Student ID is unique, subtracting the computer Student ID hash total from the manual Student ID hash total (24301 − 19751 = 4550) identifies the student whose data was not entered.

Now suppose that the data for Student ID = 4550 was missed out, but the data for Student ID = 3885 was entered twice. In that case the computer totals from the spreadsheet are as follows:

Computer Totals: Batch Total = 4
Control Total (Q1) = 19 + 20 + 20 + 22 = 81
Hash Total (Student ID) = 6502 + 3885 + 3885 + 9364 = 23636

In this case, neither the batch total nor the control total spot the mistake, but different manual (24301) and computer (23636) hash totals still indicate that there is an error. It is not as easy to work out the problem when more than one mistake has been made, but the point is that the error has been detected.

Task

Consider the previous case study. Using the front pages of the four student scripts shown, state an example of one data item which could have been used for the control total which would not have detected that student 3885 had been entered twice and that student 9364 had been omitted. What does this tell you about control totals?

12.6 Limitations of Data Validation and Data Verification

We have seen how data validation (making sure that the data is sensible and reasonable within acceptable boundaries) and data verification (ensuring that all copies of the data exactly match the original source) can detect many data input errors. However, it is important to understand that employing these methods will not eliminate all errors.

For example, someone could enter their date of birth as 31 April 2001. If the validation check was simply to ensure that the day was in the range 1..31, and the verification check was to require double entry, then neither method may pick up the error. Similarly, the methods will not detect errors in the original data. For example, the original document may contain a mistake. Even if a validation check ensures that the copy exactly matches the original, it will still be wrong.

Data users, therefore, should be aware that data validation and verification, while very useful, have their limits and cannot be relied upon to prevent all errors.

Questions

1. With reference to the table of example data below, explain the difference between data, information and knowledge.

Name	Time to complete 100 m race (seconds)
John	12.6
Harry	12.9
Sam	12.3

2. With reference to the table of example data below, explain the difference between data, information and knowledge.

Type of Fruit	Actual Weekly Sales (kg)	Target Weekly Sales (kg)
Apples	32	40
Pears	45	40
Bananas	19	20

3. List three factors which affect the quality of information.

4. A youth club wishes to record information on all its members. One of the leaders has designed the form below:

```
┌─────────────────────────────────────────────────────────────────────────────┐
│                                                                               │
│   FIRST NAME:                                    AGE:                         │
│   _____              _____       │
│                                                                               │
│                                                                               │
│   WEIGHT:                                        HEIGHT:                       │
│   _____              _____       │
│                                                                               │
│                                                                               │
│   CONTACT NUMBER:                                                             │
│   _____                           │
│                                                                               │
└─────────────────────────────────────────────────────────────────────────────┘
```

Explain what is meant by each of the following, giving an example from the form above:
(a) Irrelevant data,
(b) Incomplete data,
(c) Up-to-date data.

5. Compare and contrast the terms 'data validation' and 'data verification'.

6. Calculate the modulus 11 check digit which should be added to the following base numbers:
(a) 601
(b) 9585
(c) 41506
(d) 801

7. Explain the following terms in the context of data verification:
(a) Double entry,
(b) Proofreading.

8. Describe the type of validation check which would be used for each of the following:
(a) To ensure 26:63 is not entered as a time (24-hour clock).
(b) To check that a person's age is entered as a number rather than a digit (for example, 20 rather than "twenty").
(c) To ensure that a password of exactly 6 alphanumeric characters is entered.
(d) To ensure that a hospital number consisting of 2 letters followed by 4 digits is entered.
(e) To check that something has been entered in a field on an electronic form.

9. (a) Explain the terms batch total, control total and hash total.
(b) Demonstrate how batch, control and hash totals could be used as validation checks for the scores obtained by 20 golfers in a 9-hole golfing competition. The golfer's name, their competitor number, the score for each of the 9 holes played and the total score are recorded on each score card. The score cards of the first three competitors are shown on the next page. All details of each competitor are to be entered into a spreadsheet.

NAME: John Smith		NAME: Dermot O'Hagan		NAME: Susan Fitzsimmons	
COMPETITOR ID: 1		COMPETITOR ID: 2		COMPETITOR ID: 3	
Hole 1	4	Hole 1	3	Hole 1	5
Hole 2	5	Hole 2	4	Hole 2	4
Hole 3	3	Hole 3	3	Hole 3	3
Hole 4	4	Hole 4	6	Hole 4	5
Hole 5	6	Hole 5	4	Hole 5	3
Hole 6	6	Hole 6	4	Hole 6	6
Hole 7	4	Hole 7	5	Hole 7	3
Hole 8	5	Hole 8	6	Hole 8	4
Hole 9	4	Hole 9	4	Hole 9	3
TOTAL	41	TOTAL	39	TOTAL	36

10. A database is set up to contain data about plants in stock in a garden centre. Data for each plant needs to be recorded as follows:

- Plant identifier, 6 characters long where the first 3 characters identify the supplier. For example, "GRD345".
- Product name, for example "5-leaf Akebia".
- Cost price, for example £3.99.
- Selling Price, for example £5.99.
- Date of Purchase, for example 03/09/19.
- Sell-by Date, for example 03/11/19.

(a) With reference to the garden centre example, explain the difference between information and knowledge.

(b) Describe how 'relevance' and 'completeness' affect the quality of the data in the database.

(c) What is the purpose of data validation?

(d) Describe two different validation methods which could be used in this database.

(e) The data also needs to be verified. Describe two different verification methods that could be used.

CHAPTER 13
Architecture

By the end of this chapter students should be able to:

- describe the internal components of a computer system: processor, clock, main memory, cache memory, buses (address, data and control), input/output (I/O) controllers, registers and ports;

- describe the fetch-execute cycle;

- evaluate the factors that can influence the speed of processing: processor type and clock speed;

- explain the need for secondary storage;

- describe secondary storage media: magnetic, optical and flash; and

- evaluate the use of secondary storage media for common applications.

13.1 The Internal Components of a Computer System

Modern computing started in the early nineteenth century when Charles Babbage proposed the 'difference engine' – a mechanical machine which could calculate numbers from given inputs. Sufficient funding was not available for Babbage to realise his dream so the machine was not completed in his lifetime.

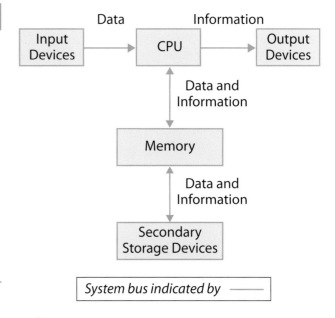

Figure 13.1: The internal, von Neumann architecture of a computer.

However, most modern computers use the **Von Neumann architecture** as shown in figure 13.1. In this machine:

- all data and instructions are stored in the **memory**;
- data and instructions are moved between components via a data path called the **system bus**;

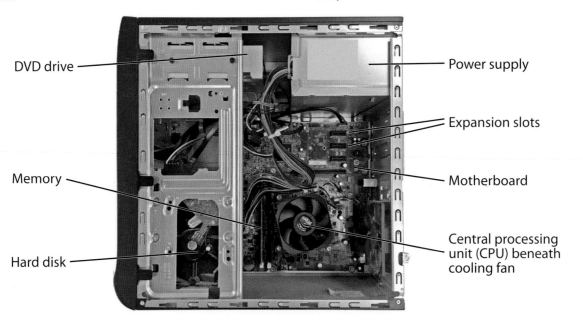

Figure 13.2 The interior of a typical computer showing the main components.

- all input and output (such as entering data or printing) is performed by **input/output devices**; and
- data and programs can be permanently stored on **secondary storage devices.**

Inside the computer (figure 13.2) is a main printed circuit board, known as the **motherboard,** which contains all the crucial electronic components and provides the connections for other devices such as keyboards and printers. The motherboard also contains **expansion slots** which allow cards that add additional functionality, such as sound cards or network cards, to be connected to the system. In the following sections we shall consider the various components inside a computer system in more detail.

Central processing unit (CPU)

The **central processing unit** (commonly called the **processor**) is the 'brain' of the computer, where most calculations take place. The CPU is the most important, most complex and most expensive component of the computer. It interprets and carries out basic instructions, stored in a program, to process the computer's data and exchanges this data with other components and peripherals. To put it another way, the CPU takes inputs from an input device, processes the input in some way and outputs the results to an output device.

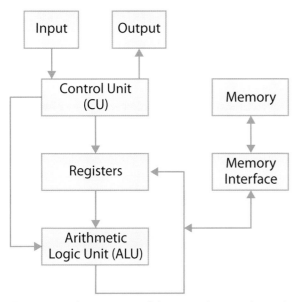

Figure 13.3: Components of the central processing unit.

The principal components of a CPU are shown in figure 13.3. They include:

- the **control unit** (CU),
- the **arithmetic logic unit** (ALU), and
- **registers**.

The **control unit** (CU) performs three tasks. Firstly, it extracts instructions from memory and decodes and executes them, calling on the ALU (see below) when necessary. This is known as the **fetch-execute cycle**, which we shall discuss in more detail in section 13.2. Secondly, it controls and monitors the hardware attached to the system to make sure that commands (sent by the application software) are executed. Finally, it controls the input and output of data.

The **arithmetic logic unit** (ALU) loads data from the input **registers**, receives instructions from the control unit on what operation to perform and stores the result in an output register. It can perform two types of task: arithmetic computations (such as addition, subtraction, multiplication and division), and logical operations (such as >, <, =, AND and OR comparisons).

Registers are temporary, high-speed storage areas which are used for data or instructions needed quickly by the control unit. Each register is a single storage location within the CPU. All data must be stored in a register before it can be processed. For example, if two numbers are to be added, both numbers are first stored in registers, the ALU performs the calculation and the result is then placed in a register. The register can also contain the address of a memory location where data is stored rather than the actual data itself.

As well as the general registers there are specialised registers, the most common of which are:

- the **accumulator** (ACC), a data register used for short-term storage of arithmetic and logic data;
- the **program counter** (PC), an incrementing counter that keeps track of the memory address of which instruction in the program is to be executed next;
- the **current instruction register** (CIR), a register for temporarily holding the instruction which has just been fetched from memory, and is currently being executed by the processor;
- the **memory address register** (MAR), holds the address in memory of the next data element to be fetched; and
- the **memory data register** (MDR), a two-way register which holds data that has just been fetched from memory or data that is waiting to be stored to a location in memory.

The movement of data in and out of registers is usually transparent to users, and even to programmers. Only low-level **assembly language** programs can manipulate registers. The compiler is responsible for translating high-level instructions (such as C# code) into low-level instructions that access registers.

Many computers now have **multi-core processors.** A multi-core processor is a single computing component with two or more independent processing units called **cores**. Multi-core processors can have two cores (dual-core), four cores (quad-core) or more. Multiple cores can have multiple programs (known as threads) running at the same time. This increases the overall speed of programs which have been written to take advantage of this ability.

32-bit and 64-bit processors

The two main categories of processors are **32-bit** and **64-bit** (sometimes referred to as having a 'word size' of 32 bits or 64 bits). The type of processor affects the overall performance of the computer and can dictate what type of software it is able to use.

In a 32-bit processor each register has a size of 32 bits, which means that the processor can work with 32 bits of data at a time. 32-bit processors (for example, the Intel 80386, 80486 and Pentium processors) are capable of working with up to 2^{32} (4 294 967 296) different memory addresses at any given time. This means that a 32-bit processor generally cannot address more than 4 GB of RAM (2^{32}).

In recent years, 64-bit processors have become more commonplace on home computers, for example, the Intel Pentium dual-core, Core i3, Core i5 and Core-i7 processors. 64-bit processors can work with up to 2^{64} (18 446 744 073 709 551 616) memory addresses, representing 16.8 million TB; but this a theoretical limit only, as it is currently impossible to physically store that amount of memory in a computer case. More recent operating systems have been developed in both 32 and 64-bit versions, for example Windows 7, Windows 8.1, Windows 10 and MacOS. A computer with a 64-bit processor can have either a 64-bit or a 32-bit operating system installed, but the 32-bit operating system would not be able to take full advantage of a 64-bit processor. Software developed for a 32-bit processor will work on a 64-bit processor, but 64-bit software will not run on a computer which has a 32-bit processor.

Clock

The processor in every computer contains a quartz **clock** which synchronises the various computer components. The processor requires a fixed number of clock ticks (or **clock cycles**) to execute each instruction. The processor has a property called the **clock speed** (or **clock rate**) which is the speed at which it executes instructions. The higher the clock speed, the more instructions the processor can execute per second.

Clock speeds are measured in cycles per second or hertz (Hz). Processor speed is usually expressed in megahertz (MHz) or gigahertz (GHz). A modern computer running at 2.7 GHz is running at 2.7×2^{30} clock cycles per second, i.e. it is carrying out 2.7 billion instructions per second.

> **Note:** 1 megahertz (MHz) = 2^{20} hertz and 1 gigahertz (GHz) = 2^{30} hertz.

Worked Example

At how many clock cycles per second does a 3 MHz processor run?

From section 11.1 we remember that one megabyte is 2^{20} bytes. In the same way, we say that one megahertz is 2^{20} hertz. Hence:

$$3 \text{ MHz} = 3 \times 2^{20} \text{ clock cycles per second.}$$
$$= 3 \times 1\,048\,576$$
$$= 3\,145\,728 \text{ clock cycles per second}$$

Main memory

Main memory (sometimes referred to as **immediate access store**) refers to the internal storage area of a computer that can be directly addressed by the processor. It holds both the programs and the data that the user is currently using. The processor reads data and programs from some form of backing storage (hard disk, flash drive etc) and stores them temporarily in memory. This is because backing storage is much too slow for running applications from directly. The processor then extracts the instructions from memory, decodes and executes them – the fetch-execute cycle.

Main memory consists of one or more chips, either on the motherboard or another connected circuit board. Computers often have memory slots on the motherboard which hold modules of memory chips. This can allow memory to be upgraded at a later date.

There are two different types of memory, **read-only memory** and **random access memory**.

The content of **read-only memory (ROM)** is permanent. It is written onto the ROM when it is first made and cannot be altered by the user. The key advantage of ROM is that it is **non-volatile**, i.e. its content is preserved when the computer is turned off. It is therefore used to store fixed programs, such as the basic instructions necessary to start up the computer and launch the operating system. ROM is also used in systems where the program will not need to be altered, for example in the small built-in computer used to control a dishwasher.

Random access memory (RAM) is used to temporarily store data and programs that are currently in use by the processor. RAM is **volatile** memory, meaning that the contents are lost when the computer is turned off. Therefore, each time the computer is turned on the data and programs must be loaded into RAM before they can be used. The size of RAM is measured in megabytes (MB) or gigabytes (GB). A computer with 4 GB (ie 4×2^{30} bytes) of memory has 2^{32} addressable locations of RAM. The more RAM a computer has, the faster it responds. Adding additional RAM to a computer can improve its performance, as it allows more data to be held in main memory. This data would otherwise need to be stored on, and fetched from, slower backing storage devices.

Cache memory

In any computer system most of the data is stored on some form of backing storage device such as a hard disk. When the processor requires that data, it is loaded into RAM because it is much faster to access data from RAM than from the hard disk. However, although RAM is much faster than a hard disk, it is still not fast enough to cope with the speed that the processor needs to deal with the data most efficiently.

The solution is to store as much data as possible as close as possible to the processor to avoid delays. This nearby storage is called **cache memory** (sometimes referred to as **CPU memory**). The cache uses a special type of computer memory which can be accessed much faster than RAM. However, it is also much more expensive than RAM. Therefore, the more cache memory available, the more expensive the processor chip will be.

Cache memory is used to hold information (such as sections of a program and its associated data) that the computer uses frequently or is likely to use next. Cache also 'reads ahead'. When the CPU first accesses a particular memory address, the contents of that address will not currently be held in cache, so the contents of that memory location will be loaded into the cache. The cache controller will then attempt to predict which addresses are likely to be accessed next and pre-fetch those values into the cache so that they are available before they are requested. This prediction can be very accurate if the requested memory address contains a program instruction, as successive instructions are usually located in adjacent memory addresses. To ensure optimal performance, the cache should be as full as possible so that the CPU has as little waiting to do as possible.

Note: Cache memory performs two tasks:
- to store frequently used instructions, and
- to 'read ahead'.

A device called a **cache controller** transfers the data from RAM into the cache. If the CPU needs to obtain information from memory, it goes through the following process, shown in figure 13.4:

1. The CPU checks whether the information is located inside the cache (A).
2. If the cache controller has been successful in predicting that the CPU would need this data, then the required information is available from a previous data reading.
3. If not, the CPU will get the information from RAM (B) and place it in the cache (C) before processing it. The cache controller

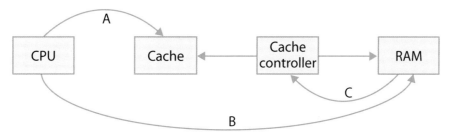

Figure 13.4: The process by which a CPU uses cache memory.

may then read further data in response to this event.

Cache memory is usually categorised into **levels** which describe its accessibility and proximity to the processor:

- Level 1 (L1) cache is extremely fast but relatively small and is usually integrated directly with the CPU chip.
- Level 2 (L2) cache may be located on the CPU or on a separate chip (a co-processor) that has its own dedicated data connection.
- Level 3 (L3) cache is generally specialised memory used to improve the performance of L1 and L2.

The relative access speeds of a hard disk, RAM and the three types of cache are shown in Figure 13.5.

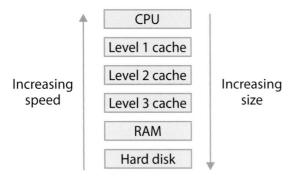

Figure 13.5: Comparison of the speed of access of various components in a computer.

Buses

Figure 13.1 showed the key components which make up a typical computer. These components need to be able to communicate with each other and this is achieved by using a **bus**. A bus is made up of a set of parallel wires along which electrical signals can pass between components. These signals represent binary values, with one bit per wire. The number of parallel wires in the bus is known as the **bus width**.

The signals on a bus can represent an address, data or control information. For this reason, the main **system bus** is made up of an **address bus**, a **data bus** and a **control bus**. Figure 13.6 illustrates the bus connections between the processor, main memory and the input/output devices. We shall consider each type of bus in turn.

Address bus

The **address bus** carries the address of the piece of memory or input/output device to be read from or written to. It is **unidirectional**, which means the address travels only one way (from the CPU to memory or input/output device). The bus width determines the number of addressable locations. For example, a 32-bit address bus can address 2^{32} (4 294 967 296) memory locations (that is, 4 GB of memory space). Most modern computers have 32-, 64- or 128-bit address buses.

Worked Example

Explain why it would not be a good idea to use a 10-bit address bus to refer to 2048 locations in main memory.

A 10-bit address bus means that it can address $2^{10} = 1024$ different locations (0 to 1023), which is less than the number of locations in main memory. This means that the computer would not be able to address locations 1024 to 2047.

Control bus

The CPU uses the **control bus** to monitor what the different parts of the computer are doing. It is **bidirectional**, which means that control signals can be transported in both directions along the bus. These signals include read requests, write requests and interrupt requests. Information about events,

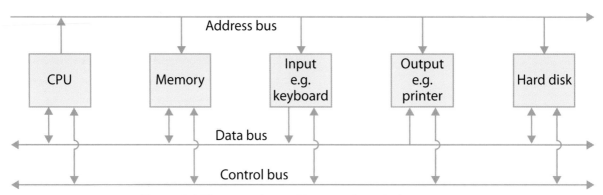

Figure 13.6: The system bus architecture of a typical computer.

such as messages to indicate that a device has been plugged in or has finished a job, are also carried along the control bus.

Data bus

The **data bus** transports data between components and is **bidirectional**. When the CPU requests some data from main memory it sends the address of the data to main memory along the address bus and the main memory then returns the data along the data bus. Most modern computers have 32-, 64- or 128-bit data buses. The width of the data bus contributes to the performance of the CPU since the wider the data bus, the more data it can carry at one time.

The maximum addressable memory (RAM) in a computer is determined as follows:

$$\text{Size of RAM (in bits)}$$
$$= 2^{\text{(address bus width)}} \times \text{(data bus width, in bits)}$$

Most computers do not come with the maximum addressable memory installed because:

- RAM is expensive,
- most programs do not require the maximum amount of RAM to be installed, and
- some addresses are allocated to input/output ports, which means those locations in main memory are not accessible. (Ports are discussed later in this section.)

Worked Example

A computer has a 32-bit address bus and a 128-bit data bus. What is the maximum addressable memory? Give your answer in GB.

$$\text{RAM (bits)} = 2^{\text{(address bus width)}} \times \text{(data bus width) bits}$$
$$= 2^{32} \times 128 \text{ bits}$$
$$= 2^{32} \times 2^{7} \text{ bits}$$
$$= 2^{39} \text{ bits}$$
$$= 2^{36} \text{bytes}$$
$$\quad \text{(since 1 byte = 8 bits = } 2^{3} \text{ bits)}$$
$$= 2^{6} \text{ gigabtyes}$$
$$= 64 \text{ GB}$$

Worked Example

A computer has a 64-bit data bus and 32 GB of RAM. What is the width of the address bus?

$$\text{RAM (bits)} = 2^{\text{(address bus width)}}$$
$$\times \text{(data bus width) bits}$$
$$32 \times 2^{30} \times 8 = 2^{\text{(address bus width)}} \times 64 \text{ bits}$$
$$2^{5} \times 2^{30} \times 2^{3} = 2^{\text{(address bus width)}} \times 2^{6} \text{ bits}$$
$$2^{38} = 2^{\text{(address bus width)}} \times 2^{6} \text{ bits}$$
$$2^{38} \div 2^{6} = 2^{\text{(address bus width)}}$$
$$2^{32} = 2^{\text{(address bus width)}}$$

Address bus width = 32 bits

I/O controllers

The CPU, memory and system bus are all internal components of a computer. Everything else is an **input** device (such as a keyboard, mouse or sensor), an **output** device (such as a screen or printer) or both (such as a hard disk), in which case we refer to it as an **I/O device** or **peripheral**. Peripherals differ in speed, operate at different voltages and have different levels of complexity, so it would not be sensible to try to design a processor capable of controlling every possible peripheral. Instead the interface between the many different devices and the internal components of the computer is managed by an **I/O controller**. The CPU uses a software interface to pass requests to the I/O controller to translate the requests into the appropriate external signals, rather than accessing the external devices directly.

The I/O controller is an electronic circuit consisting of three parts:

- an **I/O port** which allows the exchange of data between the CPU and the peripheral,
- electronics which interface the controller to the system bus, and
- electronics capable of sending signals to the device connected to the computer.

The I/O controller performs the following tasks:

- **Protocol conversion** – ensures that the external device and the computer adhere to the same protocols (i.e. the same format for commands).
- **Voltage conversion** – changes the voltage level of the external device to a value appropriate for the computer.

- **Buffering** – acts as a temporary storage of data between the external device and the computer if they operate at different speeds.
- **Data format conversion** – converts data from the format produced by the external device, for example converting the a 16-bit value produced by an I/O device to the 32-bit value required by the computer.

The I/O controller interaction is shown diagrammatically in figure 13.7. The I/O controller is commonly located on the motherboard but it can also be on an internal expansion card to provide additional input or output devices for the computer. A single I/O controller can control multiple devices, but nevertheless most computers have several I/O controllers.

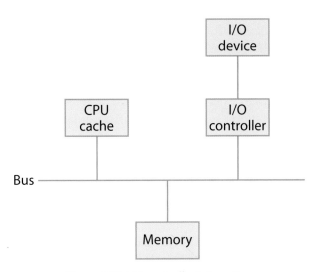

Figure 13.7: I/O controller interaction.

Ports

We have already seen that input devices (such as the mouse or keyboard) and output devices (such as printers and monitors) need to be able to connect to the computer. The actual connection point between the two is called a **port**. A cable with a **connector** at one end is plugged into the port, and the other end connected to the external device. Older computers had many different types of port, each for a specific device – power supply, keyboard, mouse, monitor, speakers etc. In the mid-1990s an industry standard, **USB** (Universal Serial Bus), was developed which defines the cables, connectors and communications protocols used in a bus for the connection, communication and power supply between the computer and peripherals. Most modern personal computers are fitted with many USB ports (symbol shown in figure 13.8).

Figure 13.8: Symbol indicating a USB port.

There are various types of USB port (1.0, 2.0, 3.0 etc) with each newer version giving improved speeds compared to previous versions. USB ports also come three sizes (standard, mini and micro), depending on the application. Standard and mini ports are designed for connections that are plugged in less than once a day, with a design lifetime of 1500 insertion-removal cycles. Micro connectors are more robust, with a design lifetime of 10 000 insertion-removal cycles, and are intended for devices such as smartphones which are plugged in frequently.

Worked Example

Match each of the following components to the numbers on the diagram below: processor, data bus, address bus, clock, ROM, RAM, keyboard port, printer port, secondary storage.

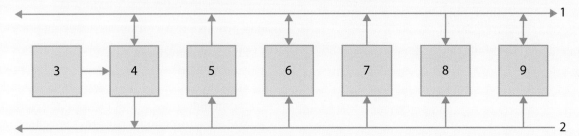

1. data bus – as this is a bidirectional bus to transport data between components.
2. address bus – as it is a unidirectional bus carrying address from the CPU to memory or input/output device.

3. clock – part of the processor.
4. processor – a bidirectional connection to the data bus and unidirectional connection to the address bus.
5. (or 7.) ROM – as data is only received from this component.
6. RAM – as data is sent to and received from this component.
7. (or 5.) keyboard port – as data is sent to the data bus.
8. printer port – as data is received from the data bus.
9. secondary storage – as data is sent to and received from a device (such as a hard disk).

Case Study

Computer specification

A shop is selling a laptop. The label describes it as having a 64-bit, 500 MHz dual-core processor with 32 GB of RAM. What does this mean?

The term 64-bit means that the word size of the processor is 64 bits. This means that it can directly access 2^{64} memory addresses.

500 MHz refers to the clock speed of the processor. 500 MHz = 500×2^{20} cycles per second, which is over 500 million.

Dual-core means there are two processors. This computer is therefore capable of carrying out two instructions at the same time (known as parallel processing) which makes programs run faster.

32 GB of RAM means that the computer has $32 \times 2^{30} = 2^6 \times 2^{30} = 2^{36}$ addressable locations of Random Access Memory. RAM is where the computer stores data and programs while they are being executed.

Enhancing computer performance

Computer performance can generally be increased in three ways:

- **Clock speed** – the faster the clock speed, the more powerful the computer, because it can execute more instructions per second. However, the faster the clock goes, the more current flows which means that the processor gets hotter. If a processor gets too hot it can burn out and need replaced.
- **Internal memory** (**cache memory**) – by increasing the size of internal memory the number of instructions or data items that can be held in close proximity to the processor is increased, so the time spent copying data in and out of memory is reduced.

- **Processor type** – upgrading the processor type from 32-bit to 64-bit or using quad-core processors will increase computer performance, as more data can be processed at once.

Benchmark tests to assess computer performance are available commercially. Sometimes such benchmarks use additional terminology over and above what has been discussed in this section. For example, the arithmetic capability of a processor is sometimes measured in MIPS (Million Instructions Per Second) or FLOPS (FLoating point Operations Per Second). These metrics are independent of other measures, such as hard disk speed.

13.2 The Fetch-Execute Cycle

The **fetch-execute cycle** refers to the sequence of steps needed for any processing to take place in a CPU. Despite its name, there are actually three steps in the process – fetch, decode and execute. This process, shown in figure 13.9, is repeated continuously by the CPU from the moment the computer is switched on until it is shut down. Before processing commences, both the data and the program (set of instructions) that act upon that data are loaded into main memory (RAM) by the operating system.

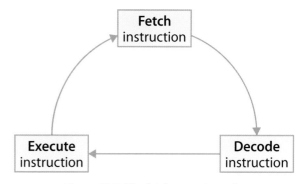

Figure 13.9: The fetch-execute cycle.

For example, when a person plays a computer game that is stored on a DVD, they first insert the disk. The program code is then loaded from the disk into main memory. Finally, to play the game, the processor repeatedly fetches, decodes and executes instructions from main memory. We will consider each of these steps in turn and then consider the concept of pipelining.

Fetch

In the first step of the cycle the CPU will **fetch** the next instruction to be processed by placing the instruction's memory address on the address bus and retrieving the memory contents from the data bus. The precise sequence of events is as follows:

1. The address of the first instruction to be read is loaded into the Program Counter (PC).
2. The contents of the PC are placed in the Memory Address Register (MAR).
3. The PC is updated to point to the location of the next instruction which must be executed.
4. The MAR places the address on the **address bus.**
5. A 'read' signal from the MAR loads the instruction into the Memory Data Register (MDR) via the **data bus.**
6. The instruction is copied into the Current Instruction Register (CIR).

Decode

The second step is to **decode** the instruction that has been placed in the CIR. The CPU is designed to understand a specific set of commands (known as the 'instruction set'). Different makes of CPU have different instruction sets. The control unit decodes the instruction by splitting it into an operations ('opcodes') and data ('operands'). It also prepares various registers for the execution of the command.

Execute

The third step, the **execute** phase, is where the actual data processing takes place. If the instruction involves some arithmetic or logic, the ALU will be used. The opcode identifies the type of the instruction (add, subtract etc). The result of the processing is stored in another register – the Accumulator (ACC).

Pipelining

In simple CPUs each instruction is executed sequentially, i.e. each instruction is completely processed before the next one is started. In more modern CPUs, the instruction cycles can overlap (i.e. run concurrently) using a process known as **pipelining.** In this process, the CPU starts fetching the second instruction once the first instruction has been passed onto the decode phase. In a simple CPU it would take three time units to execute each instruction (fetch, decode, execute). Four instructions would therefore take twelve time units. However, figure 13.10 illustrates how four instructions can be executed in six time units using pipelining.

13.3 Secondary Storage

RAM is referred to as **primary storage**, but it is volatile memory, which means that when the computer is switched off all data stored in it is lost. A computer system must have some method of storing data permanently. A **secondary storage** device (sometimes referred to as **auxiliary storage**) is a device containing non-volatile memory which can be used to store data even when the power supply is switched off. The data remains stored until it is overwritten or deleted. Secondary storage devices provide a number of additional benefits:

		Instruction 1	Instruction 2	Instruction 3	Instruction 4
Time	T_1	Fetch			
	T_2	Decode	Fetch		
	T_3	Execute	Decode	Fetch	
	T_4		Execute	Decode	Fetch
	T_5			Execute	Decode
	T_6				Execute

Figure 13.10: Pipelining in the fetch-execute cycle.

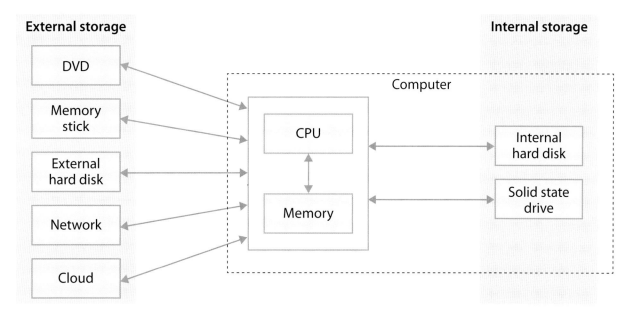

Figure 13.11: Internal and external storage.

- capacity – it has a greater storage capacity than RAM;
- portability – data can be saved and moved from one place to another;
- security – important data can be copied and stored safely (backups).

The choice of secondary storage device depends on the following factors:

- speed – how quickly the user needs to be able to access the data from the storage device;
- capacity – the amount of data to be stored;
- durability – how long the storage media is expected to last;
- portability – how far the data has to be moved (e.g. to another continent or just an adjacent room);
- reliability – assurance that the data can always be accessed reliably and in the format in which it was saved.

We shall first consider the distinction between internal and external storage devices. We shall then go on to discuss the three main types of secondary memory – magnetic, optical and flash.

Internal and external storage devices

Secondary storage devices can be either **internal** (located inside the computer case) or **external** (separate from the computer) as shown in figure 13.11. Internal storage (usually one or more hard disks) is normally used to store the operating system,

applications software and data files. External storage (portable hard disks, flash drives, CDs, DVDs etc) can be used to store backups (which can be stored off-site in case of a disaster), archive data no longer required, store data files that won't fit on the internal hard disk and so forth. External storage devices are usually connected to the computer via a USB port.

There are two main differences between internal and external storage devices, as follows.

- Access speed – internal storage devices are connected to the data bus which allows much faster access than data on an external device connected through a hardware interface such as a USB port.
- Portability – external storage devices are very portable so data can be moved easily from one location to another.

On a Windows PC, secondary storage devices appear as drive letters in the folder tree. The storage areas of a typical computer are shown in figure 13.12. This computer has a hard drive (C:), a DVD drive (D:) and external storage device (E:) called EXAM MARKS. There is a padlock icon on the external drive which shows that the drive is encrypted. This means that a password is needed to access it.

Magnetic storage

Magnetic storage is one of the most common types of computer storage. There are three main forms of magnetic storage – floppy disks, hard disks and magnetic tape.

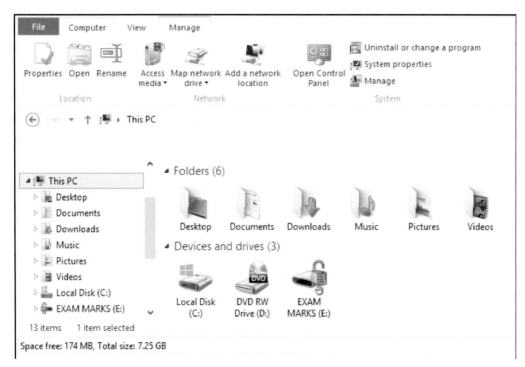

Figure 13.12: Different storage areas on a typical Windows PC.

Floppy disks

Floppy disks were the first form of secondary storage used on personal computers. They were very easy to use and were portable. The first floppy disks were 8-inch disks first available in the early 1970s. Later 5¼-inch disks were introduced which were themselves replaced by 3½-inch disks (as shown in figure 13.13) which were capable of holding up to 1.44 MB of data. Most modern computers no longer come equipped with floppy disk drives as they have a very limited capacity for today's needs.

Figure 13.13: A 3½-inch floppy disk.

A floppy disk consists of a flat, flexible ('floppy') Mylar plastic disk that rotates within a hard plastic casing. Data is stored as electromagnetic charges on a metal oxide film coating the Mylar plastic. They also contain a 'write-protect' slider that, when opened, prevents data being written to the disks. A **floppy drive** is required in order to access the data on a floppy disk. When the floppy is inserted in the floppy drive, the sliding metal shutter is opened exposing the Mylar plastic and a read-write head moves across the exposed disk to either store or retrieve data. Data is recorded on the disk in closed concentric circles known as **tracks**. Floppy disks have been largely superseded by CDs, DVDs, hard disks and flash drives.

> **Note:** Floppy disks were the original solution for personal storage on the earliest personal computers, but are now an obsolete form of secondary storage.

Hard disks

Hard disks are designed to store vast amounts of data. Modern hard disks can store gigabytes (for example, 200 GB) or terabytes (for example, 2 TB) of data. A **hard drive** (figure 13.14) consists of one or more hard disks (metal platters) mounted on a spindle, each of which has been coated with a special magnetic material to which data can be written using a magnetic head. The hard disks are placed inside a disk drive which is air-sealed to protect them. Each disk is further separated into tracks (concentric circles) and sectors (pie-shaped wedges on each track). The disks are spun many thousands of times per minute so that they rotate beneath the head.

A hard drive is provided as a standard, integral part of a personal computer or laptop, but hard drives can also be external to the computer, most often used for backup storage. Most operating systems and other frequently-used data (for example, application software, documents, pictures and video) are stored on the computer's internal hard drive.

When the operating system needs to read or write information, it looks up the **file allocation table** (FAT) to determine a file's location or available write areas. Data sent to and from the hard drive is then interpreted by a **disk controller** which tells the hard drive how to move the components within the drive to find the required area for the data. When writing data to the hard disk, the read/write head will move to the required area and the magnetic surface of the disk will be magnetised on one of two polarities representing 0s and 1s.

Figure 13.14: A hard drive, with the cover removed to show one of the platters and its magnetic head.

Note: Hard disks provide direct access, hold vast amounts of data, are relatively cheap, are very durable and are good for storing frequently-made backups.

Magnetic tape

Magnetic tape (figure 13.15) is another type of magnetic storage medium. It was used extensively for backups in the past, but in recent years has become increasingly obsolete except in large organisations or for data archiving. Magnetic tapes can store similar amounts of data to hard drives, but the reading and writing of the data is sequential which means that the tape reader has to start at the beginning of the tape and fast-forward until the required piece of data is found. There is therefore no random access (as in a hard disk) so access time can be slow. It can be used over and over again, though the quality of the tape declines if data is rewritten to it many times. The main advantage of magnetic tape is that it is very cheap for the amount of data it can store.

Figure 13.15: A magnetic tape cartridge.

Note: Magnetic tape provides serial access (the slowest of all storage media), holds vast amounts of data, is very cheap and is excellent for archiving data.

Optical storage

Optical storage works by using a laser beam to create pits in the metallic surface of a disc. A laser beam of lower intensity is used to read data stored on the disc. The optical disc must be inserted into a drive to read or write data. In the drive the disc is rotated, with the speed of rotation determining the rate at which data can be transferred to disc and vice-versa. The faster the drive, the faster data can be read from the optical disc and processed by the computer. Specialist 'burning' software is required to write data to an optical disc.

There are three main forms of optical disc – compact disc (CD), digital versatile disc (DVD) and Blu-ray disc, ranging in capacity from 650 MB for a CD, up to 128 GB for a Blu-ray disc.

Compact disc (CD)

Compact discs are small, portable and are very cheap to produce. They have a maximum storage capacity of 650 MB. Because they allow direct (random) access, they are faster than magnetic tape, but are slower than either a hard disk or flash memory. The surface of a CD can be scratched easily, which can damage the data stored. Note that the majority of DVD drives are also capable of reading CDs, so the same drive can be used for both types of disc.

CDs come in three forms:

- **CD-ROM** (CD Read Only Memory) discs have the data written to them at the manufacturing stage. CD-ROMs are mainly used for music and small software packages as the data does not need to be altered.

- **CD-R** (CD Recordable) discs come with no data on them. The user can then store ('burn') data onto the disc. However, data can only be written once, which means that once data has been burnt onto the disc, that part of the disc cannot be used for storage again, although it can be read many times. The CD drive must have appropriate burning software to write data to the disc.
- **CD-RW** (CD Re-Writable) discs can be used to save data many times. The reflective layer has a special coating which is not permanently altered when data is saved onto it, so it can be erased to accommodate new data.

> **Note:** Compact discs were the earliest form of optical storage with a capacity of up to 650 MB. They were viewed as a replacement for (and upgrade of) floppy discs, but have since been superseded by DVD and Blu-ray.

Digital versatile disc (DVD)

DVDs are also small, portable and very cheap to produce. However, they are less expensive than CDs per byte of storage because they can store much more data, up to 9 GB in a double-layer DVD. One hour of standard video needs 2 GB of storage, so a DVD is large enough to accommodate a feature-length movie. Because, like CDs, they allow direct (random) access, they are faster than magnetic tape, but are slower than either a hard disk or flash memory. They are similarly vulnerable to scratches, which can damage the data being stored.

DVDs come in three forms:

- **DVD-ROM** (DVD Read Only Memory) discs are commercially available DVDs whose contents are written at the manufacturing stage and cannot be altered, for example to sell movies.
- **DVD-R** (DVD Recordable) discs are initially blank, allowing the user to write once the data they wish to save. They can only be written once.
- **DVD-RW** (DVD Re-Writable) discs are similar to CD-RW in that they allow data to be written to the disc many times.

There is no industry standard for DVDs. They therefore come in various different formats (DVD-R, DVD+R, DVD-RW, DVD+RW) and different DVD equipment is used for the different types.

> **Note:** DVDs were originally developed by the movie industry and were originally designed to allow an entire movie to be stored on a single disc. The computer industry adopted the technology as an upgrade to the CD.

Blu-ray disc

Blu-ray discs were first released in 2006, and were designed to supersede the DVD format. Blu-ray discs have a higher storage capacity than DVDs (up to 128 GB in a quadruple-layer disc). This makes them capable of storing high-definition video, so they are used for distribution of movies and video games. The technology itself was designed to stay relevant for at least 10–15 years. The discs offer much better resistance to scratches and fingerprints than CDs and DVDs due to the provision of a hard coating on Blu-ray discs.

> **Note:** Blu-ray is an enhancement of the same optical technology used in CD and DVD, and allows much more data to be stored on a single disc.

Flash memory

Flash memory (sometimes referred to as **solid-state storage**) is a form of non-volatile data storage with no moving parts, since the electronic circuitry is built entirely out of semiconductors. The lack of mechanical movement allows for very fast access times. Although initially very expensive, flash storage has started to replace magnetic media as prices have fallen, and because it is more efficient and reliable than magnetic storage.

Memory sticks and cards

Memory sticks (sometimes called **pen drives** or **USB sticks**) are forms of flash memory external to the computer (figure 13.16). They are small, lightweight, portable devices which are connected to a computer via the USB port. They are capable of storing up to 2 TB of data, though smaller sizes of up to 32 GB are more common. Although slower than a hard disk, they have faster data transfer rates than CDs, DVDs and magnetic tape. Nevertheless, they are more expensive per byte of storage than any of these storage media. They are very durable, but the main risk is damage to the USB port.

Figure 13.16: A memory stick.

When a memory stick is inserted into a USB socket the appropriate USB driver is loaded into memory to provide the computer with code on how to read and write from the USB device. Different USB devices have different drivers. Data is read from a memory stick as follows:

1. The USB device is read, giving information on the file and folder structure (the file allocation table, or FAT) to the computer.
2. When the user attempts to read a file on the USB device, the computer sends the address required to the USB port.
3. The USB device returns the data from the required the location.

Note: When you insert a USB device, a dialogue box sometimes appears with a message "Searching for driver". If the computer does not already have a suitable driver for that device (usually on the hard disk) it needs to locate one.

Memory cards (figure 13.17) work in a similar manner to memory sticks, but come in different shapes and formats for use in small electronic devices such as cameras and mobile phones. They must be inserted into a **card reader** device in order to access them.

Figure 13.17: Three memory cards and a card reader device.

Note: Memory sticks and memory cards are small portable flash memory devices that hold varying volumes of data. They are inserted into the computer when required and removed after use.

Solid-state drive (SSD)

Unlike memory sticks or memory cards, which are external to the computer system, a solid-state drive is designed to reside inside the computer in place of a traditional hard drive. The main advantages of an SSD are as follows.

- It is smaller than a magnetic hard drive, which makes it particularly suitable for tablet computers that have insufficient space for a traditional hard drive.
- It provides faster data access than a traditional hard drive due to the absence of moving parts.
- It requires less power, which is a very important consideration for portable computers.
- It is very reliable: because there are no mechanical parts, there is less chance of it being damaged by an impact.

The main disadvantages of an SSD are as follows.

- It is more expensive per byte of storage than a traditional hard drive.
- It has a smaller capacity: at the time of writing, the largest SSD drives were 4 TB.

SSDs are becoming more common in both laptops and desktop computers as the price continues to fall and their storage capacity increases.

Note: A solid-state drive is the fastest of all secondary memory technologies. It is increasingly used as the main secondary storage device in personal computers.

Worked Example

A company has four ways to permanently store data (forms of secondary storage):

- Fixed, internal hard drives.
- Magnetic tapes.
- USB pen drives.
- CD-Rs.

Suggest which one of these devices would be most suitable for each of the scenarios below. In each case explain your reasoning. Do not use the same device more than once or give the same reason more than once.

(a) to archive 500 GB of customer sales for last year;

(b) to store a 5.3 MB word-processed file that contains sensitive information which should not be emailed as an attachment. The file is to be typed up by a secretary, but another member of staff needs to edit it.

(c) to store a promotional video (100 MB) to be sent to customers.

In each case, it is important to justify your answer or you will lose marks.

(a) Magnetic tape. It holds large quantities of data, and the data is being archived, which means there is no need to have fast access to individual files.

(b) USB pen drive. It is small and very portable. The file is small, so it can be read and written to easily.

(c) CD-R. It has enough capacity to store 100 MB, and because the data can be written to once and cannot be overwritten. CDs are also portable and hence suitable for distribution. They are flat which makes the easy to put them in envelopes.

Questions

1. The three main components of the Central Processing Unit are the control unit, arithmetic logic unit and the registers.
   (a) What three tasks does the control unit perform?
   (b) What two tasks does the arithmetic and logic unit perform?
   (c) What is the purpose of the registers in a computer?

2. Explain what is meant by the terms read-only memory (ROM) and random access memory (RAM) and explain the difference between them.

3. Using a diagram, explain how a computer makes use of cache memory.

4. Input/output (I/O) controllers are used to connect the computer's processor to peripherals.
   (a) What is a peripheral?
   (b) List the three parts of an I/O controller.
   (c) Give two reasons why an input/output (I/O) controller is required to connect external devices to a computer, rather than connecting them to the processor using the system bus.

5. A particular computer has the following configuration:

Processor Speed	1.8 GHz
RAM	16 GB
Optical Drive	CD-ROM
Hard Disk	100 GB
Data Bus Width	128 bits

   (a) Explain why clock speed alone is not considered a good measure of processor performance.
   (b) What is the address bus width for this computer?
   (c) How does the address bus width affect main memory?
   (d) Why would a user not be able to back up their data onto a CD using this computer?

6. A computer has a 32-bit address bus, a 64-bit data bus and 24 control lines with 16 MB of cache memory.
    (a) Describe the function of the address bus, the data bus and the control bus.
    (b) What is the maximum possible amount of memory this computer can address?
    (c) What is the difference between main memory and cache memory?
    (d) Why do most computers not come with the maximum addressable memory installed?
    (e) If one new line was added to the address bus, what effect would this have on the maximum addressable memory?
    (f) How would you measure the performance of the computer's processor?

7. Complete the two missing steps involved in a 'write to memory' operation:
    1. Address bus is set up with the address to be written to.
    2. …
    3. Control bus is activated with a write command.
    4. …

8. A computer has a 32-bit address bus and 64 GB of RAM. What is the width of the data bus?

9. Match the following components to the numbers on the diagram: processor, data bus, address bus, control bus, clock, main memory, keyboard, keyboard controller, mouse, mouse controller, screen, screen controller.

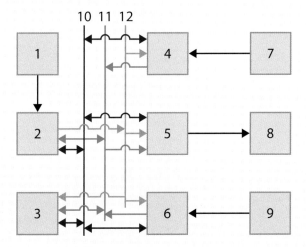

10. (a) Explain each of the three stages in the fetch-execute cycle.
    (b) Using a diagram, illustrate how three instructions can be executed in the fetch-execute cycle in the minimum number of time phases by using pipelining.

11. (a) List three benefits of using a secondary storage device.
    (b) List three factors which would influence your choice of secondary storage device.
    (c) List and explain two differences between internal and external storage devices.
    (d) How is data read from a memory stick or memory card?
    (e) What are the steps involved in writing data to a hard disk?

12. (a) Racing cars are equipped with on-board computers which record information during a race. The on-board computer has a solid-state disk. Other than robustness and cost, state two reasons why solid-state storage is used.
    (b) What are the main advantages of a solid-state drive compared to a traditional hard drive?

CHAPTER 14
The User Interface and Data Compression

By the end of this chapter students should be able to:

- describe the main features of different types of user interface: windows, icons, menu, pointer (WIMP), command line and forms dialogue;

- evaluate different types of user interface: WIMP, command line and forms dialogue;

- describe how text, sound and video can be input using a range of devices, such as personal computers, laptops, tablets or smartphones;

- explain the need for data compression;

- describe how zipping is used to compress data; and

- evaluate common data file formats: txt, wav, bitmap, Joint Photographic Experts Group (JPEG), Motion Picture Experts Group (MPEG) and Graphics Interchange Format (GIF);

14.1 The User Interface

If machines are to be useful, people need a way of interacting with them. The **user interface** is the means by which a user communicates with a computer. We meet user interfaces every day, for example the touch screen on a smart phone or at an ATM.

Good interfaces should be:

- **Simple**, with a clear, concise interface design which is easy to learn and use. It is important to strike a good balance between maximising functionality and maintaining simplicity to ensure there is no ambiguity over the way the interface works.
- **Intuitive and consistent**, allowing the user to navigate through the system easily and apply previously-learned knowledge to new tasks.
- **Responsive**, so that the user feels that the interface is 'keeping up' with their mouse activity or input from the keyboard. A slow-running interface gives the impression of poor or faulty software. The interface should always give the user feedback to indicate its current status, for example by displaying a spinning wheel or progress bar when it is working on a task.

- **Forgiving**, so that when the user makes mistakes the actions are easily reversible. The interface should also provide help and support where necessary.
- **Attractive**, providing an environment that is aesthetically appealing both in terms of typography and colour scheme. Visual appeal enhances the user experience.

In this section we shall look at various types of user interface.

Graphical user interface (WIMP interface)

A graphical user interface (GUI) is the most common type of interface used today. It is easy for the user to interact with because it makes use of pictures and colours and real-world concepts such as buttons and cut-and-paste.

A graphical user interface is also known as a WIMP interface because it makes use of:

- **w**indows, a rectangular area on the screen where applications run;
- **i**cons, pictures used to represent software applications, data files, hardware devices etc;
- **m**enus, which list options that the user can choose from; and
- **p**ointers, a symbol (usually an arrow) which can be moved around the screen (using a mouse or finger) to point to and select things, such as icons or text.

Most modern operating systems, for example Microsoft Windows, Android and iOS, use a graphical interface, often with touch interaction. An example of a GUI is shown in figure 14.1.

The main advantages of a GUI are as follows.

- It is intuitive to use.
- It is easy to navigate, as the user does not have to learn complicated commands.
- It is easy to exchange data between different software applications.
- Help guides are available for novices, and shortcut keys for experts.

Figure 14.1: The WIMP graphical user interface in Microsoft Windows.

The main disadvantages of a GUI are as follows.

- It requires a lot of memory (RAM).
- It uses much more hard disk space than other types of user interface.
- A powerful processor is required.
- It takes more time for programmers to develop applications for a GUI.

Command line interface

A **command line interface** allows the user to interact with the computer's operating system by typing commands into a window, similar to the one shown in figure 14.2. Each operating system recognises a specific set of commands. For example, the command:

```
C:\>DIR
```

is the command in the DOS operating system to display a directory listing of drive C. Many of these commands can have 'switches' – extra parameters which come after a command – to provide more specific instructions. For example, the command:

```
C:\>BACKUP C:\TIMETABLES\*.* D: /S
```

is the DOS command to create a backup of all files in the TIMETABLES directory and save the backup to drive D. The '/S' is a switch that tells the backup command to back up all the subdirectories of TIMETABLES, and not just the files that are stored in that immediate folder.

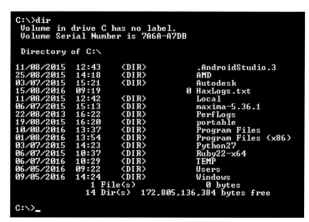

Figure 14.2: The command line interface of the DOS user interface.

In the early days of computing, command line interfaces were used by everyone. However generally only advanced users, such as systems managers, use this type of interface today since few clues are given as to the meaning of commands for inexperienced users. Systems with very limited numbers of commands many also use this type of interface.

The main advantages of a command line interface are as follows.

- Little processing power and CPU processing time is required, compared to other user interfaces.
- It uses much less memory (RAM) than other user interfaces.
- A cheap, low resolution monitor can be used.
- If the user knows the correct commands, then this type of interface can be faster than any other type of user interface.

The main disadvantages of a command line interface are as follows.

- Commands need to be typed precisely. An error will result in the command not being executed correctly and, in the worst case, could result in the loss of programs and data.
- It can be very confusing for someone who has never used a command line interface.
- It is not very intuitive, since there are a large number of commands to learn.
- It is unsuitable for novice users.

Forms interface

A **forms interface** (figure 14.3) provides the user with a limited set of choices. These interfaces typically use tools such as drop-down menus, check boxes and radio buttons to obtain data from the user. This type of interface is widely used for online user interfaces, for example when booking a holiday or buying a book.

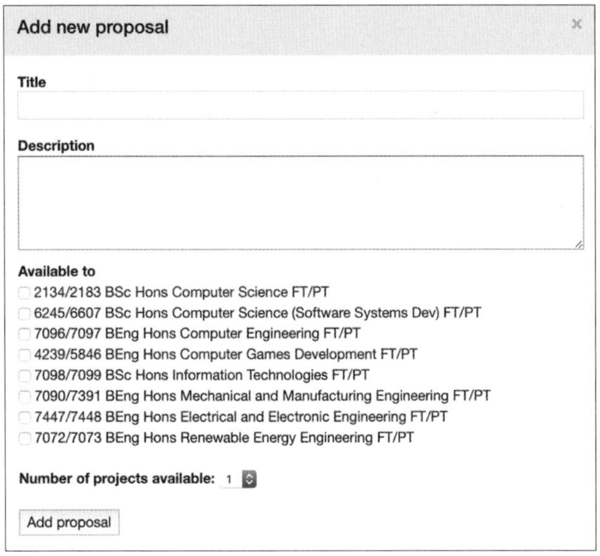

Figure 14.3: A typical forms interface.

The main advantages of a forms interface are as follows.

- It is easy to use; there is no need to learn a lot of commands.
- It is ideal for beginners as everything is displayed in a logical manner.
- Little processing power or memory is required.
- Data validation can be performed on the data as it is being entered.

The main disadvantages of a forms interface are as follows:

- Poorly designed forms may be slow to use.
- Only a limited number of options can be made available.
- Can be tedious for experts.

Dialogue interface

Note: The CCEA specification does not require you to have knowledge of the next three types of user interface (dialogue, biometric and touch-sensitive). However, because they are now common in the computing world, they are included for completeness.

A **dialogue** (or **voice**) **interface** is a way of interacting with a computer system by means of the spoken word. In some 'smart homes' lights and temperature can be controlled by voice. In the newest sat-nav devices, users can get directions to a particular location by telling the device the name of their destination. Home assistants, such as the Amazon Echo, also make use of dialogue interfaces. Because everyone's voice is slightly different, a dialogue interface usually needs to be 'trained' by the user before it can be used. Most of the intelligent assistants that are currently popular – such as Siri (Apple), Alexa (Amazon) and Cortana (Microsoft) – will work "out of the box", but performance can be improved further by repeating a series of training phrases so that the software can learn the user's speech patterns.

The main advantages of a voice interface are as follows.

- Speech input is much faster than keyboard input.
- It is good for people with dyslexia or a physical disability which makes typing difficult.
- Reduces the risk of incorrect input through typing mistakes.

CHAPTER 14 – THE USER INTERFACE AND DATA COMPRESSION

- It is hands-free, so the user can multi-task, for example speaking to a home assistant device while baking.

The main disadvantages of a voice interface are as follows.

- It takes time to train the computer to understand a particular voice.
- Background noise interferes with speech recognition.
- The computer will never be able to recognise all words and may not be able to distinguish between homonyms, such as 'there' and 'their'.
- The computer may not understand people with a strong accent or speech impediment.

Biometric interface

A **biometric interface** is a user interface that is operated by taking measurements from the human body, such as a retina scan or fingerprint. Some recent smartphones can be unlocked using a biometric interface, such as Touch ID and Face ID on Apple devices.

The main advantages of a biometric interface are as follows.

- Each individual has unique biometric characteristics, such as their fingerprints, iris or pattern of blood vessels on the retina.
- The biometric properties of an individual are part of their body and cannot be shared or lost.
- Eliminates the problem of lost IDs or forgotten passwords.
- It is difficult to forge biometric properties.

The main disadvantages of a biometric interface are as follows.

- It can be a very expensive technology.
- There are security and ethical issues with storing biometric data.
- Some biometric data, such as the iris can change due to health reasons (for example, diabetes).

Touch-sensitive interface

A **touch-sensitive interface** is one that uses finger gestures (and sometimes pressure) on a screen to provide input. They are common on small devices such as smartphones or tablets.

The main advantages of a touch-sensitive interface are as follows.

- Very intuitive to use.
- It saves space as no keyboard or mouse is required. Some touch-sensitive interfaces can provide a keyboard on the screen if required.
- Touchscreens are the fastest type of pointing devices.
- Touchscreens provide easier eye co-ordination than keyboards or mice.

The main disadvantages of a touch-sensitive interface are as follows.

- It can be difficult to read if the screen gets dirty.
- It can be difficult to select small items using finger gestures.
- Touchscreens can be scratched or broken easily.

14.2 Data Compression

Most computer files contain a lot of redundant information, i.e. the same data is repeated over and over again. Consider the following nursery rhyme:

> *Hot cross buns!*
> *Hot cross buns!*
> *One a penny, two a penny,*
> *Hot cross buns!*

Figure 14.4 shows the number of occurrences of each word:

Word	No. of Occurrences
hot	3
cross	3
buns	3
one	1
a	2
penny	2
two	1

Figure 14.4: Occurrences of words in the song Hot Cross Buns.

Ignoring case difference, more than half of the phrase is redundant. Only seven different words are used. To reconstruct the phrase, it is sufficient to store these seven words with pointers to where they occur, along with spaces and punctuation. This would require less space.

In the same way, **data compression** involves encoding information using fewer bits than the original representation. This is done for two reasons:

- to reduce file size to save storage space, and
- to reduce transmission (upload and/or download) time.

Compressing images

Images, in particular, can be very large because the colour of each pixel is stored as a binary number, often a 24-bit number. This means that an image which is 1000×1000 pixels requires 3 MB of memory:

$$1000 \text{ pixels} \times 1000 \text{ pixels} \times 24 \text{ bits (colour)}$$
$$= \quad 1\,000\,000 \times 24 \div 8 \text{ bytes}$$
$$= \quad 3\,000\,000 \text{ bytes}$$
$$\approx \quad 3 \text{ megabytes}$$

Consider a web page that contains lots of pictures of this format. Not only would a large amount of storage space be required to store the pictures, but it would also take a long time to load all of these images each time the web page was accessed. The solution is to compress the image files, to make their file size smaller so that the download time is reduced. Compression can be either **lossless** or **lossy**.

Lossless compression uses an algorithm which reduces bits by eliminating statistical redundancy, i.e. the same data is represented more concisely without losing information. For example, an image may have areas of colour which do not change over several pixels, so instead of coding "blue pixel, blue pixel, blue pixel, …[96 more blue pixels], … blue pixel" the same data could be encoded as "100 blue pixels". This technique is known as "run-length encoding" and there is no reduction in quality as the original image can be reconstructed exactly.

Lossy compression uses an algorithm where non-essential detail is removed or 'rounded off'. For example, a picture may have more detail than the human eye can distinguish. Lossy compression techniques try to match the human perception to the original by disregarding some of the image detail. The quality of the image is reduced by the process, but often not enough to be noticeable. Lossy compression techniques are often able to achieve much greater levels of data reduction than lossless techniques are.

Task

Investigate the sizes of different formats of the same image as follows.

1. Load a picture into a basic graphics package such as Paint.
2. Save the picture in TIFF format.
3. Reload the original picture and save the picture in a different format, such as JPEG.
4. Repeat step 3 several times, saving the picture in different formats such as BMP and GIF.
5. Note the file size of each of the images you have saved.

Why are they different sizes?

File Extension	Type of File	Not Compressed	Lossless Compressed	Lossy Compressed
.txt	Text	✓		
.wav	Audio	✓		
.mp3	Audio			✓
.bmp	Graphic	✓		
.gif	Graphic		✓	
.jpg	Graphic			✓
.mp4	Video			✓
.wmv	Video			✓

Figure 14.5: The types of compression used with different file formats.

Compression of other file formats

We have seen how data compression can be used to reduce the size of image files. Data compression can be used in the same way for other types of file, such as audio and video files. Figure 14.5 shows a summary of the types of compression used when creating different formats of files. We shall look at some of these file formats in more detail in the next section.

Zipping

Zipping is a lossless form of data compression which is often used for archiving data and sending email attachments. One or more files can be 'zipped' into a single file (**.zip** file extension) which allows easy storage or transmission. Any file can be 'zipped', regardless of its particular file format – it is just compressed as much as possible. Zipping can achieve good size savings with uncompressed formats such as BMP, but not much additional compression takes place when formats such as JPG are 'zipped', since they are already compressed.

14.3 Data File Formats

Data comes in different formats (such as text, audio, graphic or video) so different file types are required to store this data. We have already met some of these file types in section 14.2. In this section we shall discuss these types in more detail.

Text files

A **text file** is a sequence of lines of electronic text. Plain text files (file extension **.txt**) are recognised by all word processors and text editors and are often used where formatted text is unsuitable. Text files contain no formatting and can be opened in packages such as Notepad. Text is the most basic file format used to transfer data over the Internet as it is supported by almost all applications on most platforms.

Audio files

Sound is produced when objects vibrate, producing pressure waves in the air that can be picked up by the human ear. The intensity of these waves can be recorded and stored as a waveform, preserving the sound over a period of time. These waves are analogue signals and need to be digitised to be used in a computer application, that is they need to be changed to a series of 0s and 1s.

The digital representation of the waveform of a sound is stored on a computer system using an audio file format. The most widely used audio format is **Waveform Audio File Format** (**.wav** file extension). Data is stored uncompressed, which means the files can be large in size (around 10 MB per minute of music) but the quality is very good. Other audio file formats (such as **.mp3** files) use lossy compression to reduce the size of the audio files, but there is also a reduction in sound quality.

Graphic files

In the real world, images such as paintings are analogue in nature, i.e. tones and colours blend together in a continuous way. These images need to be digitised to store them on a computer system. The simplest way to convert an image into a binary file is to create a **bitmap** image (**.bmp** file extension). This is done by dividing the image into thousands of rectangles called **pixels** (short for 'picture element'). Each pixel has a single colour, so the more pixels there are the better the quality or **resolution**. The resolution of an image is usually measured in dpi (dots per inch, where each dot is a pixel). Graphics produced for on-screen display (such as the Web) are generally stored at 72 dpi, graphics for desktop printing should be 150 dpi and graphics used in commercial printing should be 300 dpi. Even higher resolution graphics are used by professional photographers.

Any colour can be represented as a combination of various intensities of just three colours: red, green and blue – the primary colours of computer graphics. Each pixel in a digital image is represented by a single binary number, and this binary number stores the colour of the picture as the intensity of each of these three colours at that particular location.

Different numbers of bits can be allocated to represent the intensity of each of the colours red, green and blue. The more bits that are allocated, the more colours can be represented. This is known as the **colour depth**.

As a byte has 8 bits, 1 byte could be used for each of the three colours, a total of three bytes per pixel. We describe this as **24-bit** colour depth. This means about 16.8 million different colours can be represented – corresponding to the ability of the human visual system to distinguish between different colours, shades and tones:

$$2^{24} \qquad (2^8 \times 2^8 \times 2^8)$$
$$= \qquad 16\,777\,216$$
$$\approx \qquad 16.8 \text{ million}$$

So a pixel could be represented by red, green and blue values in the range 0–255, for example red = 45, green = 125, blue = 78. These 16.8 million possible colour specifications are known as the **RGB colour space.** Some examples are shown in figure 14.6.

The bitmap image file format (file extension **.bmp**) represents the image as a series of pixels using the RGB colour space. It is not compressed and therefore can lead to very large file sizes.

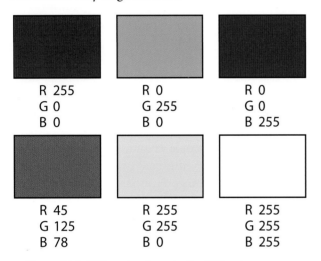

R 255   R 0   R 0
G 0   G 255   G 0
B 0   B 0   B 255

R 45   R 255   R 255
G 125   G 255   G 255
B 78   B 0   B 255

Figure 14.6: Different colours in the RGB colour space.

Worked Example

A graphics image measuring 3 inches wide and 2 inches high has a resolution of 300 dpi and 24-bit colour depth. How large is the file when stored in bitmap image format?

24-bit colour depth means that each pixel is 3 bytes

$$
\begin{aligned}
\text{Size} \quad &= \quad (3 \times 300) \times (2 \times 300) \times 3 \text{ bytes} \\
&= \quad 1\,620\,000 \text{ bytes} \\
&\approx \quad 1.62 \text{ MB}
\end{aligned}
$$

Other image file formats exist that use compression to reduce the file size. These **optimised** file formats are more suitable for use on the internet where speed of transmission is important.

The **Graphics Interchange Format** or **GIF** (file extension **.gif**) only allows 8 bits per pixel for each image. However, the colour of each pixel is chosen from that particular file's own palette of 256 (2^8) different colours which have themselves been chosen from the larger 24-bit RGB colour space, based on the characteristics of that particular image. GIF also supports animations allowing a separate palette of up to 256 colours for each frame. GIF images are compressed using a lossless data compression technique to reduce the file size without degrading the visual quality. GIF is particularly suitable for graphics that have sequences of similar colours, for example clipart.

The **Joint Photographic Experts Group** or **JPEG** file format (file extension **.jpg**) is a graphics file which has been compressed using a lossy compression algorithm. The JPEG standard defines how an image is compressed into a stream of bytes and decompressed back into an image. Although it is based on a 24-bit colour palette, these files tend to drop information when they are decompressed. The higher the rate of compression was when the JPEG file was created, the more the quality of the image will be affected when the file is decompressed (figure 14.7). The JPEG file format is most suitable for graphics with continuous changes of shade, for example photographs.

Vector graphic formats

> **Note:** The CCEA specification does not require you to have knowledge of vector graphic formats. However, you will come across them in the real world as they are very common.

As we have seen, bitmap images are collections of dots that form an image with each dot (pixel) having its own colour. Generally digital pictures and scanned images are bitmap files. However, drawings made in packages such as Adobe Illustrator are saved as **vector** graphics. The content of vector graphics is entirely described by a series of mathematical definitions of the position, appearance and curvature of each line.

Vector graphics are usually smaller than bitmap file formats as they only contain the data needed to reconstruct the lines and other objects that form the drawing. Only a vector graphic file with a very large number of objects would be larger than the equivalent bitmap image. A key advantage of vector graphics is that they can be scaled up indefinitely with no loss in quality, whereas scaling up a bitmap file can result in the image appearing 'pixelated'.

Vector graphics are becoming more popular for the creation of charts, graphs and other infographics on the World Wide Web. The SVG (Scalable Vector Graphics) standard has been incorporated into the most recent specification of HTML.

Bitmap image
File size: 289 KB

JPEG compression: medium
File size: 52 KB

JPEG compression: high
File size: 19 KB

Figure 14.7: The same image saved in JPEG format with three levels of compression.

Worked Example

A company has produced a new logo which is a bitmap graphic (stored as a .bmp file).

(a) What is a bitmap graphic?

(b) State one problem with enlarging bitmap graphics and suggest a different graphic type which would overcome this problem.

(c) The company wishes to use an optimised version of their new logo on a web page. What is meant by optimisation and give two advantages of optimised images.

(d) The company wishes to email the logo to a printing company. In its current form it is too large to send as an attachment to an email. Why would zipping the file be preferable to compressing the file using a lossy compression algorithm?

Appropriate answers are as follows:

(a) An image made up of a grid of pixels where each pixel potentially has a different colour.

(b) Problem: The image may become pixelated, i.e. there is a loss of quality as it appears "blocky". A vector graphic could be used to maintain quality.

(c) Optimisation reduces the size of the file. Optimised images allow faster upload/download to/from a web page and save on storage space.

(d) Zipping the file would compress the file without loss of quality.

Video files

Video data is often stored in the **Moving Picture Experts Group** or **MPEG** file format (file extension **.mp4**) which is designed to store an encoded data stream containing compressed audio and video information. All the information required to play back MPEG data is encoded directly in the data stream. The original MPEG standard is referred to as MPEG-1. The most recent one, MPEG-4, allows for the compression of audio-visual data so that the image and sound quality is suitable for digital distribution (either online, TV broadcast or via optical media such as DVD) without noticeable degradation of fidelity.

MPEG compression uses a lossy compression method. Compressing video data into the MPEG file format is much more complicated than decompressing it, so MPEG-based compression is a good choice when the video data only needs to be written once, but needs to be read many times, for example distributing movies, TV catch-up services such as BBC iPlayer or online video archives such as YouTube.

Questions

1. State four features that a good user interface should have.

2. State two advantages and two disadvantages of each of the following types of user interface:
   (a) WIMP
   (b) Command line
   (c) Forms

3. Why might an advanced programmer prefer a command line interface over a graphical user interface?

4. State two advantages of using data compression.

5. A photograph is to be uploaded to a web page. The photograph has been compressed using a lossy compression algorithm.
   (a) What effect will the compression have on the file?
   (b) State two advantages of using compressed files.
   (c) What difference would you expect there to be if a lossless compression algorithm had been used instead?

6. A bitmap graphic measuring 3 inches by 4 inches has a bit depth of 24 bits and a resolution of 150 dpi.
   (a) How many colours can be represented in this graphic?
   (b) What is the size (in KB) of the file?
   (c) What effect would increasing the bit-depth have on the file size of the graphic?

7. A camera has a 12 gigabyte flash card. Photographs (4 inch by 6 inch) are taken with a resolution of 1024 dpi and using 24-bit colour depth. What is the maximum number of photographs which can be stored on the card?

CHAPTER 15
Software

By the end of this chapter students should be able to:

- describe the purpose of an operating system;
- describe different types of operating system: single user, multi-user, multiprocessing, multitasking and multithreading;
- explain the need for utility programs;
- describe some common utility programs: data compression, file backup, archive software and disk defragmenters;
- explain what is meant by application software;
- explain the difference between generic software and special purpose software;
- compare the use of custom-built software with off-the-shelf software;
- explain how application software can be delivered on different platforms, for example downloaded to a device or accessed using the web;
- evaluate different methods of obtaining software: propriety and open source;
- describe batch processing and real-time processing;
- evaluate the use of batch processing and real-time processing for common applications; and
- describe the input, output and processing involved in a range of common devices: automatic teller machines (ATMs), point of sale (POS) terminals and smartphones.

15.1 Introduction

In this chapter we shall consider the two main types of software:

- **System software**, which relates to the operation of the computer itself. System software consists of the **operating system**, which manages the computer and its resources, and **utility programs** which allow the user to perform tasks related to managing the computer.
- **Application software**, designed for the end user to perform specific tasks such as word processing or playing computer games. Application software accesses the computer's resources through the operating system.

We shall conclude by looking in more detail at the different ways in which software can process data.

15.2 The Operating System

An **operating system** is a system software program that manages all the operations and resources of a computer. It acts as the interface between the hardware, application software and the end users. The operating system is the first thing that is loaded when the computer is switched on, and without it the computer is useless.

Many operating systems are available, for example Microsoft Windows, Android, iOS, macOS, Unix and Linux. However, all operating systems can be broken down into four parts as shown in figure 15.1.

- **User interface** – this is the part of the operating system which receives data from the user (for example, from the keyboard). The data is processed by the computer and returned as information to the user via the user interface. Common user interfaces include command line interfaces and graphical user interfaces, as discussed in chapter 14.
- **Application interface** – the operating system stores device drivers for every piece of hardware which is connected to, or is part of, the computer. A device driver allows the operating system to control and communicate with a particular device, as discussed in chapter 13. Manufacturers must create different device drivers for each operating system. Device drivers are stored in the operating system's **registry**.
- **Kernel** – loads/unloads applications to/from memory and seeks to manage the allocation of the computer's resources efficiently, for example memory, secondary storage and scheduling the use of the processor.
- **Hardware interface** – this is the part of the operating system which connects together the physical components of the computer, such as the CPU, memory and external devices.

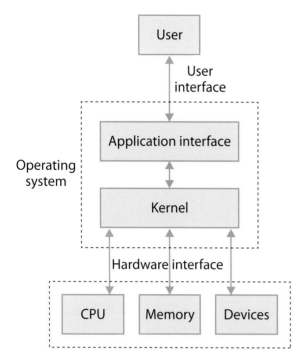

Figure 15.1: The four main components of a computer operating system.

An operating system must be designed to work with a particular processor's set of instructions. For example, Microsoft Windows is built to work with a series of processors from the Intel Corporation that share the same (or similar) sets of instructions.

Single and multi-user operating systems

Operating systems can be designed to be used by both a single user or multiple users at the same time. The three main categories are as follows.

Single user, single application operating system

In this type of operating system only one person is running one program at any given time. There are no facilities to distinguish between different users, and a user cannot run multiple applications (processes) at the same time. An example of a single user, single application operating system is a mobile phone.

Single user, multitasking application operating system

In this type of operating system several applications (or processes) can be in operation at the same time, and the user can switch between processes. The operating system allocates resources to each process.

It requires more memory than a single user, single application operating system but it is more flexible for the user.

Most desktop computers, laptops and tablets come with this type of operating system. For example, on a PC running Windows 10 the user could be downloading a file from the internet and at the same time be using a word processing package to type a document.

Multi-user operating system

This type of operating system allows multiple users to access a single computer system. This is the type of operating system found on mainframes and supercomputers. Some operating systems permit hundreds or even thousands of users to have access at the same time (concurrently). Each user has their own terminal and appears to have exclusive use of the system. Resources, such as memory, processing and data requests, must be managed while optimising the use of the processor by sharing its time between users and their tasks (an activity known as time-slicing). Data security must be maintained by the operating system, i.e. each user's data and files must be kept private from all other users.

Multiprogramming, multiprocessing, multitasking and multithreading

Many operating systems allow more than one program to be loaded into main memory at the same time. There are four main ways in which the operating system allows all these programs to operate in the same computer.

Multiprogramming

In a multiprogramming system more than one program (process) can be resident in the computer's main memory ready to execute. However, only one program is being executed at any given time. When one program is unable to execute (perhaps because of some input/output operation), the operating system will switch to another program and allow that program to run, as shown in figure 15.2.

The idea of a multiprogramming system is to optimise CPU time. When the program currently being executed, program A, gets interrupted by the operating system between tasks, control is transferred to program B. Program B will keep executing until it voluntarily gives the CPU back, or is interrupted by the operating system (for example, between tasks).

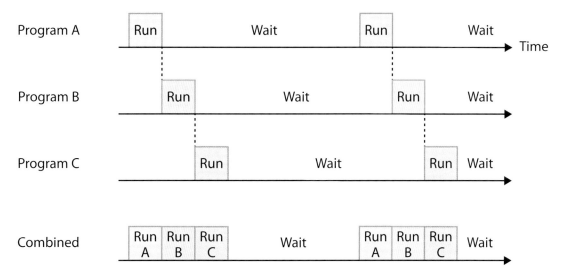

Figure 15.2: Multiprogramming with three programs.

At this point, control is returned to program A (or to another program). The objective is to keep the CPU as busy as possible for as long as there are processes ready to execute. From the user's point of view, the operating system switches seamlessly between processes, and rapidly enough to create the illusion of parallelism.

Multiprocessing

In a multiprocessing operating system a program (process) is divided up between a number of processors (or cores) so that true parallel computing can be achieved. The main advantage of such a system is speed. Note that an operating system can be both a multiprogramming system (having more than one program running concurrently) and a multiprocessing system (by having more than one physical processor).

Multitasking

The term 'multitasking' has the same meaning as multiprogramming, but in a more general sense. Here, an application program is divided into a number of processes or tasks. In a multitasking operating system, multiple tasks share a common resource such as CPU or memory. The operating system will allocate resources (for example, storage, CPU time) accordingly. Time-slicing may be used.

Multithreading

So far we have seen that multiprogramming is a way to allow multiple programs to be resident in main memory and (apparently) running at the same time. Multitasking refers to many tasks (apparently)

running simultaneously and multiprocessing refers to systems having multiple processors.

Multithreading is the ability of a process to be used by more than one user at a time, or to manage multiple requests by the same user without running multiple copies of the process on the computer. Each user runs a **thread** of execution within the process. Multiple threads can exist within the same process, executing concurrently and (at the same time) sharing resources such as memory and executable code. Each thread has a separate path of execution. For example, two programmers could be using the same compiler to compile their source code. When the compiler is loaded into memory a thread is created for programmer A to start using it. When programmer B wants to compile some code, the operating system knows the compiler process is already in memory, so a second thread is assigned to start executing compiler instructions. Both programmers are making use of the compiler, but neither is aware that the other is using it.

Multithreading is a good way to write concurrent software, i.e. where parts of the program can be executed at the same time. However, the programmer must consider the possibility of two or more threads trying to access a shared resource, where the system could be left in an inconsistent state or a state of deadlock (where two threads are each waiting for the other to do something).

15.3 Utility Programs

Utility programs are system software programs that allow the user to perform specific tasks that are usually related to managing a computer, its devices or its programs. Utility programs are often built into the computer's operating system. For example, Microsoft Windows has a built-in data compression utility which can be used to compress and decompress files or folders. Three of the most common types of utility program are as follows.

Data compression programs

Data compression – explored in detail in chapter 14 – involves encoding information using fewer bits than the original file. Data compression programs are regarded as utility programs because reducing the file size is merely a means to an end: namely, to use the resources of the computer system more efficiently by reducing storage space and file transfer times.

File backup and archive programs

Backup utility programs are used to create exact copies of files or databases. These backup copies may be used to restore the original contents in the event of data loss from the original system. An archiving program can be used to create backups. The different types of backup were discussed in more detail in chapter 7.

A file archiving program combines a number of files together into one archive file, or a series of archive files, for easy storage, transportation or convenient mailing. It often uses data compression and can also be used for data backup and recovery. A basic file archiving program will simply take a list of files and concatenate their contents sequentially into archives, storing 'metadata' such as filenames and the lengths of the files so that they can be reconstructed when necessary. More advanced archive programs store additional metadata such as access control lists (i.e. who can access each file, and what operations can be performed), file attributes and timestamps.

A system administrator can set up an archive schedule and choose which files are archived, where and how they are stored, how long they are stored for, who has access to them and so forth. The system administrator also needs to ensure they have the software needed to reconstruct the archived file (unarchiving) if necessary.

Disk defragmenting programs

When a file needs to be stored, the operating system's **file manager** will look at the FAT (File Allocation Table) to find a free area of the disk (known as a **cluster**) to start writing data to. This starting cluster

is noted in the directory table. When this cluster is full the file manager will search the FAT for the next free cluster and continue writing data to it. This continues until all the data in the file has been saved. So, a file is actually made up of a chain of clusters that may not all be in the same area of the disk.

When the user deletes a file, the actual data is not erased. Instead, the file manager starts at the first cluster and marks every cluster in the chain associated with that file as 'free'. It then goes to the FAT and flags the file as deleted. This continual saving and deleting of files on a hard disk will cause the files to 'fragment' all over the hard disk. A badly-fragmented hard disk will appear to operate much more slowly than a clean disk, so system tools have been developed to defragment a hard disk.

A disk defragmenter will shuffle the data around until a file has contiguous clusters which means it can be accessed more quickly. It also does the same for free space. A disk defragmenting procedure can take many hours as a lot of data may need to be moved around.

15.4 Application Software

Application software is a set of programs designed to allow the end user to perform specific tasks, for example word processing, database programs, accounting packages or flight simulators. Application software accesses the computer's hardware through the operating system. In this section we shall discuss different types of application software, in terms of how they are produced, installed, licensed and run.

Generic software versus special purpose software

Generic software can be used for lots of different tasks without modification. For example, the same word processor can be used to write a letter, create a set of instructions or create an invoice. In each case, the developers write the programs and then make lots of copies to sell 'off-the-shelf'.

Special purpose software, by contrast, is a type of software created to perform a unique business need. For example, car-wash equipment installed in the forecourt of a petrol station typically has in-built fault-diagnosis software. The company responsible for maintaining the equipment will need a bespoke piece of software to receive the error reports from the machines and efficiently allocate its engineers to visit and fix the equipment.

Custom-built software versus off-the-shelf software

Custom-built (bespoke or tailor-made) application software is built for a specific purpose or a specific user. It can be developed by an organisation in-house or the organisation could employ a third party to write the software specifically for it, for example military control software.

The main advantages of custom-built software are as follows.

- The organisation will get exactly what they need.
- The software will be optimised for the company's specific needs.
- Only those features required by the system will be provided (and hence storage space will not be taken up by other unnecessary and unused functions).
- The developers will be available to correct any errors which arise during initial use of the system.

The main disadvantages of custom-built software are as follows.

- It can be very expensive to develop.
- It can take a long time to develop.
- The software may not be fully tested and there may be bugs in the source code which are only

triggered by a specific event, for example the start of a new year.
- Little support will be available online via blogs or forums.

Off-the-shelf application software is generic software, such as Microsoft Office, which has been developed by a company and sold commercially.

The main advantages of off-the-shelf software are as follows.

- The software is available immediately.
- It will usually cost less than custom-built software.
- The software will be fully tested.
- A lot of support will be available online.

The main disadvantages of off-the-shelf software are as follows.

- Installation and configuration may take some time to ensure that it is aligned to the company's needs.
- There may be many features that the company does not require (and extra storage space is required for these features).
- The software may not have some features that the company requires.

Delivering application software on different platforms

The term **platform** refers to the underlying computer system that applications can be built on or run on. The term generally refers to one of the following:

- the type of processor and/or other hardware on which an operating system or application runs (hardware platform), or
- the type of operating system and/or programming environment (software platform), or
- a combination of the type of hardware and the type of operating system running on it.

For example, both the Microsoft Windows 10 and the macOS operating systems are built to work with a series of microprocessors from Intel, or compatible companies, that share the same (or similar) x86 architecture. However, these two operating systems are completely different, and therefore they are regarded as different platforms.

Historically, most application programs were written to run on a particular platform. Each platform provided a different application program interface (API) for different system services. Therefore, a

PC program would have to be written to run on the Windows platform and then re-written to run on the macOS platform. Although these platform differences continue to exist (and there will probably always be proprietary differences between them) new interfaces now allow for the development of **cross-platform** programs that are capable of running on different platforms through mediating or 'broker' programs.

The Java platform

Java is different to other software platforms in that it uses a **virtual machine** for its compiled code (known as **bytecode**) that is independent of any particular operating system. Instead of compiling into code for a specific processor, source code written in the Java language compiles into code for a 'virtual' processor. A Java Virtual Machine (JVM) is then built for each specific platform, which acts to convert the Java bytecode into instructions for that particular processor. This means that the same executable bytecode can run on all systems which implement a JVM. Java code running in the JVM has access to all the operating system services such as disk input/output. Currently, Java programs can run on Microsoft Windows, macOS, UNIX operating systems and Android. Cut-down versions of Android have been developed for devices which have fewer resources, and some of these may not fully support Java.

Web applications

Web applications (web apps) are cross-platform applications because they are accessible via different web browsers on different operating systems. A web application is generally a **client-server** software application where most of the processing is done on a remote server and the result is passed to the client, via a user interface which runs in a web browser.

Installing application software

There are a number of ways in which application software may be obtained by the end user. Traditionally, software was purchased on physical media such as CD-ROM or DVD-ROM, but most modern applications are either downloaded from an online source or used via the Web.

Downloading application software

Software obtained in this way is downloaded as an executable installation package from the publisher's website. Once downloaded, the installation package executes on the user's machine and creates a version of the application that is configured for the user's system and runs using only local resources. Software in this category is usually obtained for a one-off fee that enables the user to use the application for as long as is required. Some software, however, requires an annual renewable fee or subscription. In such cases, while the software is still installed locally, its functionality is disabled and it will not perform any of the operations expected until the subscription has been paid or renewed.

Using software via the Web

Many software packages are made available as online applications, where the software runs on the publisher's server and is accessed using a web browser. These applications service many users simultaneously and require minimal capability on the user's machine – except for a reliable Internet connection. Software in this category is often priced using a renewable licence model, where an annual payment enables the user to use the application.

Software licencing

Application software is classified as either **propriety** or **open source**.

Propriety software

This is 'closed' software, which means it is owned by an individual or a company and is distributed under a license agreement which limits any modifications to the source code (i.e. it is copyright-protected). These programs usually include regular upgrades and technical support. Virtually all of Microsoft's software, including the Windows operating systems and Office suite of programs, is propriety. The term **freeware** refers to a type of propriety software that is offered for use free of monetary charges. Nevertheless, as with other types of proprietary software, generally there are restrictions on the use of freeware and the source code is not available.

Open source software

This is software that is distributed, along with the source code, freely under a license with no limitations on making changes to the source code. The license normally stipulates that if a modified version of the software is distributed, the source code for the modified version must also be made freely available. The best-known example of open source software is the Linux operating system, developed and managed by a consortium of companies known as the Linux Foundation. Although Linux is provided free to the user, some manufacturers are able to make a return on their investment by charging for support.

15.5 Processing Systems

As discussed in chapter 12, all software applications process data in some form, outputting useful information. However, the way in which the data processing takes place can vary. The two main ways in which software can process data are **batch processing** and **real-time processing**.

Batch processing

Batch processing occurs when a group of transactions, files or databases are processed at one time. The transactions, files or databases (the 'jobs') are usually queued up to create a **batch job** which is then processed as a 'batch' at a later date. The same operation is performed on each file, the only difference being that the input and output data for each iteration may be different. Once the initial instructions (such as data file details, what to do if a job fails etc) are set up, the batch job should run without any intervention.

Examples of batch processing are as follows.

- A building supplier may collate all orders received during the day and then print all the invoices at the end of the day.

- A stock control program may store details of every item sold in a shop during that day, then calculate what needs to be re-ordered at the end of the day.

- A person may keep all receipts for work-related expenses and give them to their accountant at the end of the tax year.

- A credit card company stores all transactions for each card holder and sends out a single bill at the end of each month.

Computerised batch processing is often performed overnight when there is less activity on the system. Validation checks, such as batch/control totals (discussed in chapter 12), are usually performed as part of the procedure. Banks often run large batch processes overnight to collate the many thousands of transactions that have taken place during the day.

Real-time processing

Real-time processing occurs when files or databases are updated as transactions occur, i.e. the transaction is performed 'now'. Real-time systems are time-critical. Examples of real-time processing are as follows.

- Updating a password. This needs to take effect immediately, since it would not be a very efficient system if a user had to wait until the next day before the password was updated and they could use the system.
- Updating a bank balance after a withdrawal or

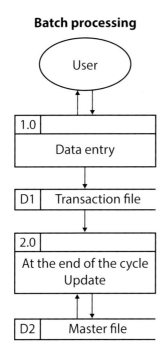

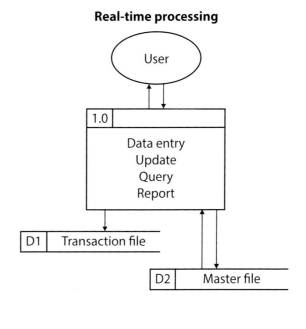

Figure 15.3: Batch and real-time data processing.

payment has been made. If the balance was only updated once per day, an account holder could spend more money than was in the account.

- Traffic lights which must react rapidly to changing volumes of traffic.
- A heart rate monitoring system which must monitor the heartbeat in real time.

In real-time processing many requests can be made to a system at the same time, so it may be necessary to prioritise these requests. In order to deal with this problem, many real-time computer systems have scheduling algorithms which allocate resources to higher-priority requests. For example, if a heart rate monitoring system wants to report that its battery is running low, and simultaneously that it has detected that the user has gone into cardiac arrest, it will prioritise the latter request.

Figure 15.3 summarises the differences between batch and real-time processing.

15.6 Data Processing Devices

Many devices, such as automated teller machines, point-of-sale terminals and smartphones, can be considered to be data processing systems with associated input and output devices.

Automated teller machines

Automated teller machines (**ATMs**) are machines which are connected to a bank's computer system. An ATM can:

- dispense cash,
- display the customer's bank balance,
- provide a receipt, and
- sometimes take deposits.

Banks supply their customers with a plastic card which the customer inserts into a card reader in the ATM. The customer must also enter a personal identification number (PIN) for authentication using a keypad. The PIN is either transmitted to the bank for verification, or if a **smart card** (a card with an integrated circuit or chip) is used, verification takes place at the ATM. PIN management is governed by international standards and, provided the card has a MasterCard/Maestro/Cirrus/Visa logo, it can generally be used at any ATM worldwide which displays that logo. Once it has successfully processed the PIN, the ATM then processes the user's request by displaying a range of options on the screen with the user providing input via either the keypad or a

touchscreen. If the user is withdrawing money, the system will check whether sufficient funds are available. When the money is dispensed the amount will instantly be deducted from the customer's balance. The output devices are the ATM screen, a cash dispenser, and a receipt printer.

Figure 15.4 shows the sequence of input-process-output events that take place when a user is

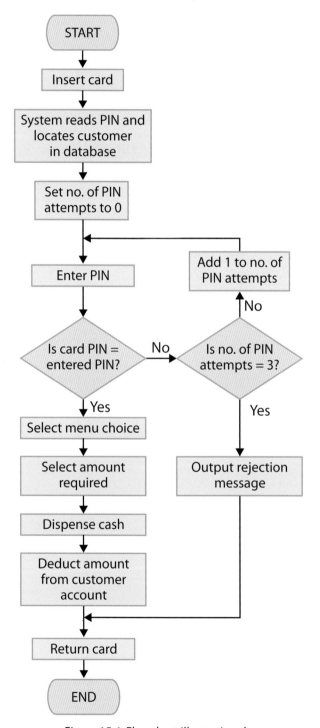

Figure 15.4: Flowchart illustrating the input-process-output events of using an ATM machine to withdraw some cash.

withdrawing cash from an ATM. It assumes only fixed amounts (displayed to the user) can be withdrawn and that there are sufficient funds to fulfil the request.

Point-of-sale terminals

A point-of-sale (**POS**) terminal is a computerised replacement for a cash register (or till) but has many more capabilities such as inventory management and the ability to record and track customer orders. For example, a fast food outlet might have a POS system which lists all items on the menu and records information such as time of order, status of order etc. POS systems can be customised to the retailers' particular requirements. Input devices such as barcode scanners, touchscreens and electronic scales can all be included in the system.

The key requirements of a POS terminal are as follows:

- ease of use,
- high and consistent operating speed,
- reliability,
- good functionality, and
- low cost.

Electronic Funds Transfer at Point of Sale (EFTPOS) is an electronic payment system which uses debit or credit cards to electronically transfer funds. This allows the user to pay for goods or services without needing to carry cash. The customer inserts the debit/credit card into an EFTPOS machine, enters a security PIN and, after reviewing the amount, confirms the purchase. The EFTPOS machine contacts the customer's bank and the funds will be transferred in a matter of seconds. Confirmation of the transaction is sent to the store and a copy is usually given to the customer.

In this case, the input devices are the card reader and keypad. The processing includes validating the PIN, calculating the amount and communicating with the bank. The output devices are the monitors to display the totals, a receipt printer and possibly some auditory feedback to indicate an error.

Smartphones

A smartphone is a mobile phone with an advanced mobile operating system which combines the traditional features of a mobile phone with the computing features of a personal computer operating system. It is a multi-purpose device and its operating system is able to multi-task, which means that it permits several applications (known as **apps** on a smartphone) to be open at the same time. However, this is not 'true' multitasking as described earlier in this chapter. Rather, a smartphone has one app running in the foreground, displayed on the screen and interacting with the user, while any other apps are maintained in a 'sleeping' state with data temporarily stored in the phone's memory. When the user switches between apps, the one currently in the foreground is put into 'sleep' mode, while the newly-selected app has its data returned from memory and is re-activated. Sleeping apps generally consume no processing resources and no battery power. However, some apps, such as those used for messaging, will be able to receive notifications while in the sleeping state and so will use limited resources.

Currently, there is a wide range of options for input, processing and output on smartphone devices, as described below.

Input

- The primary input device on a smartphone is the touch-sensitive screen that typically covers the entire top surface of the device. It can recognise a wide range of gestures such as single and multi-digit taps, swipes, pinch and reverse-pinch. The touchscreen is sometimes pressure-sensitive to enable it to distinguish between a light or heavy touch in order to select between different operations. Typed input is possible via a software keyboard that is displayed on the screen so that users can type by touching the region occupied by the characters required.
- Smartphones are able to receive data transmitted by Wi-Fi and high-speed cellular networks such as 4G and the emerging 5G.
- Smartphones also have an embedded microphone for voice commands that can activate personal assistant software such as Siri

(Apple), Cortana (Microsoft) and Google Assistant (Android).

- Some devices include a biometric fingerprint sensor, usually positioned on the top surface, to secure the device against unauthorised access.
- Smartphones also include high-resolution image sensors that enable the user to take photographs and record video. The camera can also be used as a barcode reader or for facial recognition input to prevent unauthorised access of the device.
- A gyroscope (or tilt sensor) allows the phone to automatically switch between portrait and landscape displays according to the orientation of the device in the user's hand.
- Additional sensors are often available: for example, a compass to enable the device to determine which direction it is facing, a barometer to determine its altitude and a GPS receiver to allow the precise location of the device to be determined for mapping and route-finding applications.

Processing

- The operating system on a smartphone performs the same role as that of a desktop or laptop computer. It provides an interface between the hardware and the application software and delivers an environment in which the application software (apps) can run. Two main operating systems are used on smartphones. **Android** is developed by Google and is based on the open source Linux operating system. It is popular with technology companies which require a customisable operating system for their high-tech devices. **iOS** is developed by Apple and used exclusively on Apple products, for example the iPhone, iPod touch, iPad (as iPadOS) and Apple Watch (as watchOS).

Output

- The touchscreen is also the primary output device on the smartphone. It is a full-colour display with a typical screen size of 10 to 15 cm (4 to 6 inches), resolutions ranging from 1080×1920 to 3040×1400 pixels and a pixel density ranging from 400 to 800 ppi (pixels per inch).
- A near-field communication (NFC) antenna embedded in the smartphone body allows it to

be used as an electronic payment device by wirelessly transferring details of the user's payment card across short distances (a few centimetres) to an EFTPOS system.
- Embedded speakers can be used to output audio. Alternatively, users can choose to connect headphones, either through a headphone socket or wirelessly via Bluetooth.
- A 'vibrate' feature allows the device to alert the user to incoming calls or other events even when the device has been switched into 'silent' mode.

Questions

1. What is the purpose of an operating system?
2. What is the difference between a single user operating system and a multi-user operating system?
3. Explain what is meant by each of the following types of operating system:
   (a) multiprogramming,
   (b) multiprocessing,
   (c) multitasking,
   (d) multithreading.
4. Describe the role of each of the following types of utility program:
   (a) data compression program,
   (b) file archiving program,
   (c) disk defragmenting program.
5. Application software can be custom-built or purchased off-the-shelf.
   (a) Describe two advantages and two disadvantages of custom-built software.
   (b) Describe two advantages and two disadvantages of off-the-shelf software.
6. The owner of a small computer outlet wishes to introduce a computerised system mainly for stock control. Previously the owner worked as a software developer for a large computing company, so has considerable programming experience. Both propriety and open source software stock control packages are available.
   (a) Describe the main features of propriety software.
   (b) State two advantages of propriety software.

(c) State two disadvantages of propriety software.

(d) Describe the main features of open source software.

(e) State two advantages of open source software.

(f) State two disadvantages of open source software.

(g) Suggest which type of software the shop owner should choose. Justify your answer.

7. A bank processes its cheques at the end of each day using batch processing. Describe the main features of batch processing.

8. An online business uses real-time processing to deal with all orders. Explain why real-time processing is used by businesses that accept orders online.

9. A smart card can be used to withdraw cash from an ATM. Identify two examples of input, processing and output associated with an ATM.

10. When a customer visits their local supermarket a point-of-sale terminal is usually used at the checkout.
    (a) Identify two examples of input devices used in a POS terminal.
    (b) Identify two examples of output devices used in a POS terminal.
    (c) What processing takes place at a POS terminal?

11. State two examples of input devices and two examples of output devices on a typical smartphone.

CHAPTER 16
Web Applications

16.1 Introduction

The **Internet** is the global system of interconnected computer networks, organised such that any connected device on one network can communicate with any other connected device on another network. It spans almost every country in the world and is used in all walks of life, from government, security and retail to transport, leisure and education.

According to estimates (2019), up to 27 billion devices representing 4 billion users are connected to the Internet worldwide, with the number of devices projected to rise to over 75 billion by 2025 as the 'Internet of Things' grows in prominence.

The **World Wide Web** is an open information system organised as a collection of linked **pages**, where each page has a unique address. It is the primary means by which people use the Internet in their homes, schools, workplaces or on the move through smartphones and tablets.

In this chapter we will examine the Internet and World Wide Web in detail. We will first explore the history of the Internet and show how its development and organisation is managed. We shall also consider how the Internet's addressing system allows any connected device to be uniquely identified and how changes to any device's address are automatically communicated across the network.

We will explore how the World Wide Web grew from a project in a Swiss research lab to become the most widely used network tool in the world and discuss how search engines evolved from simple indexes of content into the sophisticated intelligent tools of today.

16.2 Technical Foundations of the Internet

History

The history of the Internet begins with the development of the first electronic computers in the 1950s. From the outset, scientists realised the potential advantages of sending information from one computer to another and, in the 1960s, the United States Government's Defence Advanced Research Projects Agency (DARPA) commissioned the development of the first computer **network**, known as ARPANET, which initially connected four United States universities. The network quickly spread and 213 sites were connected by 1981.

During the same period, two important European computer networks were also developed. Firstly, the commercial network of the National Physical Laboratory (NPL) in England introduced the concept of **packet switching**, whereby files were broken up into smaller pieces, sent one at a time and put back together by the receiver. Secondly, the scientific network CYCLADES in France improved reliability by developing an **end-to-end protocol** which made a virtual connection from sender to receiver. This means that the communication link operates as if it were a dedicated physical channel with all details regarding the division into packets, routing through the network, handling packet loss and/or damage and re-construction of the data hidden from both the sender and receiver.

ARPANET, NPL and CYCLADES each made important contributions to the development of what we know as the Internet, but initially they were incompatible with each other. In 1971, the American scientist Vint Cerf led the development of **TCP/IP** (Transmission Control Protocol/Internet Protocol), a set of rules that specifies how all communications from one network to another must be performed. TCP/IP was adopted by the early networks and, with all networks following the same rules, any computer on one network could now communicate reliably with any computer on another network. The term coined for connecting networks using TCP/IP was **internetworking** and, as a result, the collection of networks joined in this way became known as the **Internet**.

The initial users of the Internet were scientists and researchers, who used it to exchange data and messages. However, in 1989 Tim Berners-Lee, a British scientist at the European Organisation for Nuclear Research (CERN) in Switzerland, proposed the development of an information resource, where documents would be stored on a central computer and retrieved on request. Furthermore, the collection of documents would be linked via a page of readable text which, when the links were clicked, would cause the linked document to be retrieved and displayed. Berners-Lee proposed that the central storage of documents would reside on a collection of computers distributed across the Internet. He coined the term **WorldWideWeb** (initially all one word) to refer to this collection of linked content.

When Berners-Lee published a description of the project in 1991, other research agencies were quick to develop their own implementations of his idea. Furthermore, when CERN announced in 1993 that the 'Web' would be free of charge for anyone to use and contribute to, universities and large corporations across the world were quick to connect to the fast-growing network. From CERN's initial website in 1991, the network quickly grew to 17 million sites by 2000, to 200 million by 2010 and almost 2 billion websites worldwide by 2019.

Internet Protocol addresses

The guiding principle of the Internet is that every device connected to it must be uniquely addressable. An **Internet Protocol address** (**IP address**) is a numeric value assigned to each device that is guaranteed to refer *only* to that device. Sometimes the IP address will be assigned each time the device connects to the Internet (a **dynamic** IP address) or the address can be permanently assigned (a **static** IP address).

The designers of the Internet Protocol originally specified the address as a 32-bit value that provides 4.7 billion unique addresses and this version, known as **IPv4**, is still in use today. However, the growth of the Internet has been such that IPv4 no longer provides enough unique addresses, so a 128-bit version, known as **IPv6**, was developed in 1995. IPv6 provides more than 34 trillion trillion addresses. IPv6 was launched worldwide in 2012 as a long-term replacement for IPv4 and by 2019 just over 25% of all Internet-connected devices were using IPv6 addresses.

Computers, of course, represent **IPv4** addresses in binary. However, when they need to be written in human-readable form the 32 bits are usually grouped into four chunks of 8 bits, with each chunk written as its decimal equivalent, and the chunks separated by a full stop. Hence the 32-bit IPv4 address:

11010001110000101010001100110001

would be divided into four chunks as:

11010001.11000010.10100011.00110001

and then written in decimal as:

209.194.163.49

In **IPv6**, the 128-bit values are grouped into eight chunks of 16 bits, with each chunk expressed in hexadecimal (base 16) and separated by colons. An example IPv6 address therefore appears in the form:

13d5:8c3:5631:ab40:d:456:5da2:30ff

Domain names

Because IP addresses are difficult for humans to remember, on the Internet, the IP address is usually represented by a **domain name**, a human-readable combination of words separated by full stop characters which maps onto an IP address. Typically, the domain name consists of between two and five parts with the parts at the beginning of the sequence representing the name or purpose of the device and the later parts representing the location or type of the device's organisation.

Case Study

Domain Names

You can derive information about an organisation or web site based on its domain name. Some example domains names are as follows.

www.ebay.com
the web server (www) belonging to eBay (ebay) who are a commercial company (com).

www.bbc.co.uk
the web server (www) belonging to the BBC (bbc) who are a company (co) in the United Kingdom (uk).

ccea.org.uk
the web server belonging to the Council for the Curriculum, Examinations and Assessment (ccea) who are a non-profit organisation (org) in the United Kingdom (uk). Note that it is often unnecessary to specify the 'www'.

www.tcd.ie
the web server (www) belonging to Trinity College Dublin (tcd) which is an organisation based in Ireland (ie).

In the examples presented in the case study, the final part of the domain name (.com, .uk, .ie) is known as the **top-level domain** (TLD) while the other parts are **sub-domains**. So, for example, www.ebay.com is a sub-domain of ebay.com which is itself a sub-domain of the .com top-level domain.

In practice, there are few rules regarding the composition of a domain name. Web servers usually begin with www, but it is not a requirement. In addition, while the last part of the domain name often identifies the country in which the server is located (for example, .uk, .ie, or .fr) this is not always the case. For example, the Northern Ireland television company UTV uses the country domain identifier of the Pacific island of Tuvalu – so providing the domain name u.tv. Other countries have stricter rules. For example, it is only possible to get a .ie (Ireland) domain name if you can show that your organisation is based on the island of Ireland.

A domain name provides an easy way for a human user to refer to a device on the Internet, but this must be translated back to its corresponding IP address so that the device can be contacted. A **Domain Name Server** (**DNS**) provides this translation service by maintaining a dictionary of domain names and IP addresses. As IP addresses may change over time (for example, you may be assigned a different IP address each time you connect the device to the Internet) the Internet contains multiple Domain Name Servers which continually exchange information with each other to ensure that the most up-to-date IP address is always associated with the correct domain name.

Web standards

The Internet and the World Wide Web continue to develop at a rapid pace, which means it is vital that new protocols and standards are defined and developed in line with changing communications and processing technologies. A number of standards bodies (sometimes with competing interests) are involved in setting and managing Web and Internet standards. These include:

- **IETF (Internet Engineering Task Force):** Established in 1986, the IETF is the primary body for Internet standards. They are a volunteer group and has been responsible for some of the most widely used standards, including IPv4, IPv6 and standards for email, domain names and network management.
- **ITU (International Telecommunication Union):** The ITU oversees many of the technologies that carry data across the Internet, including satellite, fixed line and radio transmission. The ITU standardisation sector (ITU-T) contributes to web standards by specifying the way in which communication takes place between devices on the Internet. This includes the specification of digital security certificates used in e-commerce, how digital video, sound and images are encoded, the underlying packet switching architecture, the electronic transmission of information across a communications medium and other technical aspects of electronic data exchange.

- **W3C (World Wide Web Consortium):** The W3C was founded by, and is still led by, Sir Tim Berners-Lee, and is made up of a number of organisations that develop standards for the World Wide Web. They are responsible for the notations and languages used to specify Web content (such as HTML and CSS), the protocols used to request Web resources and the format used to represent data in Web-based applications. The W3C standards ensure that web pages can be viewed in different browsers and that each browser will interpret the code that specifies the page in the same way.

Essentially, the ITU manages the standards concerned with the format and communication of data while the W3C manages the standards concerned with the specification of information to be displayed on a web page.

16.3 Using the World Wide Web

Connecting to the Internet

In order to connect to the Internet and the World Wide Web, individuals and companies use the services of an **Internet Service Provider (ISP)**. ISPs act as an interface between the user and the Internet by providing access to a Point of Presence (POP), as shown in figure 16.1. A POP is the connection point for the particular geographic area that an ISP covers, so ISPs that operate on a national or international basis may have multiple POPs. Home and business users can connect to their local POP via a modem, leased line or satellite link. Where users want to connect multiple devices, a router can control the link to the POP so that the traffic to and from each device is correctly managed. Often, the router and modem facilities are combined into a single unit.

Universal Resource Locators

As we have seen, the World Wide Web is a collection of connected **web servers**, which store and manage the content. Users request individual content items (**web pages**) by using a **web browser**. A web browser is an application program that allows the user to request a specific page, retrieve that page from its hosting web server on the Internet and display the page graphically on the computer screen.

Specific pages are identified by their **Universal Resource Locator (URL)**, often referred to simply as their **web address**. URLs are typically composed of three elements:

- the **protocol** to be used in retrieving the page (usually HTTP, the HyperText Transfer Protocol, which we shall consider later in this section),
- the **domain name** of the Web server on which the page is located, and
- the **file name** of the page to be retrieved.

These components are combined using colons and forward-slashes in the form:

<protocol>://<domain name>/<file name>

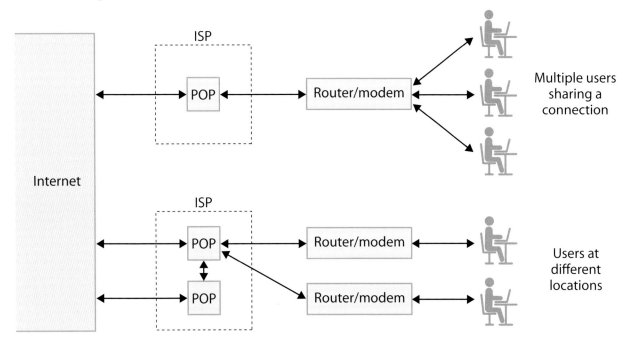

Figure 16.1: End users can access the Internet via an ISP.

165

So, for example, the URL:

http://www.ulster.ac.uk/index.html

specifies that the file with the name *index.html* should be retrieved from the web server with the domain name *www.ulster.ac.uk* using the *HTTP* protocol.

Sometimes the file name can be located within the directory or folder structure of the server, in which case the URL might take a form such as:

http://www.myserver.com/stories/first.html

meaning that the file *first.html* should be retrieved from the folder or directory called *stories* on the server with domain name *www.myserver.com* using the *HTTP* protocol.

HyperText Transfer Protocol

The **HyperText Transfer Protocol** (HTTP) is the protocol developed by Tim Berners-Lee to retrieve web pages. HTTP is an example of a **stateless protocol**, which means that each request to the server is an independent transaction that is completely unrelated to any previous request. This helps to make HTTP simple to implement and improves the efficiency of the network communication, the two key advantages of the protocol.

However, there are times when the context of a request is very important, and it is vital for the Web server to retain some knowledge of the state of an operation.

Consider the example of online banking. Before gaining access to their account information, a customer is required to log in using their secure username and password. Once the login details have been authenticated, the user is permitted to access their account and make a transaction. However, in a stateless system such as HTTP, the request for a transaction would have no knowledge of the previous, authenticated login. Therefore, we need to store details of the successful login and make sure that this information is available to the server so that it knows whether or not it should grant access to the transaction request. This can be achieved in one of two ways.

- **Cookies** are small pieces of text data, sent *from* a website and stored on the user's computer. Each time the user requests a web page, the browser sends the cookie to the server so that it knows the context of the operation. In the case of the online banking example, the successful login would cause a cookie to be written to the user's computer, with content

that confirms details of the login event. When the request for a transaction is made, the cookie is also sent to the server, which recognises the cookie as permission to service the request.

> **Note:** In recent years, cookies have become controversial as users became more aware that websites were using them to store data related to users and their browsing history on the user's computer. Since 2011, EU legislation known as the 'Cookie Law' requires websites that use cookies to receive explicit permission from the user before cookies can be stored.

- **Session variables** are values held *on the Web server* and maintained throughout a user's interaction session with the website. They provide a means by which state information can be transferred from one page to another. Once again, in the case of the online banking example, the successful login would cause a session variable to be stored on the server, recording that the user has been authenticated. This time, when the request for a transaction is made, the server checks the value of the session variable to determine whether the transaction should be allowed. Session variables are regarded as more secure than cookies as they reside on the server rather than on the user's computer, where they may be more vulnerable to unauthorised access.

Another disadvantage of the stateless nature of HTTP is that each request for a page is satisfied in full, regardless of whether all or some of the page content has already been supplied to the user's computer. Consider a user who spends an extended period on a single website, browsing from page to page. It is very likely that elements of the page (for example menus, logos, banners, graphics, etc.) will be the same on each page visited – yet they will all be transmitted across the network each time a new page is requested, generating unnecessary network traffic and associated time and cost. In addition, returning to a page already visited in the current session will require that the entire page is re-transmitted – even though it has been previously downloaded in full onto the user's computer.

This problem is reduced by using a **cache**, a temporary storage location for Web content that attempts to satisfy requests for content before having to retrieve it from the Web server. The cache can be on the user's computer (a **browser cache**), which stores copies of content items that have been previously retrieved by that user, or it can be implemented as a separate, shared server (a **proxy cache**) serving a large number of users by storing content that is frequently accessed by a number of people within an organisation. When a user requests an item from a Web server, the browser first checks the cache to see if the request can be satisfied from there. If successful, then the cached copy is re-used. This avoids having to make another HTTP request to the Web server, saving network traffic. There is a potential issue with caches where a fixed URL may contain information that changes frequently over time, such as news headlines or latest sports results. Websites can avoid this pitfall by adding a note to the page specifying to the browser that it is not to be cached at all or only cached for a specific period of time.

Web hosting

While an ISP provides a means to connect to the Internet, creating and managing your own website requires a **Web hosting** service. Web hosts are companies that lease space on a server to individuals and companies, who can then use the space to store the content of their website. Web hosts usually also provide support services to website owners. The range of support services provided varies according to the hosting company and the cost of the package purchased, but they normally include:

- a fixed amount of space on which to locate a website,
- an upper limit on the number of requests and/ or the volume of data that can be requested in a fixed period (known as the **traffic** to the site).
- one or more email addresses,
- domain name registration,
- database support,
- backup and data security services, and
- traffic analysis tools.

Once connected to the Internet, a website owner can upload content onto a web host by using the **File Transfer Protocol** (FTP). FTP is a standard network protocol that allows one computer to connect to another and to transfer files between them. Users identify themselves by a username and password which are authenticated before the connection is allowed. If the target machine does not require user authentication, then we have **anonymous FTP**, which allows any user to connect. Anonymous FTP is only used when an individual or organisation wants to make a collection of data files freely available for download. It is not used for upload of files to a server.

Note: FTP is a protocol for the transfer of any file to or from a server whereas HTTP refers specifically to a request by a browser for a web page. In general, web pages are loaded to the server via FTP and then viewed in a browser via HTTP.

Searching the Web

In the early days of the World Wide Web, all pages were indexed by hand. A list of Web servers was maintained by Tim Berners-Lee and made available as a list on the CERN website. However, as the number of servers grew, it became impossible to keep this list up-to-date and some automatic system for indexing and searching was required.

Early efforts involved reading the directory listings of each Web server to generate an index of web pages and the servers on which they were located, but in 1994 **WebCrawler** became the first **search engine**, a tool which allows users to search for any word on any web page. WebCrawler was followed by many others, including **Magellan**, **Alta Vista**, **Yahoo!**, **AskJeeves**, **Infoseek** and **Lycos**. However, around 2000 **Google** rose to prominence due to its innovative **PageRank** algorithm which provided better results than any previous search engine, and Google soon came to dominate the search engine market.

All modern search engines, including Google, consist of three key elements:

- **Web crawler** – The aim of a Web crawler is to visit every page on the Internet. It starts from a 'seed' page and collects all of the links on that page. All of these links are then visited in turn, collecting all of the links to pages that have yet to be visited and adding these to the list of pages to visit. The process continues until every page has been visited.

- **Index** – As the Web crawler visits each page, it gathers information about the page, including the text it contains, any images or video on the page and any descriptive information (known as metadata) provided in the page header. All this information is stored in a dictionary structure so that the content is associated with the page on which it is found.
- **Query engine** – This provides an interface through which the user can search for some specific text. The search engine compares the user's request against the contents of the index and returns the list of pages on which this text is found. The list of matching pages is sorted according to some criteria (in the case of Google, this is its PageRank value: see Case Study below) so that the 'best' matches are returned at the top of the list.

Note: The term **metadata** means data that describes other data. In the context of a web page, it refers to information that describes the page but which is not visible content. Metadata is used by search engines to determine when and where to include the page in search results. Search engines also display the metadata to potential website visitors who will read it when deciding which page best suits their needs.

Case Study

PageRank

PageRank was developed by Google founders Sergey Brin and Larry Page. Every webpage on the Internet is given a PageRank score, which is the sum of the PageRank scores of all pages that link to that page. The premise is that 'good' pages will be those that have most incoming links, and that these will therefore have the highest PageRank scores.

By using this algorithm, when the user requests a search for a certain term, the top page returned is the page with the highest PageRank score of all those pages that contain the term, and which is more likely to be a 'good' page.

16.4 Providing Web Services

In recent years, the World Wide Web has come to play a central role in many areas of everyday life. Many of the services that would previously have been paper-based, and activities that would have required us to be physically present at a particular location, can now be carried out through a web browser. In this section we shall classify the various types of Web-based applications and give examples of each.

E-services

E-services are services provided using electronic communication, usually the Internet. The term covers a diverse range of activities including online shopping (both Internet-only services such as Amazon, and online versions of high street stores such as supermarkets), online banking and other financial services such as insurance, online helpdesks (including live chat) and digital editions of newspapers and magazines.

The main benefit to the consumer is convenience, but there are also to the service provider. These include access to a wider customer base, provision of an alternative communications channel to customers, ability to offer an increased range of products and services, potential for increased knowledge about customers and their likes/dislikes and potential for a competitive advantage over competitors. Retailers who operate only online may also benefit from reduced costs through not needing to maintain a physical shop.

E-government

E-government refers to the electronic delivery of government services to citizens, businesses and other organisations. This can involve online publication of information (such as policy documents, regulations and calendars of events), transaction-based services (such as vehicle licensing and tax returns) and active governance activities (such as consultation, representation and polling).

The main advantage of e-government services is increased efficiency over a more traditional paper-based system. Businesses and citizens are able to receive information and assistance faster and more conveniently, with potential savings in workforce costs and physical resources. However, government services must be available to all citizens and therefore adequate provision must be made to ensure that those without the technical ability to interact online, and those without the necessary equipment and Internet connectivity, are not disadvantaged.

Portal services

A **portal service** is a website (or single web page) that provides links to a number of connected services in a consistent manner. Portal content is often organised into groups of links (sometimes known as **portlets**) which can often be re-arranged by the user so as to have the links they use most often provided in the most convenient and accessible location. An **enterprise portal** is a portal where the links refer to online services provided by an organisation for the benefit of its staff or clients, as shown in figure 16.2.

Our responsibilities

Road improvement schemes

How the public road network is managed, maintained and developed, as well as delivery of wider transport projects ... more

Transport initiatives

Belfast Rapid Transit - Glider, Belfast on the Move and the Department's transport plans for Northern Ireland ... more

Roads

Roads policies and legislation including the process and licencing requirements for road openings carried out by utility companies ... more

Public transport

The Department's role in bus, rail and ferry travel including relevant legislation and our supported travel programmes ... more

Active travel

Sustainable transport policies, primarily focused on cycling and walking in Northern Ireland. ... more

Waterways

Inland Waterways, the Lagan Towpath and the Department's work with, the cross-border body, Waterways Ireland. ... more

DfI Roads procurement

Procurement activities, ranging from supplies and services, and small-scale works to major road maintenance and high value capital construction projects. ... more

Road users

Promoting and improving road safety via education, licensing and regulation of transportation. ... more

Water and sewerage services

Ports

The Department's role in air and

Figure 16.2: The Department for Infrastructure website contains an enterprise portal linking to the various services that it provides (©DFI, used under the terms of the Open Government License.)

Intranets

An **intranet** is a private network that is contained within an organisation and can only be accessed by members of that organisation. The term is most often used to refer to a 'private' Web of online services. Intranets allow individuals to communicate and collaborate, but within a secure area that cannot be accessed by anyone outside the authorised group of users.

Use of an intranet can bring many advantages to an organisation, as follows.

- Information for employees can be made available online. This may include health and safety guidelines, company policies, internal forms, staff directory, training manuals and other material that would otherwise exist as printed documents. Where documents are updated, only the most recent version will be available and outdated material will no longer be accessible.
- Information is only made available to those to whom it is relevant. Employees are required to identify themselves with a username and password and different groups of users can be presented with different links and documents.
- Internal communication within a company can be enhanced by the use of messaging applications, wikis, blogs and discussion boards.
- Online tools for activities such as holiday requests and meeting scheduling can also help organise tasks that might otherwise be problematic.
- Employee morale can be monitored and enhanced by use of tools to survey opinion and involve staff in decision making.

Intranets also have some potential disadvantages, as follows.

- There is a significant setup and maintenance cost. As it is essential that the information is kept up-to-date it may be necessary to employ additional staff specifically for this role.
- Data privacy has become a significant issue with the advent of the General Data Protection Regulation (GDPR) in 2018 which gives individuals control over how their personal data is stored and used – as well as the right to withhold their data without prejudice.
- If an employee uses a password that is easy to guess, there is potential for a rogue user to gain access to confidential and business-sensitive material. This threat is increased if users are able to access the intranet from outside of the organisation.
- Where an organisation has a high degree of dependence on its intranet, there is a significant risk that business will be severely disrupted if the intranet is rendered unavailable by a technical or connectivity issue.

16.5 Security Issues

Much of the traffic on the Internet is in the form of human-readable text, including email messages, the content of web pages and other computer files that may be sent from one user to another. Sometimes this information can be of a private or sensitive nature, so steps need to be taken to ensure that the information can only be read by the intended recipient. There are a number of tools that can be used to achieve this aim.

Encryption

Encryption techniques encode information so that it is unintelligible to anyone who is not the intended recipient.

Public key encryption is a technique that uses two key values (essentially long, random numeric sequences) that are connected by a mathematical formula such that data encrypted using one of the keys can only be decrypted by using the other key.

The key used for encryption is known as the **public key** and is made freely available, while the key used for decryption is known as the **private key** and is available only to the individual to whom it belongs. For example, if user Alice wishes to send a private message to user Bob she encrypts the message using Bob's **public key**. The message can only be decrypted using Bob's **private key**, which only Bob has access to. In this way, even if the message is intercepted during transmission, it cannot be decrypted and read.

Secure Sockets Layer and HTTP Secure

Sometimes the primary security concern is the connection between the user's access point (for example, their computer or smartphone) and the server to which they are connecting. **SSL (Secure Sockets Layer**, also known as **Transport Layer Security** or **TLS**) is a security protocol that establishes an encrypted link between devices. This is useful in cases such as a person using a web browser to sign in to their email provider, or a user establishing an FTP connection to upload a file to their Web host, where they do not want the content to be read by anyone as it is being transmitted.

SSL operates as a 'digital passport' which verifies the identity of both parties. The process is performed using **digital certificates**. An SSL certificate is purchased from a trusted online vendor and has an expiration date after which it must be renewed (usually every year). The certificate contains a public key and a private key as well as a serial number and the owner's name. Establishing an SSL connection is a four-step process as follows:

- The device sends a 'hello' message to the server, containing a proposal for the data encryption algorithm to be used and a random 32-byte data sequence.
- The server selects an encryption technique from those offered and returns its own 32-byte random sequence together with its public key.
- The device generates the key for the communication session by combining both its and the server's 32-byte values, and encrypts it using the server's public key. This key is sent to the server.
- When the server receives the encrypted key, it decrypts it using its own private key. If the expected pair of 32-byte values are returned, the secure connection has been established.

SSL encryption can also be used to request and return web pages from a server. This combination of SSL and HTTP is known as **HTTPS (or HTTP Secure)**.

Digital signatures

SSL and HTTPS are used to secure the connection between devices, but sometimes we need to be able to verify the authenticity and integrity of a file or message that we receive from the Internet. One way to achieve this is to use a **digital signature** to 'stamp' the document to give an assurance of its origin or status.

A **digital signature** (not to be confused with a digital certificate) is created by generating a numeric hash value from the electronic data to be signed and encrypting the hash using the entity's private key. The encrypted hash is the digital signature and it is transmitted along with the document. When the document is received, the receiver decrypts the digital signature using the sender's public key. It then performs the same hash calculation and compares the result with the digital signature. If the hashes match, then the document has been delivered intact. If even a single character of the original document was altered in transit, then the hashes would not match, and the document could be discarded.

Questions

1. Which of HTTP and FTP would be used in each of the following situations? Explain your answer.
   (a) Uploading a web page to a server.
   (b) A web browser requesting a page from a server.

2. Explain the meaning of the following terms and describe the relationship between them.
   (a) World Wide Web
   (b) Web server
   (c) Website
   (d) Web page

3. The guiding principle of the Internet is that each device connected to it should be uniquely addressable. Explain how IP addresses and domain names achieve this.

4. Identify the subdomains of the URL http://www.ulster.ac.uk

5. What are the two key advantages of the stateless nature of the HTTP protocol?

6. What is the role of a Domain Name Server (DNS) in the operation of the World Wide Web?

7. Explain how an intranet differs from the Internet.

8. List any five services you would expect to be provided by an Internet Service Provider (ISP).

9. Describe the three main components of a search engine.

10. What is the difference between public and private keys in data encryption?

CHAPTER 17
Website Development

17.1 Introduction

A **website** is a collection of linked web pages that is retrieved and displayed by a web browser. A **web page** is a formatted collection of page elements, described in a notation called **Hypertext Markup Language (HTML)**. Page elements are content items such as paragraphs, headings, lists, images and links to other pages. The appearance of each content item is controlled by its style properties. The style elements are attributes such as colour, size, position and spacing. Style values are described using a notation called **Cascading Style Sheets (CSS)**. In this chapter, we shall explore how to create web pages using HTML and CSS code. We shall conclude with a further discussion on Web applications with a focus on client-side and server-side processing.

17.2 Hypertext Markup Language

Structure

In HTML, the content of a web page is **marked up** with elements (called **tags**) which consist of keywords contained within pairs of angle brackets, i.e. < and >. These tags describe the structure of the web page and how it is to be displayed in a browser.

The first tag in an HTML document is the html element itself which tells the browser that this web page is encoded using HTML. Therefore, every HTML document begins with a start tag of <html> and terminates with an end tag of </html>. An end tag has the same keyword as the start tag, except that a forward slash is placed before the keyword.

HTML tags are not case sensitive, although it is good practise to be consistent in the way in which tags are specified. Also, it is important to note that white space (spaces, tabs and new lines) is insignificant in determining the layout of a web page. Any consecutive white space characters in the HTML source of a document are collapsed to a single space character. If we want multiple spaces, tabs or new lines, then we must use the appropriate tags, described later in this section.

Within the <html> tags, an HTML document is comprised of **head** and **body** sections. These are denoted using the <head> ... </head> and <body> ... </body> tags to open and close each section. The head contains various elements relating to the document as a whole, such as the document's title (indicated within the <title> ... </title> tags), but other head elements will be introduced later in this chapter. The **body** contains the actual content to be displayed by the browser.

Figure 17.1 shows an example of a simple web page, which contains a single sentence welcoming the reader. The HTML code for this page is shown below. Note how the browser uses the information contained in the <title> to identify the tab containing the page.

```
<html>
<head>
   <title>My First Web Page</title>
</head>
<body>
   Welcome to my first Web page
</body>
</html>
```

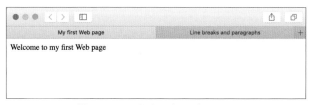

Figure 17.1 A simple web page.

Basic text formatting

HTML provides a number of ways to format the text on a web page. By default, the text on a web page is displayed in a top-to-bottom, left-to-right order, where the width of the browser window determines when a new line of output is started. If we want to force content to be displayed on separate lines, we can use the
 (line break) tag.

> **Note:** The
 (line break) tag is one of the few tags that stands alone, i.e. it does not have an associated end tag. Tags such as this are known as **empty tags**, while those with opening and closing elements, such as <html> ... </html>, are known as **container tags.**

Where we have a large quantity of text information, we may want to organise the text into paragraphs. The HTML paragraph tags <p> ... </p> provide a container into which we place the paragraph text. Figure 17.2 illustrates the effect of using line breaks and paragraphs to organise text on a web page. The HTML code for this page is shown below.

```
<html>
<head>
  <title>Line breaks and paragraphs</title>
</head>
<body>
  <p>This is the first paragraph. All of this
     information will be displayed in a
     continuous flow, with a new line taken
     only when required.</p>
  <p>This is the second paragraph. Note
     the default space between paragraphs.
     We will see later how to over-ride
     this default. <br> This sentence is
     presented on a new line within the same
     paragraph.Note the difference between
     line spacing and paragraph spacing.</p>
</body>
</html>
```

This is the first paragraph. All of this information will be displayed in a continuous flow, with a new line taken only when required.

This is the second paragraph. Note the default space between paragraphs. We will see later how to over-ride this default.
This sentence is presented on a new line within the same paragraph. Note the difference between line spacing and paragraph spacing.

Figure 17.2: Line breaks and paragraphs.

Headers are a simple method of text formatting that changes the size of the text based on the level (of importance) of the header. HTML specifies six levels of header, with Level 1 for the most emphasis (the largest text size) down to Level 6 for the least emphasis. Figure 17.3, and the equivalent HTML

code below, illustrates how to specify the six header styles using the appropriate HTML tags.

```
<html>
<head>
  <title>Header styles</title>
</head>
<body>
  <h1>Header level 1</h1>
  <h2>Header level 2</h2>
  <h3>Header level 3</h3>
  <h4>Header level 4</h4>
  <h5>Header level 5</h5>
  <h6>Header level 6</h6>
</body>
```

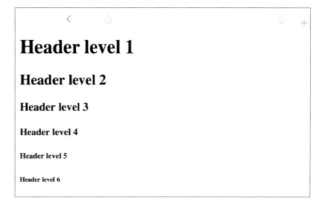

Figure 17.3: Header styles.

HTML makes special provision for the insertion of characters which are either difficult to type on a standard QWERTY keyboard (such as ©, ½ and accented characters like é), or which have a special meaning in HTML (such as < and >). Such characters can be obtained by using their ASCII code. For example, the ampersand character, &, has the ASCII code 38h and can be specified in HTML by typing &$38;. In some cases, an abbreviation of the character name can be used. For example, typing © will display the copyright symbol ©, ½ will display the fraction ½, and é will display the accented character é. Note the use of the semicolon in each case.

List structures

HTML provides alternative methods for presenting information in the form of lists – the **unordered list** and the **ordered list**.

An **unordered list** creates a list where each item is preceded by a bullet mark. The list must be enclosed in <ul> ... </ul> tags and, within those tags, each list element is enclosed within <li> ... </li> tags.

Figure 17.4, and the HTML code below, illustrates the definition of a simple unordered list.

```
<html>
<head>
  <title>Unordered Lists</title>
</head>
<body>
    <p>The following programming languages
       are available</p>
    <ul>
        <li>JavaScript</li>
        <li>C++</li>
        <li>Prolog</li>
        <li>Visual Basic</li>
    </ul>
</body>
</html>
```

The following programming languages are available

- JavaScript
- C++
- Prolog
- Visual Basic

Figure 17.4: An unordered list.

An **ordered list** is defined by the <ol> ... </ol> tags. Each list item is enclosed in <li> ... </li> as before. Now, instead of the bullet, each item is numbered. Figure 17.5, and the HTML code below, illustrates the definition of a simple ordered list.

```
<html>
<head>
  <title>Ordered Lists</title>
</head>
<body>
    <p>The following programming
       languages are available
    </p>
    <ol>
        <li>JavaScript</li>
        <li>C++</li>
        <li>Prolog</li>
        <li>Visual Basic</li>
    </ol>
</body>
</html>
```

The following programming languages are available

1. JavaScript
2. C++
3. Prolog
4. Visual Basic

Figure 17.5: An ordered list.

Tag attributes

The meaning of many HTML tags can be further refined by adding one or more **attributes** to them. An attribute is specified within the angle brackets of a start tag in the form:

```
[attribute name] = [value]
```

For example, by default, ordered lists use decimal sequence numbers (1, 2, 3, 4, …)., However, by setting the type attribute of the <ol> tag the style of numbering can be modified. For example, the tag <ol type='A'> would result in uppercase numbering in the form A, B, C …, while <ol type='I'> would display uppercase Roman numerals in the form I, II, III, IV.

Hyperlinks

The World Wide Web is made up of connected pages, where each page includes clickable links (**hyperlinks**) to other pages, either on the same server or elsewhere on the Internet. Links are specified in HTML using the **anchor** tag <a> ... </a>. A typical anchor tag to specify a link to another page might be as follows:

```
<a href=
"http://www.webserver.com/nextPage.html">
Click here</a>
```

where the value of the href attribute is the URL of the destination of the link and the text between the <a> ... </a> tags is the clickable text.

A hyperlink can also trigger an email message rather than a jump to another page by using a mailto: value for the href attribute. For example, the following HTML fragment will provide a link which, when clicked, will open the default mail program to compose a message to the quoted address.

```
Click
<a href="mailto:someone@somewhere.com">
here</a> to send me an email.
```

Tables

Note: The CCEA specification does not require you to know how to construct tables using HTML. However, they are one of the most common and versatile HTML elements and are included here for completeness.

The **table** is one of the most flexible and useful features of HTML. A basic table consists of a head and a body, each of which may be further subdivided into rows and columns, and a caption. Figure 17.6 illustrates a basic table displayed in a web browser. The equivalent HTML code is shown below.

```
<html>
<head>
  <title>Table Structures</title>
</head>
<body>
  <table>
     <caption>Class President Results
     </caption>
     <thead>
        <tr> <th>Candidate</th>
        <th>Percentage</th> </tr>
     </thead>
     <tbody>
        <tr> <td>Amy Adams</td>
        <td>35%</td> </tr>
        <tr> <td>Barry Bigger</td>
        <td>30%</td> </tr>
        <tr> <td>Carol Cates</td>
        <td>20%</td> </tr>
        <tr> <td>David Dixon</td>
        <td>15%</td> </tr>
     </tbody>
  </table>
</body>
</html>
```

Class President Results	
Candidate	**Percentage**
Amy Adams	35%
Barry Bigger	30%
Carol Cates	20%
David Dixon	15%

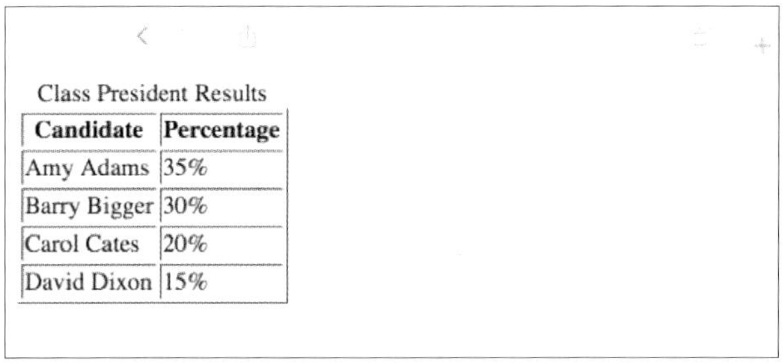

Figure 17.6: A basic table structure displayed in a web browser.

A table is defined inside the `<table>` ... `</table>` tags. The `<caption>` ... `</caption>` is an optional element that inserts a text heading directly above the table in the browser window. HTML differentiates between the head and body of a table. The head should always be specified first, using `<thead>` ... `</thead>` tags, and usually contains a single row of titles for each of the columns of information. The remaining rows are part of the body, specified within `<tbody>` ... `</tbody>` tags.

A **table row** is used for formatting the cells of individual rows. Within a row we then have **cells** – the smallest units of table information. All the cells of a row belong within the `<tr>` ... `</tr>` tags for that row. There are two types of cell: **table header cells**, specified by `<th>` ... `</th>` tags, which are used in the table head to give a title to each column, and **table data cells**, specified by `<td>` ... `</td>` tags, that usually contain the actual information.

Images

HTML supports the inclusion of images on web pages by the `<img>` tag. Figure 17.7 shows an image displayed in a web browser. The equivalent HTML code is shown below.

```
<html>
<head>
  <title>Images</title>
</head>
<body>
  <h1>Learning HTML5</h1>
  <img src="html5.gif" alt="The HTML5 Logo">
</body>
</html>
```

Learning HTML5

Figure 17.7: Using images.

In this example, we specify that an image file *html5.gif* is to be placed on the page. The `alt` attribute specifies alternate text to be used if the browser is unable to display the image. The value of this attribute is also used by many browsers to generate a tooltip when the viewer's cursor is located on top of the image, and in browsers designed for the visually-impaired. Where the image file is not located in the same directory as the HTML page, then the full path to the file needs to be specified.

Note that we can also specify an image as the anchor for a hyperlink, so that the user clicks on the image to get to the required page. This is done by including the `<img>` tag within the `<a>` ... `</a>`, such in the following example which will send the user to the HTML5 specification when they click on the logo.

```
<a href="https://dev.w3.org/html5/spec-LC">
   <img src="html5.gif" alt="The HTML5 Logo">
</a>
```

17.3 Cascading Style Sheets

Cascading Style Sheets (CSS) allow us to specify the appearance of page elements (colours, spacing, margins, etc) separately from the structure of our document (headers, body text, links, images etc). This separation makes it much easier to manage the appearance of our website. The term **style sheet** refers to the section of a web page where the style information is described.

Specifying style information

The style sheet information can be specified in one of three places:

- **inline**, i.e. associated explicitly with the element to which it applies, or
- **global**, i.e. gathered together in the head of the HTML document, or
- in an **external style sheet** file and linked to the pages to be affected.

Inline styles

Figure 17.8 shows a web page where the text appears in three different styles. This has been achieved using **inline** style definitions, where the appearance of an element is described using the style attribute of the `<p> … </p>` tag. The HTML code is shown below.

```
<html>
<head>
  <title>Inline Style Definition</title>
</head>
<body>
  <p>Text in the default style</p>
  <p style="font-size: 20pt">
    Some more text</p>
  <p style="font-size: 15pt; color: red">
    Even more text</p>
</body>
</html>
```

Figure 17.8: A web page with text using inline style definitions.

Let us consider each line of text in turn.

- The first line of text, with no style information specified, appears in the browser default colour, font and size.
- In the second line, the style attribute of the paragraph tag specifies that it should be rendered using 20-point text. All other text attributes on this line will be displayed using the browser defaults.
- The third line of output is displayed in red, using 15-point text, as specified by the font-size and colour properties of the style attribute. Any number of style properties can be set for an element by separating the style definitions with semicolons, as shown in the code.

Global styles

Inline style definitions are easy to use and understand, but they must be defined for each element to which they are applied. A better approach is to define **global** style rules in the head of the document and then to refer to these rules in specific elements, as required. The code below illustrates this approach. The appearance of the resultant web page is shown in figure 17.9.

```
<html>
<head>
    <title>Using the Style Element</title>
    <style type="text/css">
       h1   { background-color: yellow }
       p    { font-family: Arial; color: red }
    </style>
</head>
<body>
    <h1>A heading with a yellow
    background</h1>
    <p>A paragraph in red text in
    the Arial font </p>
</body>
</html>
```

Figure 17.9: A web page with text styled using the global `<style>` element.

The `<style>` element in the head of the document is the container for the style sheet. The `type="text/css"` attribute specifies that what follows is a set of CSS style definitions.

The body of the style sheet contains the CSS rules for this document. In this example, we have specified rules for the `<h1>` and `<p>` tags, so that all instances of `<h1>` and `<p>` in the document will now be displayed in the stated manner.

External style sheet files

The third method of specifying style sheet information is to use a separate, **external style sheet file**, which is linked to the HTML document. This is the most flexible of the three methods discussed, as it allows us to use a single style sheet definition across multiple web pages. In addition, a single change to the CSS file will be reflected immediately on all pages to which the file is linked. CSS is thus a very important tool in managing a large collection of web pages, such as the website for a business, as a single change in the style sheet (for example, to change a colour scheme) will automatically be reflected across all pages in the website. This helps to maintain consistency across the website as well as minimising the maintenance required. The code below shows the contents of a CSS style sheet document called *styles.css*.

```
h1  { color: red }
p   { font-size: 10pt; color: navy }
li  { text-indent: 1cm }
```

Figure 17.10 shows a web page that has been specified using this external CSS file. The HTML code shown below illustrates how to connect this CSS file to an HTML document.

```
<html>
<head>
    <title>Using an External Stylesheet
    </title>
    <link rel="stylesheet" type="text/css"
    href="styles.css">
</head>
<body>
    <h1>My Pets</h1>
    <p>A list of my pets, demonstrating an
      external style sheet</p>
    <ul>
        <li>Cat</li>
        <li>Hamster</li>
        <li>Fish</li>
    </ul>
</body>
</html>
```

Figure 17.10: A web page with styles defined using an external style sheet.

The style sheet is linked to the HTML page by the `<link>` tag, which has attributes `rel` (relationship – in this case "`stylesheet`"), `type` ("`text/css`" as used in the `<style>` element earlier) and `href` (the path/name of the external CSS file). (Note that the `<link>` tag does not have an associated end tag.) The effect of the style sheet is to specify the colours to be used for the `<h1>` and `<p>` elements, the font size of the `<p>` element, and the indentation of each `<li>` element.

Using colours

The `color` property specifies the colour to be used when rendering (creating an image of) text elements. Note the American spelling is used (i.e. color, not colour). There are three ways to specify colour values. In each example given below, the colour being specified is bright yellow.

- By using one of 126 standard colour identifiers. For example:
  `color: yellow`
- By specifying the red, green and blue primaries that make up the colour, with each primary being a value in the range 0–255. For example:
  `color: rgb(255,255,0)`
- By specifying the amount of red, green and blue as hexadecimal values, with each colour being two digits in the range 00 to FF. The six digits are preceded by a hash (#) symbol. For example: `color: #FFFF00`

The `backgound-color` property specifies the coloured background of any element that occupies browser space, including paragraphs, table rows and cells, headings, and the page body itself.

Resolving style conflicts

It is clearly possible for styles to be specified within other styles. As a general principle, style rules defined for 'parent' elements are also applied to 'child' elements, whereas rules redefined within 'child' elements take precedence over the 'parent' definition. In short, each page element is displayed using the closest available style information. Where no style information is available, then browser defaults are used.

Figure 17.11 shows a website that contains three paragraph elements that illustrate the key concepts of **precedence** and **inheritance** that arise from these principles. The HTML code is shown below.

```
<html>
<head>
    <title>Precedence and Inheritance</title>
    <style type="text/css">
        p     { font-family: arial; color:
                blue }
        span { background-color: yellow }
    </style>
</head>
<body>
    <p>Demonstrating <span>inheritance</span>
        in action</p>
    <p>Specifying
        <span style="font-weight: bold">
            additional</span> style properties</p>
    <p>Demonstrating <span style="background-
        color: lime"> precedence</span>
        in action</p>
</body>
</html>
```

Figure 17.11: Demonstrating precedence and inheritance.

Note: The `<span>` ... `</span>` HTML tag used in this example has no physical characteristics of its own, but provides a container that allows us to apply style information to part of the content of its parent element.

The first paragraph will be displayed using the style rules specified for the `<p>` and `<span>` elements in the document `<head>`. No inline style is specified in this case. As the `<span>` element is contained within the `<p>`, then the contents of the `<span>` element will **inherit** the style rules of the `<p>`, and will be displayed in **blue**, **Arial** text on a **yellow** background.

In the second paragraph, an additional inline style rule is specified for the `<span>` element. This rule adds to the existing, inherited rules, so the `<span>` element is displayed in **bold**, **blue**, **Arial** text on a **yellow** background.

The additional inline style rule in the third paragraph re-defines the inherited `background-color` rule. The rule of precedence states that the closest definition takes priority. Therefore, the text in the `<span>` element is displayed in **blue, Arial** text on a **lime** background.

The principles of precedence and inheritance are clearly defined and predictable, giving rise to the term 'cascading'.

17.4 Client-side and Server-side Processing

As we saw in chapter 16, a Web application is a computer program (or set of related programs) which is accessed through a web browser and which requires some processing or computation. This is distinguished from a static web page which requires only the retrieval and presentation of information and requires no further input from the user and no computation or calculation. Often, Web applications will involve some kind of offline storage such as a database or file store, so that the state of the application can be modified as it is used. One example is an online facility for purchasing airline tickets. The system maintains a database of seats available and modifies this as each purchase is made.

In Web applications, it is important to differentiate between processing carried out by the browser (**client-side**) and that carried out by the server (**server-side**).

Client-side processing

Client-side processing is computation that can be performed by the browser, without any additional resources. Typically, this will involve responding to user input and generating error or warning messages or modifying the appearance of the page.

For example, in our airline ticket example, the user may complete the purchase by providing his or her credit card details. Once the details are provided, the information will ultimately be sent to the server, but a level of verification can be carried out before this happens. In particular, the following checks can be made:

- Has the user provided information in all of the required fields? Certain details can be left blank (for example, you sometimes do not need all of the fields to specify your full address), but the user must, at a minimum, provide a name, credit card number and expiry date.
- Are the data values provided valid? Credit card numbers consist of 16 digits, so the browser could check that the length of the value entered by the user is correct and that each character is a digit. It could also check that any date values are in the correct format and in the correct range.
- Is the input still timely? When purchasing tickets online, users are often given a fixed time period in which to complete the transaction. If the time limit has expired, then the user should be informed.
- Has the correct combination of fields been completed? Some credit cards have an 'issue number' that should be provided as part of the payment process. It is important that the system checks that an issue number has been entered if the relevant type of credit card has been selected.

All of these checks can be carried out by the browser, on the client-side. If any of the validation checks fails, then the user is informed and invited to change their selections or values entered. Only when all validation tests are passed is the data submitted to the server.

Server-side processing

The role of **server-side processing** is to accept the data passed from the browser, carry out whatever transaction has been requested, and generate an appropriate web page to be returned to the browser to inform the user about the result of the transaction. Often, a transaction involves a number of phases, such as the following sequence for the airline ticket example.

1. The data is accepted from the browser and analysed to identify the transaction required. This might be a request to purchase a ticket on a particular flight.
2. Any information required from the database is fetched so that the transaction can be performed. In this example we need to retrieve the current number of seats remaining on the flight so that it can be reduced accordingly.
3. The computation is performed. Here, we subtract the number of seats being booked from the number remaining.
4. The database is updated in preparation for the next transaction. In this case, we write the new number of seats remaining, as well as recording the passenger details for the seats booked in this transaction.
5. The payment is processed. This will involve opening a connection to the user's credit card company and invoking the financial transaction.
6. A response page is generated. This will usually be a page confirming that the transaction has been completed and that the seats are reserved. However, if there has been a problem in any of the previous stages (for example if the card is declined or it has not been possible to reserve the requested number of seats), then the database is rolled back to its previous state and a page informing the user of the problem is generated.
7. The generated page is returned to the browser and displayed to the user.

Figure 17.12 illustrates the sequence of actions as well as the communication between the browser, the server, the database and the online payment system.

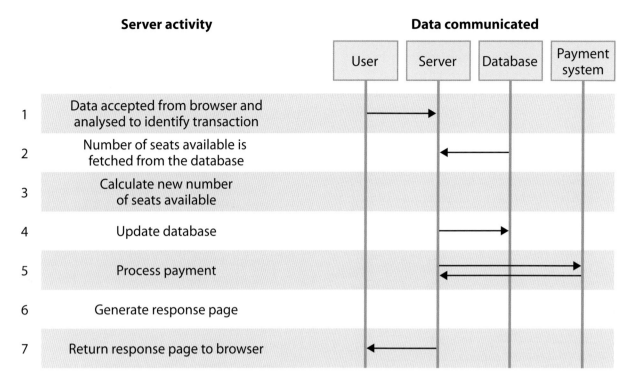

Figure 17.12: The sequence of interactions involved in an online payment system.

Questions...

1. What is the difference between an empty tag and a container tag in HTML? Give one example of each.

2. A web page for a school contains the following text:

> # Welcome to the Model School
>
> We prepare students for the following subjects:
>
> - Technology
>
> - Languages
>
> - Sciences
>
> <u>Click here to continue to our further information page.</u>

    (a) Write some HTML code that will display this section of the page.

    (b) How would you change the code to display a numbered list rather than bullet points?

    (c) The school now wants to add an image displaying the school crest at the top of the page, before any other content. Provide the code to achieve this, assuming that the crest is in the file *modelschool.png* which is in the same directory as the HTML page.

3. What is the purpose of CSS in web page development? How does CSS differ from the role of HTML?

4. Linked style sheets are often used in website development. Explain what this means, and discuss the main advantages of using a separate linked file for the CSS rules.

5. Consider the following extract from the source code of a web page.

```
<style type="text/css">
        p { font-family: arial;
        color: blue }
</style>
<p style="color: red">Paragraph 1</p>
```

    (a) Describe how the text "Paragraph 1" will be displayed in a web browser.
    (b) If the style rule were removed from the <p> element, what effect would this have on the text displayed in the browser?

6. When signing into an online banking application, the user is prompted to enter their username and password and then click an 'Enter' button. If the correct username and password have been entered, the browser then displays details of their account.

    Making reference to this scenario, distinguish between client-side and server-side processing.